Vedic Science and Technology

Dr. Sadasiva Biswal
Dr. Bidyut Lata Ray

D.K. Printworld (P) Ltd.
New Delhi

Cataloging in Publication Data — DK
[Courtesy: D.K. Agencies (P) Ltd. <docinfo@dkagencies.com>]

Biswal, Sadasiva, 1945-
Vedic science and technology / Sadasiva Biswal, Bidyut Lata Ray.
p. cm.
Includes bibliographical references (p.)
Includes index.
ISBN 13: 9788124604656 (HB)
ISBN 13: 9788124604663 (PB)
ISBN 10: 8124604657 (HB)
ISBN 10: 8124604665 (PB)

1. Science — India — History. 2. Technology — India — History. 3. Vedas and science. 4. Science in literature. 5. Technology in literature. 6. Vedic literature — History and criticism. I. Ray, Bidyut Lata, 1947-, joint author. II. Title.

DDC 509.34 22

ISBN 13: 978-81-246-0465-6 (HB) ISBN 10: 81-246-0465-7

ISBN 13: 978-81-246-0466-3 (PB) ISBN 10: 81-246-0466-5

First published in India in 2009

Published & printed by:
D.K. Printworld (P) Ltd.
Regd. Office: 'Sri Kunj', F-52, Bali Nagar
Ramesh Nagar Metro Station
New Delhi - 110 015
Phones: (011) 2545 3975; 2546 6019; *Fax*: (011) 2546 5926
E-mail: dkprintworld@vsnl.net
Website: www.dkprintworld.com

Preface

THE word "Science" has its derivation in the Latin word *Scientia,* meaning "to know." Knowledge obtained through science should not be solely factual but should advance understanding of phenomena. Obviously, any knowledge is not called science now-a-days. Science means today what is called *systematized and formulated knowledge.* It has been classified according to certain principles. In order to understand these principles we have to remember that our universe consists of matter, energy and life. These are all collectively called the *nature.* So, *natural philosophy* or *natural science* concerns all the phenomena in nature, the phenomena being partly *physical* and partly *biological.*

According to I.I. Rabi,[1]

> Science is an adventure of the whole human race to learn to live in and perhaps to love the universe in which they are. To be a part of it is to understand oneself, to begin to feel that there is a capacity within man far beyond what he felt he had, of an infinite extension of human possibilities — not just on the material side. . . .

Rabi proposes that science be taught "with a certain historical understanding, with a certain philosophical understanding, with a social understanding and a human understanding." The study of the history of philosophy, on the other hand, shows that materialism is the earliest philosophy. Therefore,

1. I. I. Rabi, Address given at the AAAS meeting of the Educational Policies Commission, 27 December 1966, Washington, D.C.

it is said that science begins from philosophy and finally it ends in philosophy. An enquiry into the origin and nature of ancient Indian materialism shows that the materialism has been blended with the philosophical thoughts. Oriental idealism is commonly contrasted with occidental materialism as if there were races of men either naturally materialistic or naturally idealistic. In fact, a survey of Indian philosophical system clearly points out that materialism was never unknown to our thinkers and "it undoubtedly had its day in India."[2] Indian philosophy has had an extremely long and complex development — much more complex and probably a longer history of continuous development than any other philosophical tradition. Thus, here we find varieties of thoughts — scepticism, materialism, pluralism, dualism, naturalism, along with idealism of different forms. Philosophy being man's quest after the ultimate reality, every philosophical tradition, including that of India, is characterized by so many divergent viewpoints.[3] After surveying the history of materialism, Lange[4] declares that not only materialism is as old as philosophy, but the latter itself started its career as the former. Thus, it would be correct to say that materialism is the oldest known philosophy.

Russell[5] goes a step further and identifies this earliest philosophy with science.

Man has an inquiring mind. The earliest history of man reveals his attempts to understand his environment — attempts made not just to satisfy his curiosity but also to assure his

2. Radhakrishnan and Moore (eds.), *A Source Book of Indian Philosophy*, p. xxiii.

3. U. Gupta, *Materialism in the Vedas*, Classical publishing Company, New Delhi, 1987, pp. 1-2.

4. Lange, "Hisoty of Materialism" quoted in Uma Gupta's book, *Materialism in the Vedas*, op. cit., p. 16.

5. Russell, *A History of Western Philosophy*, p. 21.

survival in a sometimes hostile world. Like the primitive man, the modern man still feels the need to understand the world around him, and the cause-and-effect relationships which will enable him to predict events and, to a certain degree, control his environment. Formerly, Vedic people, in the absence of acceptable explanations of phenomena, developed their own "informal science" based on magico-religious speculations which subsequently gave birth to true scientific observations in the theoretical and experimenal perspectives. Our three Ṛgvedic *sūktas*, viz. *Pṛthvī, Agni* and *Savitṛ* correspond to Matter, Energy and Life needed for the genesis and growth of any culture. Vedic literature records the thoughts of the most ancient Indian tradition and culture. The magico-religious phenomena described in the Vedic literature gave rise to the growth of ancient Indian science.

The thoughts contained in the Brāhmaṇas have been regarded by eminent scholars like Levi, Oldenberg, Schroeder[6] and Renou[7] as containing "pre-scientific" knolwedge. Winternitz designates them as "priestly pseudo-science."[8] Likewise, Keith[9] also regards the magical thoughts and practices of the Vedic priests of the *Atharvaveda* and the Brāhmaṇas as the forerunners of science or the primitive science of man. This is because there is an intimate relationship between magic and science. Tracing the history of science, it has been shown by such scholars as Dampier, Needham, Sarton, Singer and Throndike that "Science did not germinate and grow on an open and healthy prairie of ignorance, but in

6. M. Winternitz, *A History of Indian Literature,* trans. S. Ketkar, vol. I, Calcutta University Press, Calcutta, 1927, p. 187f.

7. L. Renou, *Vedic India,* Sushil Gupta Ltd., Calcutta, 1957, p. 31.

8. M. Winternitz, op. cit., p. 187.

9. A. B. Keith, *The Religion and Philosophy of the Vedas and Upaniṣads,* Harvard University Press, Cambridge, Mass., 1925, pp. 380-81.

the noisome jungle of magic and superstition."[10]

The primitive man was a hardboiled realist and a tough-minded materialist. Hence his belief in and practices of magic are the expressions of the most primitive materialistic thoughts which can properly be called the archaic materialism. Ostensibly, this archaic materialism, finding its first expression in the magico-religious phenomena, is bound to contain the germs of science. It, therefore, may justifiably be called the nascent science or pre-science.

The Vedic conception of *ṛta,* implying some consciousness of the law-bound universe and the belief in the magical efficacy of *mantra* and *yajña* as the means to have control over the courses of nature and even over gods, underlie an attitude of the Vedic Āryans akin to that of science. Frazer, in fact, describes magic as the "next kin to science" because both have in common "the general assumption of a succession of events determined by law." Both start as a necessity for man's survival in the struggle for existence. Both represent man's reaction to and interpretation of nature and both aim at discovering causes of natural events and controlling them by human will. The distinction between them lies in the fact that magic has no theoretical background other than analogy or symbolism. Being the product of an immature phase in the evolution of human reason, it fails to discover the real causal connection among natural events; in other words, it fails to distinguish between causes — imaginary and real. Science, on the other hand, has been able to do so only through a process of unfolding of the reasoning faculty of man along with the accumulation of the a posteriori facts of experience in the course of a long period of history. Again, man, in the primitive stage, was too close to his immediate environment to have a detached view and wide comrehension of nature. Hence, in his interpretation of nature, though he starts with the rational

10. U. Gupta, op. cit., p. 127 and fn. 322.

laws of causality and uniformity of nature, he commits the fallacies of mal-observation and non-observation. Thus, his investigation of the natural phenomena consists of an illusory technique instead of the real one. Such illusory technique of magic is a necessary stage for the development of the real technique of science. Needham[11] points out that in its earliest phase, science was indistinguishable from magic; hence, he calls the latter "pre-science" or "proto-science." According to him, this significant phase of the "magico-scientific" tradition, which in its beginning "crystallized around the nucleus of primitive shamanism,"[12] has left its unmistakable imprint on the people not only in ancient and mediaeval periods but even after the birth of modern science.

The present treatise consisting of 10 chapters throws light on the ancient knowledge of the Vedic people *vis-à-vis* modern scientific theories. Earlier, people belonging to other disciplines, especially from linguistics, mathematics, physics and astronomy have tried to interpret the Vedas from the point of view of their particular discipline. Here, in this study, attempts have been made to analyse the Vedic verses in scientific terms. In the *Ṛgveda,* man did not postulate a scientific theory but it is equally clear that he was aware and self-conscious of the principles on which scientific theories are based, and moreover he was accurately perceiving the phenomenon of life and nature.

In the Vedic literature, we come across innumerable myths to transmit the *truths* to the masses in an interesting and easily memorizable manner, and to explain what was not yet really and fully understood. In all cultures, myths and legends were also created to engrave in the collective memory the traditions and history of a people, of a clan or a race. The hypotheses

11. J. Needham, *Science and Civilization in China,* Cambridge, London, 1956, vol. I, pp. 108-209.

12. Ibid., pp. 93, 117, etc.

and the speculations of the Vedic seers go a long way in exploring the scientific causes and effects created every moment in nature. The Vedic deities symbolize the natural phenomena which the human beings come across in their day-to-day life. The present analysis contains the significant aspects of Vedic science and technology keeping coherence between the thoughts of the Vedic bards reflected in the hymns and the modern scientific theories developed later. It is, thus, revealed that the modern scientific theories and practices have their bases in the most ancient tradition and culture. Various branches of knowledge, such as Astronomy, Astrology, Cosmology, Cosmogony, Space-time Continuum, Mathematics, Chemistry, Physics, Meteorology, Seismology, Botany, Zoology, Medicine, Agriculture, Geology, Environmental Science and Ecology, and Science and Technology have been discussed here in accordance with speculations of the Vedic bards reflected in the hymns. Many more scientific explanations of the Vedic words and terms can no doubt uncover the real ideas of the seers underneath the hymns. The present attempt is a very small beginning for a large building to be erected for explaining the Vedic verses in the true sense of the scientific knowledge.

"Knowledge dispels ignorance."

Rathayātrā
8 July 2008

S. Biswal
B. L. Ray

Acknowledgement

THE present Volume is the outcome of the cultivation of new thoughts and insights in the study of Vedic literature in its microscopic character over a macroscopic system. Such an analysis goes a long way in compensating the earlier Vedic studies, particularly in their scientific aspects. In this respect, we have highly benefited from the vast field of Vedic studies undertaken by the eminent scholars of India and abroad and to whom we owe our indebtedness.

A study, an interpretation, a formulation, an observation or a conception goes in vain if it does not attract the readers who are the real judges of the works done. So, we render all our findings here in the hands of our learned readers and evaluators who could taste the sweetness and the sourness of the facts. We are thankful to all of them. They are our real inspirations.

We express our sincere thanks to all those friends and colleagues who have activated our norms to take up a study like this.

We are highly indebted to our parents and in-laws whose support and advices have paved the ways for our study and investigations.

Words are inadequate to express our sincere thanks to our two *putra ratna*s Saumya and Shaunak and *Sukanyā* Shashwatee Swagatica, who have created the congenial atmosphere at home for our studies and writings. They are the silent observers of our works.

Lastly, we are highly obliged to Mr Susheel K. Mittal, Director, D.K. Printworld (P) Ltd., New Delhi, for bringing out the monograph in a magnificent get-up and alluring style.

Sadasiva Biswal
Bidyut Lata Ray

Contents

	Preface	v
	Acknowledgement	xi
	Transliteration Chart	xvii
1.	General Introduction	1
	Ṛgveda	2
	Sāmaveda	4
	Yajurveda	5
	Atharvaveda	6
	Brāhmaṇas	7
	Āraṇyakas	9
	Upaniṣads	9
	Vedāṅgas	11
2.	Facets of Vedic Science	15
	Astronomy	18
	Astrology	19
	Calculation of Time	20
	Cosmology	22
	Cosmogony	24
	Water Theory	24
	Golden-egg Theory	25
	Space-Time Continuum	29
	Time	30
	The Cosmic order Ṛta	34
	Mathematics	36
	Chemistry	39

	Metallurgy	42
	Physics	43
	Meteorology	53
	Water	58
	Cloud-formation – Lightning and Thunder – The Rains	
	Air	63
	Fire	65
3.	SEISMOLOGY	67
	Causes	67
	Effects	70
	Symptoms	71
	Modern Method of Forecasting an Earthquake	72
	Classification	73
	Vedic Theroy of Predicting Deep Shock Earthquakes	73
4.	BOTANY	77
	Vedic Flora: A Study	77
	Plants	78
	Water-plants and Weeds	81
	Herbs and Grasses	82
	Grains and Creepers	83
	Flowers, Fruits and seeds	85
	Trees	86
5.	ZOOLOGY	89
	Vedic Fauna : A Focus	89
	The Animals	90
	The Cattle	95
	The Birds	97
	The Insects	99
	Reptiles	101
	The Serpents	101
	The Worms	102
6.	MEDICINE	105

Introduction 105
Characteristics of Vedic Medicine 110
Process of Healing 112
Mythology in the Vedic way of Healing 113
Vedic Physicians and Practice of Medicine 114
Diseases 116
Internal diseases 116
Diseases Related to Yakṣmā and/or Takmān 117
General Treatment of Internal Diseases Related to Yakṣmā and Takmān 130
Diseases not Related to Yakṣmā and/or Takmān 131
External Diseases 140

7. AGRICULTURE 153
Introduction 153
Farmers 155
Land under Cultivation 156
Irrigation 157
Preparation of Ploughshares and their Use 159
Use of Manure 161
Types of Grain 162
The Harvest 163
Livestock of the Farmers 166
Management of Cattle Farms 170
Precautions in Cattle Breeding 172

8. GEOLOGY 175
Introduction 175
Geophysical Phenomena 177
Vedic Theory of the Earth 185
Vedic Heliology 188
Vedic Selenology 189
The Effects of Eclipses 189
The Effects of the Stars 190
The Geological Agents 191

The Age of the Earth 192
Shape of the Earth 193
Dimensions of the Earth 193
Constitution of the Earth 195
Movements of the Earth 198
Conclusion 199

9. ENVIRONMENTAL SCIENCE AND ECOLOGY 201
Part I : Environmental Science 201
Introduction 201
Oceans in Ṛgveda 202
Rivers and Lakes in Ṛgveda 203
Countries, Cities, Towns & Holy Places in Ṛgveda 207
Mountains and Forests in Ṛgveda 209
Flora and Fauna in Ṛgveda 211
Climate 216
Fire, Air and Water 216
The Earth in *Ṛgveda* 217
Part II : Ecology 218
Introduction 218
Ecology of Matter, Energy and Life 219
Relationship of Organic Matter with Environment 221
Man and Biosphere Relations 221

10. SCIENCE AND TECHNOLOGY 225

BIBLIOGRAPHY 233

INDEX 247

Key to Transliteration

VOWELS

अ *a*	आ *ā*	इ *i*	ई *ī*	उ *u*	ऊ *ū*	ऋ *ṛ*	ॠ *ṝ*[1]
(Roman)	(palm)	(it)	(police)	(put)	(rule)	(rig)	
ऌ *ḷ*	ॡ *ḹ*[1]	ए *e*	ऐ *ai*	ओ *o*	औ *au*		
(able)		(there)	(aisle)	(no)	(loud)		

CONSONANTS

Guttural	क *ka* (skate)	ख *kha*[2] (blockhead)	ग *ga* (gate)	घ *gha*[2] (ghost)	ङ *ṅa* (sing)
Palatal	च *ca* (chunk)	छ *cha*[2] (catch him)	ज *ja* (john)	झ *jha*[2] (hedgehog)	ञ *ña* (bunch)
Cerebral	ट *ṭa* (start)	ठ *ṭha*[2] (anthill)	ड *ḍa* (dart)	ढ *ḍha*[2] (godhead)	ण *ṇa* (under)
Dental	त *ta* (path)	थ *tha*[2] (thunder)	द *da* (that)	ध *dha*[2] (this)	न *na* (numb)
Labial	प *pa* (spin)	फ *pha*[2] (philosophy)	ब *ba* (bin)	भ *bha*[2] (abhor)	म *ma* (much)
Semi-vowels	य *ya* (young)	र *ra* (drama)	ल *la*[3] (luck)	व *va*[4] (vile)	
Sibilants	श *śa*[5] (shove)	ष *ṣa*[5] (bushel)	स *sa* (so)	ह *ha* (hum)	
Others	क्ष *kṣa* (*kṣatriya*)	त्र *tra* (*triśūla*)	ज्ञ *jña* (*jñānī*)		

अं (ं) *ṁ anusvāra* is a nasal off-glide that immediately follows the pronunciation of a vowel as in *saṁskṛti.*

अः *visarga* = *ḥ* consists in abrupt release of breath after a vowel as in *prātaḥ*.

ऽ *Avagraha* shows non-pronunciation, that is, deletion of "a" after "e" or "o" as in *ime 'vasthitāḥ*. In Vedic ṣanskrit, it can also show word division.

HINDI LETTERS (extras)

ँ = m̐ (*candrabindu*)	ं = ṅ (*anusvāra*)	ड़ = *ṛa*	ढ़ = *ṛha*

---

1 Longer form of the preceding vowel.

2 Aspirated forms of the preceding consonants. The compound words given as examples should be pronounced without a syllabic break at the underlined places. "tha" and "pha" should not be pronounced as fricatives.

3 retroflexed and written as "L *la*" in certain phonetic contexts.

4 Pronounced like "w," without aspiration.

5 "śa" is palatal; "ṣa" cerebral or retroflex.

1

General Introduction

THE Vedas are the primordial sources of human civilization and culture. Out of the four Vedas, namely *Ṛg, Sāma, Yajur* and *Atharva,* the earliest specimen of Indian literature is the *Ṛgveda,* an anthology of hymns in ten books, I-X. Evidently, Vedic literature is the most ancient and marks the beginning of Indian literature. It is also the first full-length religious and literary account of the Indo-European people. Being the earliest record of human civilization, the Vedas deal with various aspects of human life, the Vedic people came across or experienced. It is quite encouraging to record here that copious branches of Vedic studies are now opened up by our readers, interpreters and research scholars. Besides history, tradition, culture and literature, we find elaborate and lucid descriptions of the "creation." Vedic Cosmology and Cosmogony describe the genesis of the universe, the earth, the water, air and life. The ecology and the environment depicted in the Vedas include all the natural provisions made for human existence. Vedic flora and fauna, rivers, lakes, seas, oceans, climate, mountains, forests, etc. provide the physical pictures of the surroundings in which the Vedic people were living. The names of cities, towns and holy places have also been traced in the sacred hymns of the Vedas. Society, polity, education, science and technology in the realm of Āyurveda and warfare mark the significance of Vedic hymns. Above all, Matter (Pṛthvī), Energy (Agni) and Life (Savitṛ) are conceptually extolled in the Vedic *sūkta*s. Ostensibly, we have a comprehensive and coherent account of the Vedic people — their life, ethos, thoughts and beliefs.

If the Vedas mark the very beginning of human knowledge and civilization adhering to all such branches of studies like history, archaeology, cultural anthropology, sociology, comparative religion and mythology, linguistics and philosophy, cosmology, ecology, environment, science of healing and the theory of the creation, then what the Veda really is?

The term *veda* means "knowledge *par excellence*," that is sacred and all-pervading. The Veda represents the religion that the Āryans brought with them into India and developed during ancient times on Indian soil. In fact, the term refers to a series of texts of various contents and forms which are believed to be derived from a "hearing" (*śruti*) that is a revelation. Common beliefs go in favour of the term that the Vedic narrations have emanated from *Brahman*. The human authors of the Vedas were the *r̥ṣis* or inspired sages who were able to receive the Vedic *mantras* by "direct vision."

The Vedic texts, include the Saṁhitās or "collections" which generally present hymns, prayers and ritual formulae. Other Vedic texts are the Brāhmaṇas, the Āraṇyakas (forest texts), the Upaniṣads, the Vedāṅgas (i.e. the auxilliary limbs of the Veda) and the Kalpa-Sūtras. The subsidiary works of exegesis, explanation are not the part of the Veda in the narrow sense. In this, context, they are no longer *śruti* but *smr̥ti* (memory). In fact, the most ancient form of Brāhmanism is the Vedism established by the four Vedas and the Vedic texts.

The R̥gveda

The span of Vedic literature from the Saṁhitās to the Vedāṅgas not only marks the beginning of Indian literature but also stands as the first full-length text of the Indo-European religion and culture. Our knowledge of pre-Āryan influence on the Āryans is wholly conjectured for the *Ṛgveda Saṁhitā* period. The *Ṛgveda,* being the earliest specimen of Indian literature, is an anthology of hymns in ten books. These Saṁhitās are nothing but the bulk of poetry of praise and prayer addressed to the gods. Though these prayers are mostly crude and uninspired, they contain the anthropomorphic description of the life, culture and tradition of the most ancient people in the form of their social structure and style. Their language, literature, forms, dresses, ornaments, food and drink, weapons, business, transport, commerce, feats and bounty, etc. are at once gleaned from the poetry of the *Ṛgveda.* Besides these, a variety of subjects such as doxology, war songs, legends, ballads, intoxication-songs (9th *Maṇḍala* of *Ṛgveda*), repentance of the sinner (the gambler's song), song of desire (*yama-yamī*), wedding song (*sūryā* hymn), intrusion of a new cult (*Vṛṣākapi*) panegyrics of donors (*dānastuti*), dialogue hymns, devotional, philosophical and cosmogonic hymns including hymns of pure doubt and groping constitute the forms of the *Ṛgveda.*[1] Vedic people were depending on agriculture and the domestic animal like cow. With the development of agriculture, iron ploughshare was introduced in due course. Consequently, there was improvement in trade and commerce. In place of barter system, rudimentary coinage was introduced. This is quite evident from the word *niṣka* mentioned in the latest section of the *Ṛgveda.* There was mention of 100 *niṣka*s and 100 horses for a certain payment in the *Ṛgveda.*[2] Thus, *niṣka* was the name of the coin used.

In course of time, metals like copper, iron, bronze, etc. were discovered. This led to the genesis of the science of metallurgy which in turn brought about the development of crafts and trade. Gradually, Vedic people felt the importance

1. S. Bhattacharji, *Literature in the Vedic Age,* vol. I, Calcutta: K. P. Bagchi & Company, 1984, p. xiii.
2. *Ṛgveda,* I.12.2; I.126.2; VIII.2.41.

of time for ploughing, sowing and harvesting and this led them to discover a calendar for their routine. The introduction of the calendar governed agriculture. Hence, there were considerable changes in the social ethos with the rise of kingship. Territorial autonomy became the desire of the rulers. The priests capitalized on the king's ambition of political security. There was the emergence of sacrifices like the *Vājapeya, Rājasūya* and *Aśvamedha* which were performed for the prosperity and military success of the rulers.

The age of the composition of the *R̥gveda* is still in illusion though considerable debate has been continuing for a very long time. Macdonell[3] opines that the *R̥gveda* is undoubtedly the oldest literary monument of the Indo-European language. But, the exact period when the hymns were composed is a matter of conjecture. All that we can say with any approach to certainty is that the oldest of them would date back to earlier than the thirteenth century BCE. From astronomical considerations, one Sanskrit scholar places the oldest Vedic hymns in 3000 BCE while another puts them as far back as 6000 BCE. Tilak[4] observed that the oldest period in the Āryan civilization may be referred as the pre-Orion and one can fix its date as 6000–4000 BCE.

From the point of view of S. Sastry,[5] the Haṛappan culture is a development over the Vedic culture. Obviously, the Indus Valley civilization owes its origin to the Vedic civilization and hence it is most probable to ascertain the age of the Vedas sometime of the order of 8000 to 7000 BCE.

The Sāmaveda

The *Sāmaveda* is the Veda of *sāmans* (melodies). It has three

---

3. A.A. Macdonell, *A Vedic Reader for Students,* Oxford Press, 1976.
4. B.G. Tilak, *The Orion,* Pune: Messers Tilak Brothers, 1972, p. 243.
5. S.S. Sastry, *Harappa and Mohanjo-Daro in Bhāratīya Saṁskr̥ti Darśana,* ed. A.N. Krishna Rao, Bangalore, 1962, pp. 9-18.

recensions, namely Kauthuma, Raṇayaṇīya and Jaiminīya or Talavakāra. The last one contains larger collections of melodies than the Kauthuma. Sāyaṇācārya commented on this Veda in the fourteenth century CE. According to S.V. Ganapati,[6] this Veda consists of nearly 1875 *mantras*. But, Renou[7] counts it as 1810 and views that the verses are borrowed for the most part from the *Ṛgveda*, often with variants of a verbal character or due to the necessities of musical transcription. These *mantras* had their special place in the *Soma* ritual. Again, the first group of verses of the *Sāmaveda* is noticed in its Ārcika section while the last group of verses forms the Uttarārcika section of this Veda. It is obvious that the Uttarārcika was compiled after the Ārcika.

The verses of the *Sāmaveda* are primarily intended to be sung. The present-day music is a derivation from it. As the *sāmans* are in the musical form, they are easily committed to memory. The entire Veda is devoted to two subjects, viz. (i) evolution and (ii) operation of human mind and sense-organs in offering the prayers to the gods and goddesses. All these *mantras* are chanted for one's own welfare and prosperity.

The Yajurveda

The hymns of the *Yajurveda* are employed for the performances of sacrifices like *Rājasūya, Aśvamedha, Somayāga* and *Agniṣṭoma*. Two recensions of this Veda are available. They are *Kṛṣṇa Yajurveda* and *Śukla Yajurveda*. The first one contains both prose and poetry in its *mantras* while the second one has only poetry. Again, the *Kṛṣṇa Yajurveda* is divided into five *kāṇḍas*, and the *Śukla Yajurveda* is noted to have only forty *adhyāyas* and 1,975 *mantras*.

Out of 85 *śākhās* of the *Kṛṣṇa Yajurveda*, only four are available now. These are Taittirīya, Maitrāyaṇī, Kaṭha and

6. S.V. Ganapati, (ed.) *Sāmaveda*, Delhi: MLBD, rpt., 1992, p. xix.

7. L. Renou, *Vedic India*, Delhi: Indological Book House, 1971, p. 17.

Kapisthala. Two *śākhās* of *Śukla Yajurveda* are known. These are Yājñavalkya and Vājasaneyī. Also, two traditions of the *Śukla Yajurveda,* namely, Kāṇva and Mādhyandina are prevailing. The former tradition is prevalent in the south while the latter is followed in north India.

The *Yajurveda* contains interesting features of ancient mathematics and geometry in its *iṣṭividhāna* and *citi nirūpaṇa* epithets. Murthy[8] holds that the fifth hymn of *Vasordhārā* includes *rudra camaka praśna* which is significant from the geological point of view and more so for its metallurgical attributes.

The Atharvaveda

This Veda was a later addition to the Vedic literature. This Veda bears the names of the great worshippers of Agni, Atharvan and Aṅgiras. The *Atharvaveda* is also called the *Brahmaveda.* The recensions of the *Atharvaveda* have two roots, each of which has nine divisions. One group contains Paippala, Dānta, etc. and the other group contains Paippalāda, Taudāyana, etc. However, of these, only two, Paippalāda, and Śaunakīya are available. The *Atharvaveda* presents the following subjects of diverse nature :

(i) charms to cure diseases and possession by demons (*bhaiṣajyāni*),

(ii) prayers for the long life and health (*āyuṣyāni*),

(iii) imprecations against demons, sorcerers and enemies (*ābhicārikāni* and *kṛtyā-pratiharaṇāni*),

(iv) charms pertaining to women (*strīkarmāṇi*),

(v) charms to secure harmony, influence in the assembly and equal status (*sāmmanasyāni*),

8. S.R.N. Murthy, *Vedic View of the Earth,* New Delhi: D.K. Printworld (P) Ltd., 1997, p. 35.

(vi) charms pertaining to royalty (*rājakarmāṇi*),

(vii) prayers and imprecations in the interest of brāhmaṇas,

(viii) charms to secure prosperity and freedom from danger (*pauṣṭikāni*),

(ix) charms in expiation of sin and defilement (*prāyaścittāni*),

(x) cosmogonic and theosophic hymns,

(xi) ritualistic and general hymns,

(xii) hymns of marriage and funeral rites, etc.

(xiii) hymns of the 20th *kāṇḍa*, and

(xiv) the *kuntāpa* hymns.[9]

The *Atharvaveda* is noted to be the foundation of the science of Indian medicine. This Veda is also the source of the science of Indian archery (Dhanurveda).

Thus, the four Vedas comprise various branches of knowledge like mythology, philosophy, religion and science, etc. As mentioned earlier, all the streams of education and learning are blended in one. There was no education other than the Veda required at that time, and the Vedas used to be learnt from a *guru* (teacher) for not less than 12 years, the period even extendable up to 32 years.

The Brāhmaṇas

The Brāhmaṇas were composed after the closure of the last section of the *Ṛgveda*. The primary concerns of the Brāhmaṇas are sacrifices. These are the guidebooks for the priests to perform sacrifices and rites. Besides, the Brāhmaṇas preserve a fuller picture of society than we have in the Saṁhitās. The Brāhmaṇas in their earliest stage present a cultural homogeneity which disintegrates, even in the later Brāhmaṇas themselves, so that they reflect increasingly smaller and

9. B.S. Kharade, *Society in the Atharvaveda*, New Delhi: D.K. Printworld (P) Ltd., 1997, p. 2.

smaller areas of social reality.[10] The Brāhmaṇas contain the ritual details to guide officiating priests. They preserve a number of myths and legends which are religious, popular and secular. The Brāhmaṇa myths do not appear as records of gods' acts. They are rather justifiable for carrying brisk priestly activity.

In the Brāhmaṇa literature, myths form, as it were, the forte of this literature. The language in which the Brāhmaṇa literature depicts these myths is poetic and has all the freshness and beauty. The episodes of *dharma, dāna* and *dayā* as narrated in the Brāhmaṇas form the basis of every philosophy. Most of these myths and legends have survived even to date in one form or other, whether it is the story of the conflict between the *deva*s and the *asura*s or the story of Manu and the Fish.

Prof. N.V. Gadgil[11] opines that the beginning of the caste system is to be noticed in a crude form in the *Ṛgveda Saṁhitā* and it came to maturity during the Brāhmanic age. It is interesting to record here that the Brāhmaṇa literature bear mixed opinion about women. The forces of nature, which govern the human beings, have been well treated in the Brāhmaṇas. The interpretation of *satya, vāc, nāma* and *anna* in the Brāhmaṇa literature attaches sociological significance to it. The technical procedures of the performance of sacrifices are described in this literature in great detail. All matters connected with sacrifice, such as altar, priest, initiation, observance of the initiated, Agnihotra, etc. are dealt with. Here, mythology appears to have connections with sacrifice. Ostensibly, the Brāhmaṇas form a bridge between the Saṁhitās on the one hand and the Upaniṣads on the other.

---

10. S. Bhattacharji, op. cit., p. xvi.
11. G.V. Devasthali, *Religion and Mythology of the Brāhmaṇas,* Foreword by Prof. N.V. Gadgil, University of Poona, 1965, p. ii.

The Āraṇyakas

The Āraṇyakas or the "forest texts" consist of abstruse works having magical power.[12] So, they are always kept away from the public and read in isolated places, very often in forests. These are mostly composite works having *mantra,* Brāhmaṇa and even elements of *sūtra.*

Aitareya, Kauṣītakī and *Taittirīya* are the three significant Āraṇyakas available. Besides, there exist some chants which bear the temper of the Āraṇyaka texts. As literature, the Āraṇyakas and the Upaniṣads continue the tradition of the best metaphysical sections of the Brāhmaṇas. But the difference is that the Āraṇyakas tend for the quest of knowledge and asceticism while the Upaniṣads follow clear doctrines. The *Mahāvrata* rite reinterpreted in the *Aitareya* and *Śāṅkhāyana* serves as a bridge between ritual and knowledge epochs of the Vedic religion. The physical, cosmic, academic, familial and philosophical materials are traced in the Āraṇyakas in addition to the ritual elements. The conception of time in the *Taittirīya Āraṇyaka* is different from other schools of thought. Here, the time is treated as indivisible and eternal.

The Upaniṣads

The Upaniṣads are based on the *jñāna-mārga* while the other Vedic texts follow the *karma-mārga.* The paths of Upaniṣadic knowledge are more scientific than religious. As the magical aspect is presented here in the dialogues, the Upaniṣads may be defined as dialectic on a magical basis.[13]

There are mainly two types of Upaniṣads, prose Upaniṣads and metrical Upaniṣads. The first group includes *Bṛhadāraṇyaka, Chāndogya, Aitareya, Kauṣītakī, Keṇa, Taittirīya* and *Īśāvāsya.* The second group consists of *Kaṭha, Śvetāśvatara, Mahānārāyaṇīya,*

---

12. H. Oldenberg, *The Religion of the Veda,* Berlin, 1890.

13. L. Renou, op. cit., p. 34.

Muṇḍaka, Praśna, Māṇḍūkya and *Maitrāyaṇīya.*

The subject matter of the *Bṛhadāraṇyaka Upaniṣad* spreads over cosmology, eschatology, ethics, etc. The *Chāndogya Upaniṣad* is based on *sāman* mysticism. It contains doctrines attributed to cosmology and metaphysics. The *Aitareya Upaniṣad* depicts the creation of the world by the *ātman,* the triple birth of the *ātman* and its pantheistic essence. We find the reflection of contemporary social customs in the *Kauṣītakī Upaniṣad.* Besides, this book presents the interpretation of dreams, reincarnation, the theory of breath and that of the *ātman.* The *Taittirīya Upaniṣad* deals with semi-mystic relationships in cosmic, astronomical, intellectual, physical and spiritual elements. The *Iśāvāsya Upaniṣad* treats the four stages of life and teaches the inefficacy of works. Its doctrine lays stress on the knowledge of the *ātman* which is present in all essences and overcomes all differences.

The *Kaṭha Upaniṣad* describes the Yama-Naciketā story. It is observed that the story of Naciketā is a derivation from a legend of *Taittirīya Brāhmaṇa* and seems to refer to an initiation into the mysteries. The episode of Rudra-Śiva has been depicted in the *Śvetāśvatara Upaniṣad.* According to Barth,[14] this book is a Śaiva *Bhagavad-Gītā.* It treats psychology and metaphysics in the Sāṁkhya way.

It also treats creation as an evolution. The *Muṇḍaka Upaniṣad* eulogizes the "high knowledge" of the *Brahman,* from which this world has emanated. Prajāpati as the source of creation is mentioned in the *Mahānārāyaṇīya Upaniṣad.* Accordingly the discourses on the theory of creation have been analysed here. The *Praśna Upaniṣad* tends to explain the theory of creation and the existence of life on the earth in a metaphysical way. The *Māṇḍūkya Upaniṣad* belongs to the *Atharvaveda* and establishes the fundamental doctrines of the

---

14. A. Barth, *The Religions of India,* London: Kegan Paul, Trench, Trubner and Company, 1932, also, cf. L. Renou, op. cit., p. 36.

later Vedānta philosophy. The *Maitrāyaṇīya Upaniṣad* deals with material of diverse nature in its sixth Chapter that throws adequate light on the social and religious life of the period. This book presents Sāṁkhya and Yoga in a comprehensive way and mentions the triad of Brahmā, Viṣṇu and Śiva, and their three different *guṇa*s and three different cosmic actions. The book carries a number of lessons delivered by the sage Śakayanya to the prince Bṛhadratha on the origin of life and of consciousness.

Bhattacharji[15] holds that the Upaniṣadic religion and philosophy was strictly exclusive, confined to the intelligentsia, the socially and culturally respected elite. The period of the Upaniṣads was followed by the composition of a set of completely different texts called the Vedāṅgas or the Sūtras which were recognized as human writings.

The Vedāṅgas

The Vedāṅgas have six divisions, namely:

(i) *Śikṣā* (phonetics),

(ii) *Vyākaraṇa* (grammar),

(iii) *Chanda*s (prosody),

(iv) *Jyotiṣa* (astronomy),

(v) *Nirukta* (etymology), and

(vi) *Kalpa* (religious ceremonies)

Again, *Kalpa* is divided into four sections, such as

(i) *Śrauta* (liturgy for collective sacrifice),

(ii) *Gṛhya* (familial, domestic rites),

(iii) *Dharma* (social), and

(iv) *Śulba* (geometry for altars, etc.)

15. S. Bhatacharji, op. cit., p. xxvii.

In addition to these, some ancillary texts like *prāyaścitta* (expiatory), *pariśiṣṭa* (complementary) and *śrāddha* (propitiatory), etc. are also available.

In both nature and temper, the Vedāṅgas are clearly distinguished from the Vedas and other Vedic texts. However, the six Vedāṅgas have a common form, i.e. they are composed in terse, prose formulas with a maximal economy of words. They are all closely connected with the sacrificial rituals. They also signify the inception of certain technical procedures and scientific principles which include grammar, etymology, astronomy, geometry and prosody. The correct procedures for the performance of the sacrifices are laid down in the texts of the Śrauta-Sūtra (liturgy), Śulba-Sūtra (ritual geometry) and Jyotiṣa (astronomy). On the other hand, Śikṣā, Nirukta, Chandas and Vyākaraṇa are used for correct pronunciation, recitation and comprehension of the hymns. The Gṛhya-Sūtras codify the ritualistic behaviour of the Āryan family. The Dharma-Sūtras contain the customs and rules emerged due to the interaction of family and society. The Dharma-Śāstras or the Smṛti literature came to exist due to the genesis and growth of the above Sūtras.

The knowledge of the Vedic Saṁhitās and the Brāhamaṇas of the respective schools are found reflected in the Kalpa-Sūtras. Moreover, a number of sacrifices narrated in the Kalpa--Sūtras are derived from the Brāhmaṇas. In this respect Ram Gopal[16] opines that the Kalpa-Sūtras simply record the rituals and traditions current in their respective schools and don't give any explanation and rationale.

Thus, the vast bulk of the Vedic literature presents the stages of changes in the life of the Āryans through their social, economic, cultural and political development. This record

---

16. Ram Gopal, *India of Vedic Kalpasūtras*, 2nd edn., Delhi: MLBD, 1983, p. 2.

marks the progress of ancient Indian life and thought over 1500 years. It is also the first full-length document of the religious and cultural life of the Indo-Europeans and hence requires serious and critical studies not only on a macroscopic standpoint but also on a microscopic notion. New insights are to be given in interpreting the Vedic hymns to extract the real subject matter from the verses.

2

Facets of Vedic Science

THE magical thoughts and practices of the Vedic seers are latent in the Vedic hymns. Such beliefs and practices of magic reveal the most primitive materialistic ideas of Vedic people. This is because magic has an intimate relationship with scientific exercises. As the Vedic verses are blended with magical thoughts, these contain "pre-scientific" knowledge. Eminent scholars like Levi, Oldenberg, Schroeder[1] and Renou[2] opine that the thoughts contained in the Brāhmaṇas possess scientific temper. Winternitz[3] calls it "priestly pseudo-science." According to Keith[4], the magical thoughts and practices gleaned from the hymns of the *Atharvaveda* and the Brāhmaṇas symbolize the scientific mind of the most primitive man. From the studies of the scholars like Dampier, Needham, Sarton, Singer and Throndike on the history of science, it is known that science has its origin in the noisome jungle of magic and superstition.[5] It has not evolved and developed on an open and healthy prairie of ignorance.

---

1. M. Winternitz, *A History of Indian Literature,* vol. I, tr. S. Ketkar, Calcutta: Calcutta University Press, 1927, p. 187f.
2. L. Renou, *Vedic India,* Calcutta: Sushil Gupta Ltd., 1957, p. 31.
3. M. Winternitz, op. cit., p. 187.
4. A.B. Keith, *The Religion and Philosophy of the Vedas and Upaniṣads,* Harvard University Press, Cambridge, Mass 1925, pp. 380-81.
5. U. Gupta, *Materialism in the Vedas,* New Delhi: Classical Publishing Company, 1987, p. 127.

The materialism prevailed in the Vedic literature has its first expression in the magico-religious phenomena and it surely contains the germs of science. Hence, magic, religion and science were threaded together into a complex of magico-religious phenomena which, arising from the practical necessities of life, was the first attempt of man to understand and interpret nature and quest for causes of natural phenomena. Actually, the Vedic people were great lovers of nature. They were born in the midst of nature, they were brought up in nature and they lived on nature. They meticulously observed the happenings in nature, the changes brought about in nature and thereby experienced with the cosmic law (*ṛta*) that governs the natural phenomena. From such experiences of the most primitive man, the nascent science or pre-science evolved. All the three qualities, magic, religion and science were blended together into one called magico-religious phenomena that arose from the practical necessities of life as mentioned above. There is no clear-cut demarcation between magic, religion and science. Initially, scientific ideas were expressed in terms of metaphysical perceptions. According to Uma Gupta,[6] the belief in the magical efficacy of *mantra* and *yajña* as the means to have control over the courses of nature and even over gods, underlie an attitude of the Vedic Āryans akin to that of science. Comparing magic with science, Frazer[7] marks an equivalance between the two, i.e. both have in common "the general assumption of a succession of events determined by law"; both start as a necessity for man's survival in the struggle for existence; both represent man's reaction to and interpretation of nature and both attempt to discover the causes of natural phenomena and tend to regulate the courses of nature. The distinction between magic and science is that

6. Ibid., p. 128.
7. J.G. Frazer, *The Golden Bough*, Abridged edn., London: Macmillan, 1960.

the former has no theoretical background and it fails to distinguish between causes — imaginary and real — while the latter is capable of doing so through a process of "why and how" with the accumulation of the a posteriori facts of experience in the course of a long period of emergence and development of science. However, it is true that the illusory technique of magic is the real foundation for the genesis and growth of scientific knowledge and techniques. Needham[8] calls magic as "pre-science" or "proto-science" since magic and science were indistinguishable from each other in the most primitive period. Further he points out that the "magico-scientific tradition" in its early phase "crystallized around the nucleus of primitive shamanism," has left its right impression on the people of ancient, medieval and even of modern age.

It is true that science was originated from practical problems. It is, thus, a "problem-solving" mechanism that prevails all over the history of science. The early phases of science is characterized by the absence of theoretical knowledge leading mostly to empirical results. In solving the vital problems of human life, both magic and science come together. Though the earlier phase "magic" was quite imperfect in understanding the nature and natural phenomena, still it was a necessary step towards exploring the correct one. Ostensibly, Sarton remarks that science emerged out of man's quest for solving innumerable problems of his life. The earliest solutions were no doubt mere expedients but were the foundations for improvement. Obviously, perfectibility is achieved on the basis of imperfect ones.

The philosophy, religion, magic and science went together in the Vedic period and this led to the origin of the different branches of science even in that period. According to Sircar's view, the ancient Indian sciences were rich in quality, quantity

---

8. J. Needham, *Science and Civilization in China,* vol. 1, Cambridge, London, 1956, pp. 108-209.

and variety. Those can be equated with those of the ancient Greeks.[9] It is also quite evident from the Vedic germs that the Indian sciences of the period under consideration took their origin from the Vedas themselves. We will now discuss briefly the scientific achievements of the Vedic people in the light of the Vedic elements. Such achievements laid down the foundations of astronomy, cosmology, cosmogony, metallurgy, chemistry, mathematics, biology and medical sciences, etc. All of these branches of Vedic science represent the knowledge *par excellence*[10] that the most primitive ancient Indian culture had.

Astronomy

During the period of the Vedas, Astronomy was in a very elementary stage. The naked-eye astronomers of this time meticulously observed the movements of the sun, the stars and the moon. Weber points out that the observations of the sky was only confined to a few fixed stars, especially to 27 or 28 constellations (*nakṣatra*s) and to various phases of the moon.[11] The Vedic concept of *nakṣatra*s also expresses a lunar Zodiac or a system of lunar mansions.[12] The *Ṛgveda*[13] itself mentions the

9. B.K. Sircar, *Hindu Achievements in Exact Science,* New York: Longmans Green and Co., 1918.

10. B.H. Seal, *Positive Sciences of the Ancient Hindus,* London: Longmans Green and Co., 1915; G. Mukhopadhyaya, *History of Indian Medicine from the Earliest Ages to the Present times,* vols. 1-3, Calcutta University, 1911; P.C. Ray, *History of Hindu Chemistry,* London, 1907; P. Ray (ed.), *History of Chemistry in Ancient and Medieval India,* Calcutta: Indian Chemical Society, 1956; B.K. Sircar, op. cit.; H. Zimmer, *Philosophies of India,* London: Routledge and Kegan Paul, 1951; L. Renou, *Vedic India,* Delhi: Indological Book House, 1971, p. 1.

11. A. Weber, *The History of Indian Literature,* London, 1878, p. 246.

12. Ibid., p. 248; A.A. Macdonell, and A.B. Keith, *Vedic Index of Names and Subjects,* vol. 2, p. 158; A.B. Keith, *Cambridge History of India; Ancient India,* vol. 1, India, 1955, p. 124.

13. *Ṛgveda,* X.85.13; V.59.13; X.64.8.

names of some of the lunar mansions. Besides those mentioned in the *Ṛgveda,* the earlier *Atharvaveda*[14] gives the names of four others while a complete set of 28 lunar mansions is noticed in the later *Atharvaveda.*[15] These 28 lunar mansions are invariably associated with the *Maitrāyaṇī Saṁhitā,*[16] There is mention of 27 *nakṣatras* in *Taittirīya*[17] and *Kāṭhaka*[18] Saṁhitās of the *Yajurveda.*

The Vedic deity Savitṛ stands for the sun which effects the day and night due to its movements in the sky. According to Macdonell,[19] there is no direct reference to the sun passing below the earth. The other probabilities seem to favour the view that the luminary was supposed to return towards the east in such a way that the darkness covers the earth during the return journey.[20] A doubt is expressed regarding what happens to the stars during the day time but no conjecture is made.[21]

Astrology

Astronomical claculation based on the movements and positions of the planetary bodies are the other aspects of the *Yajurveda.* Such calculations in the Vedic period had become a matter of specialized profession called *jyotiṣa-vidyā.* Moreover, a distinct section of the Vedic literature evolved out of it. This is known as Jyotiṣa-Vedāṅga. The *Yajurveda* mentions the

---

14. A.A. Macdonell, and A.B. Keith, *Vedic Index of Names and Subjects,* vol. 1, p. 411.
15. *Atharvaveda,* XIX.7.
16. *Maitrāyaṇī-Saṁhitā,* II.13.20.
17. *Taittirīya-Saṁhitā,* IV.4.10.1-3.
18. *Kāṭhaka-Saṁhitā,* XXXIX.13.
19. A. A. Macdonell, *Vedic Mythology,* Delhi: MLBD, 1981, rpt., p. 10.
20. Ibid.
21. Ṛgveda, I, 24.

nakṣatra-darśa or "star-gazer"[22] and the *gaṇaka* or "calculator."[23] According to Weber,[24] astronomical observations were required for the regulation of the solemn sacrifices — of those offered in the morning and evening, of those at the new and full moon, and finally, of those at the commencement of each of the three seasons (*cāturmāsya*).[25]

In order to fix the proper times for the sacrifices, there was the need of preparing a ritual calendar. This, in turn, made it necessary to record the changes in the celestial phenomena which played an important part in the Vedic system, tradition and culture. In response to this need, the Jyotiṣa-Vedāṅga,[26] attributed to Lagadha, was compiled. The Jyotiṣa deals with the positions of the moon and the sun at the solstices and lays down the methods of calculating the positions of the full and new moons in relation to the cycle of 27 mansions (*nakṣatras*). The divisions of time, the names of the *nakṣatras* and the astrological facts are given in a short and recent work of the *Atharvaveda*, called the *Ātma-Jyotiṣa*.[27]

Calculation of Time

The *Ṛgveda* mentions the year consisting of 360 days split into 12 months of 30 days each.[28] The Vedic year is a solar year but not a lunar year though it is nearly 5¼ days shorter than the scientific solar year.[29] Basing on the sun's course, the length of

22. *Ṛgveda*, I.2; *Vājasaneyī-Saṁhitā*, XXX.10, *Taittirīya-Saṁhitā*, III.4.4.1.
23. *Vājasaneyī-Saṁhitā*, XXX.20.
24. A. Weber, op. cit., p. 30.
25. U. Gupta, op. cit., p. 133.
26. L. Renou, op. cit., p. 49.
27. Ibid.
28. *Ṛgveda*, I.164.11.
29. A.A. Macdonell and A.B. Keith, op. cit., vol. 2, p. 158; A.B. Keith, op. cit., p. 124.

the day was calculated accurately.[30] Uma Gupta[31] points out that even in the *Ṛgveda*[32] attempts have been made to detect the discrepancy in calculation and hence, intercalation seems to exist. However, in the period of the later Saṁhitās, the system was slightly improved with the naming of the 12 months spread over 6 seasons.[33] From the Vedic ritual of *cāturmāsya* or "four-monthly" festival, it is evident that the year was divided into 3 seasons of 4 months each.[34] However, the Brāhmaṇas mention 12 months named after 12 of the *nakṣatras*.[35]

Lagadha in his *Vedāṅga Jyotiṣa* mentions the cycle of 5 years while the *Sūrya Siddhānta* of Varāhamihira takes 4.32 million years as a cycle of *mahāyuga*.[36] This large number of solar years constituting the *mahāyuga* is given to the common factor derived from the revolutions of planets in that period.[37] They are as follows:

Saturn	146564
Jupiter	364220
Mars	2296824
Venus	7022388
Mercury	17937000

---

30. A. Weber, op. cit., p. 30.
31. U. Gupta, op. cit., p. 132.
32. *Ṛgveda,* I.164.
33. *Taittirīya-Saṁhitā,* IV.4.11.1; *Kāṭhaka-Saṁhitā,* XVII.10; XXXV.9; *Maitrāyaṇī-Saṁhitā,* II.8.12; *Vājasaneyī-Saṁhitā,* XIII.25.
34. A. Weber, op. cit., p. 30.
35. U. Gupta, op. cit., p. 132.
36. S.R.N. Murthy, *Vedic View of the Earth,* New Delhi: D.K. Printworld (P) Ltd., 1997, p. 238.
37. G. Thibaut, and S. Dwivedi, *Pañcasiddhānitikā of Varāhamihira,* Varanasi, 1968.

One of the most spectacular results of the Ṛgvedic studies is the evolution of the Hindu calendar. The time reckoned in terms of five components called *pañcāṅgas* of the time, namely, *tithi, vāra, nakṣatra, yoga* and *karaṇa* each with its specific effects, is caluclated ahead of every year and circulated for the service of the people in social, religious, meteorological, agricultural and other purposes. According to Anon,[38] about 50 almanacs are now prevailing in India for the use of the common mass. This Hindu calendar seems to be fully based on the movements of the heavenly bodies. The entire system of formulating time dwells well on the motion of the earth with respect to the movement of the celestial bodies. Therefore, it appears to be scientific.

The Vedic seers recognized 5 types of years, viz. the solar, the lunar, the *sāvana* (360 days), *nakṣatra* and *bārhaspatya.* The last one is formulated on the basis of the movements of the planet Jupiter and probably in vogue from the time of Varāhamihira.[39]

Cosmology

The Vedic seers describe that the Universe is composed of three domains, namely, the earth, the air (atmosphere) and the heaven.[40] The sky is regarded as the space above the earth surrounding the entire universe. The heaven is considered as the abode of light and the dwelling place of the gods. The *Ṛgveda* repeatedly speaks of the earth, the air and the heaven.[41] The vault (*nāka*) of the sky is considered as the limit dividing the visible upper world from the third or invisible world of

38. Anon. (in Kannada), New Delhi: The Calendar Reform Committee, Government of India, 1973, p. 263.
39. S.R.N. Murthy, op. cit., p. 246.
40. A.A. Macdonell, *Vedic Mythology,* Delhi: MLBD, 1981, rpt., p. 8 and fn. 1 and 2.
41. *Ṛgveda,* VIII.10 and 90.

heaven. The *Atharvaveda*[42] mentions that the "vault of the sky" comes between the triad of the earth, the air, the heaven and the world of light, which thus forms a fourth division.

The *Ṛgveda* depicts the glory of a number of deities who wove various materials into a pattern[43] and hence shaped the universe by blasting and smelting.[44] The universe was compared to a house and the *Ṛgveda* alludes to various stages in the construction of this universal house.[45] The *Ṛgveda,* while referring to Viśvakarmā, the great designer of the universe, says that the building material of the universe is nothing but the cosmic dust.[46]

The earth (*pṛthvī*) is regarded as circular, being compared with a wheel.[47] The *Śatapatha Brāhmaṇa* calls it *parimaṇḍala* or circular in shape.

Macdonell marks that the heaven (*div*) also stands for *vyoma,* sky or as pervaded with light, the "luminous space," *rocana* (with or without *divaḥ*). The term *dyāvāpṛthivī* couples both the heaven and the earth.[48] In the *Ṛgveda,* there is no mention of the distance by which the heaven and the earth are separated from each other. But, the *Atharvaveda*[49] says that the two wings of the yellow bird (the sun) flying to heaven are "1000 days" journey apart. The *Aitareya Brāhmaṇa*[50] also holds the same notion saying that "1000 days" journey for a

42. *Atharvaveda,* 4.14; *Vājasaneyī-Saṁhitā,* 17, 67.
43. *Ṛgveda,* X.130.
44. Ibid., X.72.2 (Griffith's tr.), p. 496.
45. H.W. Wallis, *The Cosmology of the Ṛgveda,* p. 17.
46. *Ṛgveda,* X.81 and X.82; I.22.17 and X.72.6 (Griffith's tr.).
47. *Ṛgveda,* X.89.
48. Ibid., II.27.
49. *Atharvaveda,* 10.8.
50. *Aitareya Brāhmaṇa,* 2.17.

horse is the distance of the heaven from the earth. In the *Pañcaviṁśa Brāhmaṇa*,[51] it is said that the heavenly world is as far from this world as 1000 cows standing on each other.

The air or intermediate space (*antarikṣa*) is described as the region of mists and clouds and it is also called *rajas* meaning watery.[52] Three divisions of the atmosphere has been mentioned. These are *uttama*,[53] *parama*[54] and *tṛtīya*.[55] The two lower divisions are within the range of our perception, but the third belongs to Viṣṇu.[56] The atmosphere is often described as sea (*samudra*) as the abode of the celestial waters. The *Ṛgveda*[57] also conceives the lower atmosphere as one situated on the other side of the earth, to account for the course of the sun (*Savitṛ*) during the night.

Cosmogony

It is observed that two theories of the creation of the Universe persist in the Vedic and post-Vedic literature. First one is the water-theory and the second one is the golden-egg theory.

WATER THEORY

This theory states that there was only water in the beginning, and every object of this material world sprang from this water. In the philosophical hymns of the *Atharvaveda*, it is said that the gods originated first from the water. The gods are mostly connected with the element of water.[58] After creation of the

51. *Pañcaviṁśa Brāhmaṇa*, 16.8; 21.1.
52. *Ṛgveda*, I.124; V.85.
53. Ibid., IX.22.
54. Ibid., III.30.
55. Ibid., IX.74; X.45 and 123.
56. Ibid., VII.99 and I.155.
57. Ibid., VI.9; VII.80; V.81.
58. Scherman, *Philosophische Hymnen*, p. 32.

gods, the material world was created by them.[59]

GOLDEN-EGG THEORY

This theory holds that the creation started from a cosmic nucleus, known as Prajāpati,[60] the maker of the universe. This nucleus is often named as *hiraṇyagarbha* or golden-egg, which is considered as the source of the existence of all mundane and heavenly entities because it contained fire (heat) within itself. In a philosophical hymn of the *Ṛgveda,* the sun is regarded as an important agent of creation. Thus, he is called the soul (*ātmā*) of all that moves and stands.[61] In other hymns,[62] the sun is equated with the supreme god (Prajāpati), later known as Brahmā. Ostensibly, the sun is once glorified as a great power of the universe under the name of the "golden embryo," *hiraṇyagarbha.*[63] In the last verse of this hymn, he is called Prajāpati, "lord of the created beings," the name which appeared in the Brāhmaṇas as the chief god.

The *Aitareya Brāhmaṇa* gives a more detailed account of the theory of creation on the same line. It says, "Prajāpati desired to be propagated and multiplied." As Ali[64] explains, Prajāpati exhibited fervour and created the worlds, the earth, the atmosphere and the sky. He (Prajāpati) brooded over the worlds from which Agni (fire), Vāyu (air) and Āditya (sun) were born. Agni sprang form the earth, Vāyu from the atmosphere and Āditya from the sky. Then the luminaries were created by Him. After that, the Vedas took shape. The *Ṛgveda* sprang from Agni, the *Yajurveda* from Vāyu, the

59. A.A. Macdonell, op. cit., p. 14.
60. *Ṛgveda,* X.121.7.
61. Ibid., I.115.
62. Ibid., I.164; X.114.
63. Ibid., X.121.
64. S.M. Ali, *The Geography of the Purāṇas,* New Delhi: People's Publishing House, 1983, 3rd edn., p. 187.

Sāmaveda from Āditya, etc.[65] According to *Kauṣītakī Brāhmaṇa,*[66] heat was produced by Prajāpati when He underwent penance. There evolved Agni, Vāyu, Āditya, Candramā (moon) and Uṣā (dawn). Prajāpati then ordered each of them to undergo penance for His propagation.

The well-known Puruṣa-Sūkta of the *Ṛgveda*[67] accounts for the formation of the world from the body of a giant. It suggests that the disintegration of the primeval body (*ādi-puruṣa*) is the cause of this creation. Consequently, *ādi-puruṣa* is the soul and nucleus of the birth of this material world. It is conceived as an embodiment of the Supreme Spirit. The earth, the sky, the wind, the moon and the sun, and all terrestrial elements were the outcome of the dismemberment of the *puruṣa* — as a part of sacrificial ceremony. The interpretation given in this hymn itself is pantheistic on the ground that *puruṣa* is "all this, both what has become and what shall be." Similar interpretation is marked in the *Atharvaveda*[68] and in the *Muṇḍaka Upaniṣad,*[69] where the "high knowledge" of the *Brahman* has been extolled to explain that the world has emanated from Him. In the *Chāndogya Upaniṣad,*[70] *puruṣa* has also been pantheistically treated to mean Brahma. *Śatapatha Brāhmaṇa* holds that the *puruṣa* is the same as Prajāpati, the creator.

Two hymns of the *Ṛgveda* (X.72, and X.129), however, treat the theory of the origin of the universe in a different manner. Both of these cosmogonic hymns explain the origin of the universe as a kind of evolution of the existent (*sat*) from the non-existent (*asat*). *ṚV* X.72 explains that Brahmaṇaspati forged

65. *Aitareya Brāhmaṇa,* V.32; cf. Keith's *Ṛgvedic Brāhmaṇa,* p. 256.

66. *Kauṣītaki Brāhmaṇa,* VI.1.

67. *Ṛgveda,* X.90.

68. *Atharvaveda,* X.17.

69. *Muṇḍaka Upaniṣad,* 2.1.

70. *Chāndogya Upaniṣad,* 1.7.

together this world like a smith. The existent sprang from the non-existent. Thence in succession evolved the earth, the space, Aditi with Dakṣa; and after Aditi, there born the deities; who brought forward the sun. As Macdonell[71] points out, three stages can be distinguished in this hymn — first the world is produced, then the gods, and finally the sun.

The song of creation, i.e. *ṚV* X.129, 1-4 eulogizes that nothing existed in the beginning, all being void. There was neither being (*sat*) nor non-being (*asat*). Darkness and space enveloped the undifferentiated waters.[72] The space was empty but for a unit which was born by its own nature perhaps due to its inherent heat energy. This heat has been explained by Wilson[73] as austerities, but it may conveniently be taken as a physical action in the process of formation of the universe. Macdonell also explains in the like manner. He says that the one primordial substance (*ekam*) was produced by heat. Then evolved the desire (*kāma*) which is the first and foremost seed of mind (*manas*). Another short hymn of the *Ṛgveda* (*ṚV* X.190) provides a more general theory of evolution of the universe. It says that the cosmic cycle (*ṛta*) was produced from heat (*tapas*); then came night, the ocean, the year; the creator (*dhātā*) brought about the sun and the moon, the heaven and the earth, the air and the ether in succession.

Similar to the *ṚV* X.129, the *Taittirīya Brāhmaṇa*[74] declares that nothing existed in the beginning, neither heaven nor earth nor the atmosphere, which being non-existent resolved to come into being. In the general cosmogonic view of the Brāhamṇas, Prajāpati or the personal Brahmā is taken as the creator, who is not only the father of the gods, the men, and the demons,

---

71. A.A. Macdonell, op. cit., p. 13.
72. *Ṛgveda,* X.82 and X.121; *Atharvaveda,* II.8.
73. H.H Wilson, *Ṛgveda Saṁhitā,* 7 vols., Delhi: Nag Publishers, 1990.
74. *Taittirīya Brāhmaṇa,* 2.2.9.

but also the entire creation. Prajāpati is here an anthropomorphic representation of the desire (*kāma*) that is the first seed spoken of in *R̥V* X.129. The account presented by the *Chāndogya Brāhmaṇa*[75] is that not-being became being; the latter changed into an egg, which after a year resolved into heaven and earth; whatever was produced is the sun, which is *Brahma*.[76]

The *Br̥hadāraṇyaka Upaniṣad*[77] holds that Death concealed everything in the beginning. Water was produced from this first existent "Death" by way of worshipping. Gradually this water was solidified forming the crust of the Earth on which Death toiled and produced fire and light. Then, Āditya (sun) and Vāyu (air) sprang from the same body of Death. Likewise, *Chāndogya Upaniṣad*[78] mentions the non-existent in the beginning. In due course, this non-existent gave birth to existent and then grew. Then, it turned into an egg (*aṇḍā*). The egg, after lying quiescent for one year, broke into two halves, one of silver and the other of gold. The former took the shape of the earth and the latter turned into the heaven; the thick membrane became mountains; the thin changed to clouds; the small veins became rivers; and the fluid became the sea.

Thus, the fundamental ideas of Vedic cosmogony came down to the years, days, hours and the moments with some local or regional variations, though attributed to the mythological and philosophical strains, it adheres to some logical thoughts which are more scientific and also relevant to the present-day context of modern science. Moreover, the most

75. *Chāndogya Brāhmaṇa*, 5.19.

76. *Chāndogya Upaniṣad*, 3.19; Also, A. Weber, *Indische Studien*, vol. I, p. 261.

77. *Br̥hadāraṇyaka Upaniṣad*, I.2.1-3.

78. *Chāndogya Upaniṣad*, VI.32-33.

legendary *avatāra,* Viṣṇu[79] is also mingled with the cosmogonic myth of the Brāhmaṇas describing the evolution of the submerged earth by a boar. This concept belonged to post-Vedic mythology and developed the *avatāra-tattva.*

Space-Time Continuum

The word *antarikṣa* in the Vedas means the space extending outward from the earth. The Vedic bards considered the duo of the earth and sky when they spoke of Dyāvā-Pṛthivī in many *sūktas*. A relation between the earth and the space or sky is prevalent in the Vedic literature from the inception of the Vedic thought. The sky is regarded as the whole space above the earth. This space is the region of air, mists and clouds. It is also called *rajas,*[80] because of its water-vapour content. It is dark and hence called "black."[81] The space has three divisions, viz. *uttama,*[82] *parama*[83] and *tṛtīya.*[84] In space, the waters and *soma* are present. Celestial *agni* is produced here. The third space, which is a "mysterious" one, is not within the perception of human beings. It belongs to Lord Viṣṇu.[85] In general, twofold divisions of space are referred to. One is the terrestrial (*pārthiva*) and the other is heavenly (*divyam* or *divaḥ*) space.[86]

The *Ṛgveda* mentions heaven and earth as "father" and "mother," who never grow old. They are great, broad and

---

79. A.A. Macdonell, *JRAS,* 1895, pp. 178-89.
80. *Ṛgveda,* I.124 and V.85.
81. Ibid., I.35 and VIII.43.
82. Ibid., IX.22.
83. Ibid., III.30.
84. Ibid., IX.74; X.45 and X.123.
85. Ibid., VII.99 and I.155.
86. Ibid., I.62; IV.53.

vast.[87] They have been conceived as divine bowls. The *Taittirīya Upaniṣad,* while discussing the *adhilokam,* speaks of the earth as the earlier form and the sky as the later form, which are connected by space having air and atmosphere.[88] Redefining space, Murthy[89] holds that the space is the medium which accommodates the manifest universe. According to *Taittirīya Upaniṣad,* it is characterized by the quality of sound. It is noted to give rise to the earth through *vāyu, agni* and *āpas.*

TIME

The word *kāla*[90] in Vedic literature generally means time. In the *Artharvaveda,*[91] *kāla,* gives the sense of time as fate. The word is frequent in the Brāhmaṇas,[92] superseding the earlier use of the word *ṛta* (season). The more general division of time is into "past" (*bhūta*), "present" (*bhavat*) and "future" (*bhaviṣyat*).[93] Other divisions of time like *ahan,*[94] *māsa,*[95] *pakṣa,*[96]

---

87. A.A. Macdonell, *A Vedic Reader for Students,* Oxford Press.
88. S.R.N. Murthy, *Vedic View of the Earth,* New Delhi: D.K. Printworld (P) Ltd., 1997, p. 99.
89. Ibid.
90. *Ṛgveda,* X.42.9.
91. *Atharvaveda,* XIX.53.54.
92. *Śatapatha Brāhmaṇa,* I.7.3.3; II.4.2.4; III.8.3.36; VII.2.2.21; etc.
93. *Sāṅkhāyana Āraṇyaka,* VIII.20.
94. *Ṛgveda,* IV.16.19; VIII.26.3; cf. *Atharvaveda,* X.7.42.
95. *Ṛgveda,* I.25.8; IV.18.4; V.45.7; VII.91.2; etc.; *Atharvaveda,* VIII.10.19; *Taittirīya-Saṁhitā,* V.5.2.2; *Pañcaviṁśa-Brāhmaṇa,* IV.4.1; *Taittirīya-Brāhmaṇa,* I.4.9.1.
96. *Śatapatha Brāhmaṇa,* V.4.5.21; *Bṛhadāraṇyaka Upaniṣad,* I.1.1; II.8.9; etc.

saṁvatsara[97] or *parivatsara,*[98] *muhūrtta*[99] and a larger time interval *yuga*[100] are used in the Vedic literature. *Ahan* denotes a day; *māsa,* the month; *pakṣa,* half a month; *saṁvatsara* or *parivatsara,* the year; *muhūrtta,* an hour of 48 minutes; and *yuga,* the age. In the *Ṛgveda,*[101] the sense of "moment" is used for *muhūrtta.* The sense of "moment" is also common in the Brāhmaṇas.[102] We come across the words *doṣā* (evening), *nakta* (night), *nimruc* (sunset), *prabudh* (sunrise), *prātar* (early morning), *mādhyaṁdina* (midday), *mahāhna* (afternoon), *mahārātra* (advanced night), *rātri* (night), *vastu* (early morning), *pūrvāhna* (forenoon), *paurṇamāsi* (full moon night), *prapitva* (close of day), *saṁgava* (forenoon), *saṁdhi* (twilight), *sāyaṁ* (evening), *svasara* (morning), *hyas* (yesterday), *hāyana* (year) and *sīnivāli* (new moon day) in the Vedic literature in connection with time of various sorts.[103] Besides these, the names of different seasons like *nidāgha* (summer),[104] *varṣā* (rainy season),[105] *śarada* (autumn),[106] and *himā* (winter)[107] are found mentioned. The cold

97. *Ṛgveda,* I.110.4; I.140.2; I.161.13; VII.103.1,7; etc. *Atharvaveda,* I.35.4; II.6.1; III.10.2; IV.35.4; VI.53.3; etc.
98. *Ṛgveda,* X.62.2; *Taittirīya Brāhmaṇa,* I.5.5.6.
99. *Taittirīya Brāhmaṇa,* III.10.1.1; III.9.7; III.12.9.6; *Śatapatha Brāhmaṇa,* X.4.2.18, 25, 27; X.4.3.20; XII.3.2.5; X.4.4.4; etc.
100. *Ṛgveda,* I.139.8; III.26.3; VI.8.5; VI.15.8; VI.36.5; IX.94.12.
101. Ibid., III.33.5; III.53.8.
102 A.A. Macdonell, and A.B. Keith, *Vedic Index of Names and Subjects,* vol. II, MLBD, Delhi, 1995, rpt., p. 169.
103. Ibid., vols. I & II; cf. English Index of vol. II, pp. 589-90.
104. *Śatapatha Brāhmaṇa,* XIII.8.1.4.
105. *Atharvaveda,* VI.55.2; *Taittirīya-Saṁhitā,* I.6.2.3; II.6.1.1; V.6.10.1; *Vājasaneyī-Saṁhitā,* X.12; etc.
106. *Ṛgveda,* VII.101.6; X.161.2; *Atharvaveda,* I.35.1; VIII.2.2; VIII.5.21.
107. *Ṛgveda,* I.64.14; II.33.2; V.54.15; VI.48.8; *Atharvaveda,* II.28.4; XII.2.28; *Taittirīya-Saṁhita,* I.6.6.3; *Vājasaneyī-Saṁhitā,* II.27.

weather is denoted by the word *hima*.[108] The name of the season *hemanta*[109] is also traced.

A month of 30 days is established by the conclusive evidence of numerous passages in which the year is given 12 months and 360 days.[110] This month is known from the earliest records, being both referred to directly and alluded to.[111] It is the regular month of the Brāhmaṇas,[112] and must be regarded as the month which the Vedic Indians recognized. The Brāhmaṇa literature does not mention any other month. It is only in the *sūtras*[113] that months of different length occur. The solar year of 366 days is first known to *Jyotiṣa*[114] and to Garga.[115] A number of references to the year having 12 or 13 months are found in the Vedic texts.[116] Macdonell and Keith point out that the names of the months are, curiously enough, not at all ancient.[117] The *Yajurveda*, while dealing with the building of

108. *Ṛgveda*, I.116.8; I.119.6; VIII.32.26; etc.; *Atharvaveda*, VII.18.2; XIII.1.46.

109. *Ṛgveda*, X.161.4; *Atharvaveda*, VI.55.2; VIII.2.22; XII.1.36; and also in later texts.

110. A.A. Macdonell, and A.B. Keith, *Vedic Index of Names and Subjects*, vol. II, p. 158.

111. *Ṛgveda*, II.14.48; X.189.3; X.190.2; *Atharvaveda*, IV.35.4; X.7.6; X.8.23; XIII.3.8; etc.

112. *Aitareya Brāhmaṇa*, IV.12; *Kauṣītakī Brāhmaṇa*, III.2. cf. Macdonell & Keith, op. cit., vol. II, p. 159; Weber, *Naxatra*, 2.288; Thibaut, *Astronomic, Astrologic* and *Mathematik*, p. 8.

113. Macdonell & Keith, op. cit., p. 159.

114. *Jyotiṣa*, verse 28.

115. Cited in the commentary on the *Jyotiṣa* 10.

116. *Taittirīya-Saṁhitā*, V.6.7.1; *Kāṭhaka-Saṁhitā*, XXI.5; XXXIV.9; *Maitrāyaṇi-Saṁhitā*, I.10.8; *Kauṣītakī-Brāhmaṇa*, V.8; *Kauṣītakī-Upaniṣad*, I.6; *Śatapatha Brāhmaṇa*, II.2.3.27; III.6.4.24; V.4.5.23; VII.2.3.9; etc.; *Jaiminīya Upaniṣad Brāhmaṇa*, I.10.6.

117. Macdonell & Keith, op. cit., vol. II, p. 161.

the fire-altar, gives the names of the months in their clearest form.[118]

The concept of space and time is significant in Astronomy and Astrology. Pandurangi[119] has discussed the relative importance of space and time in Indian philosophy. Space and time are taken as separate entities by the Nyāya-Vaiśeṣika school. Both are eternal and all-pervasive. They are co-extensive with the entire matter, all events and actions. In Pūrva-Mimāṁsā, space is used in the sense of a substance that is an evolute of sound. The term *ākāśa* is not used in the sense of space in both these systems.

There are two views in Sāṁkhya about space and time. According to one view, there is neither space nor time as separate entity or they do not exist as aspects of matter. Space, Time and Matter all have sprung from one cosmic and primordial source called *prakṛti*. The other view predicts two levels of space and time, viz. *akhaṇḍa* and *sakhaṇḍa*. The *akhaṇḍa* is one continuous block of time and space while the *sakhaṇḍa* is the divisible space and time. The first represents the nature of *prakṛti* while the second symbolizes *ākāśa* under certain conditions.[120] The first view is similar to the Advaitic notion. The Sāṁkhya school considers that space and time are separate entities which originated from the primordial matter. In the thoughts of Dvaita and Viśiṣṭādvaita schools, the primordial matter has been taken as the basic category of being. But, the first school accepts space as a separate entity from which the time is derived, while the second holds the just opposite notion. The concept of *akhaṇḍakāla* is not accepted by Dvaita School. As illustrated by Murthy, each moment is all-pervasive but

118. Ibid., p. 161 and fn. 34.

119. K.T. Pandurangi, "The Concept of space and time in Indian philosophy" in *Scientific Heritage of India*, Bangalore: Mythic Society, 1988, pp. 244-47.

120. S.R.N. Murthy, op. cit., p. 100.

not eternal. Every moment perishes to make room for the next moment. Time is envisaged as a close associate of continuous evolution of matter and is known intuitively.[121] Explaining the meaning of the word *avidyā* in the light of the thoughts of the Advaita School, it can be said that both space and time are not real as *avidyā* and its effects are not real. The space is the product of *Brahman,* which is taken to be real and the most fundamental thing in Indian philosophy. Ostensibly, the reflection of *Brahman* is the space.

Modern science defines space as a medium for light to propagate and that bends near celestial objects.[122] The concept of space as gleaned from the theory of relativity of Einstein, it is four-demensional (x, y, z, t) where time has been taken as one of the dimensions, i.e. space is dependent on time. Hence, the space-time continuum is the most fundamental concept that holds the modern scientific thoughts and explanations. This is the object that generates and destroys the material or visible universe.

THE COSMIC ORDER R̥TA

The word *r̥ta* stands for the cosmic order or Law prevailing in nature.[123] Keith points out that the word *r̥ta* has been used in a "triple sense" — the physical order of the universe, the religious order of the sacrificial rites and the moral order of right behaviour.[124] The first sense goes in favour of the creation and its existence. It is also the fundamental basis of a materialistic religion and a naturalistic ethic.[125]

---

121. Ibid.
122. S.W. Hawking, *A Brief History of Time,* New York: Bantam, 1994, p. 198.
123. A.A. Macdonell, op. cit., p. 11.
124. A.B. Keith, *The Religion and Philosophy of the Vedas and Upaniṣads,* Harvard Oriental Series, HUP, Cambridge, Mass, 1925, p. 83.
125. U. Gupta, op. cit., p. 158.

The concept of *ṛta* in the Veda is similar to the thought of the Greek pantheon. The two thoughts are very close to each other and are also scientific in nature. Cornford[126] has established the fact that the Greek Materialism or "the scientific tradition" had its foundation in the Moira or the inviolable law. Firrington holds that a pronounced "secular note" in the *Iliad*, where Homer "emancipated man from the tyranny of the gods," formed the foundation of Greek Scientific thought.[127] An eminent philosopher of the world, Dr. S. Radhakrishnan also admitted that *ṛta* "originally" meant a physical order.[128] According to Hopkins,[129] *ṛta* has also dynamic implications. *Ṛta* is the cosmic law governing this universe. *Ṛta* is the permanent reality which remains unchanged in all the welter of mutations. It is the universal law of gravitation that holds the sun, the stars, the moon, the earth and all other material objects together in equilibrium. The force of attraction between any two material bodies in this universe is the gravitational force that holds them together. Kepler[130] gave his famous laws of planetary motion in the years 1605 and 1619. In 1605, he published his first two laws in the book *New Astronomy* and his third law was published in 1619 in the book *World Harmony*. Newton interpreted the Kepler's laws as a consequence of his universal law of gravitation.[131] His treatise

---

126. F.M. Cornford, *From Religion to Philosophy*, London: Edwin Arnold and Co., 1912.

127. B. Farrington, *Science in Antiquity*, London: Oxford, 1947, pp. 33-40.

128. S. Radhakrishnan, *Indian Philosophy*, vol. 1, New York: Macmillan, 1951, p. 79.

129. E.W. Hopkins, *The Religions of India*, London: Grinn and Co., 1895.

130. K. Samal, et al., *Higher Secondary Physics*, vol. 1, Cuttack: Vidyapuri, 1992, pp. 266-67.

131. Ibid.

principia is an immortal gift to posterity. The Vedic seers accepted the universe as a law-governed system like the scientists of later years. Even *ṛta* in the *Ṛgveda* has been taken as one superior to the will of the gods.[132] The *Ṛgveda* depicts the gods as being born of *ṛta* and following the ordinances of *ṛta*. Accordingly, it says that the Maruts come from a distance, from the seat of order.[133] Agni sprung from the Law,[134] and is also addressed as "Child of Order."[135] Soma is born with Law and hath waxen mighty by the Law.[136] The Martus are born spotless after sacred Law.[137] Mitra and Varuṇa proclaim loudly the Holy Law.[138] Indra says that he surpasses everything that exists in greatness, and "the Holy Law's commandments make me mighty."[139] Ostensibly, *ṛta* is an independent authority,[140] and also superior to gods. *Ṛta* is that which regulates the course of the universe. It is the universal gravitational law that sustains the material world.

Mathematics

Vedic Mathematics has been well treated by His Holiness Jagadguru Śaṅkarācārya Śrī Bhāratī Kṛṣṇa Tīrtha of Govardhana Maṭha, Purī (1884-1960). This great work enlightens the sixteen simple mathematical formulae given in the Vedas. The author has compiled the following sixteen *sūtras* from the stray references in the text of the Vedas:

---

132. E.W. Hopkins, op. cit.
133. *Ṛgveda*, IV.21.3.
134. Ibid., I.36.19.
135. Ibid., III.20.2.
136. Ibid., IX.108.8.
137. Ibid., V.61.14.
138. Ibid., I.151.4.
139. Ibid., VIII.89.4.
140. A.B. Keith, op. cit., p. 84.

Sūtras

1. *Ekādhikena Pūrveṇa* with a corollary.
2. *Nikhilaṁ Navataścaramaṁ Daśataḥ.*
3. *Ūrdhva-tiryagbhyāṁ.*
4. *Parāvartya yojayet.*
5. *Śūnyaṁ Sāmyasamuccaye.*
6. *(Ānurūpye) Śūnyamanyat.*
7. *Saṅkalana-Vyavakalanābhyām* with a corollary.
8. *Pūrṇāpūrṇābhyām.*
9. *Calana-Kalanābhyām.*
10. *Yāvadūnam.*
11. *Vyaṣṭisamaṣṭiḥ.*
12. *Śeṣāṇyaṅkena Carameṇa.*
13. *Sopāntyadvayamantyam.*
14. *Ekanyūnena Pūrveṇa.*
15. *Guṇitasamuccayaḥ.*
16. *Guṇakasamuccyaḥ.*

Besides, there are also thirteen sub-*sūtras* or corollaries, which have been derived by the author of *Vedic Mathematics.*[141] These Vedic mathematical formulae can be applied to solve concretely the complicated mathematical problems.

There was a highly developed numerical system from the early Vedic period.[142] Vedic numerical system is based on *Daśan* or ten (10). Macdonell and Keith opine that the numerical

---

141. *Vedic Mathematics*, Delhi: MLBD, rpt., 1998.

142. *Ṛgveda*, III.6.15; IV.32.18; VIII.1.15; VIII.2.41; VIII.21.18; *Atharvaveda*, VII.2.22; VII.8.7; X.8.24.

system was developed unprecedently in the most ancient times.[143] Probably, the Vedic Indians had the knowledge of signs of numerals.[144] Arithmetical computations involving addition, subtraction, multiplication and division bear unique features in the realm of Vedic *sūtras*. Some fractions like *ardha, pāda, śapha* and *kalā*, denoting ½, ¼, $^1/_8$ and $^1/_{16}$ respectively, were known in the Vedic period.[145] The *Ṛgveda*[146] mentions the word *tripād* meaning ¾.

Some methods were devised by the Vedic people to fix the units of measurement of length, mass and weight, etc. The Vedic Āryans were exchanging their commodities on the principle of barter system. In such a system, the cow was employed as a unit of value.[147] The *niṣka*, originally a gold ornament,[148] at a later time[149] became a unit of value. In the period of the later Saṁhitās, the *māna* became a measure of weight equivalent to the *kṛṣṇala* (the berry), which was a unit of weight.[150] One hundred *kṛṣṇala*s were equivalent to a piece of gold in weight called *śatamāna*, which generates the idea of a currency. Scholars are of the opinion that the *niṣka* and the cow continued to prevail as the units of value for a longer period.[151]

143. *Vedic Index*, vol. I, pp. 342-44.
144. *Ṛgveda*, X.62.7.
145. *Vedic Index*, vol. I, pp. 342-44.
146. *Ṛgveda*, X.90.4.
147. Ibid., IV.24.10.
148. Ibid., V.19.3.
149. Ibid., I.126.2.
150. U. Gupta, *Materialism in the Vedas*, New Delhi: Classical Publishing Company, 1987, p. 136.
151. V.M. Apte, "Religion and Philosophy," The *Vedic Age*, ed. R.C. Majumdar, and A.D. Pusalkar, George Allen and Unwin, London, 1952, pp. 360-83 and 438-48; A.B. Keith, *Cambridge History of India*, vol. I, India, 1955, p. 124.

The Vedic way of factorization, finding the highest common factor (HCF), solving simple equations, complex mergers, simultaneous simple equations, quadratic equations, cubic equations, bi-quadratic equations, multiple simultaneous equations, simultaneous quadratic equations and finding the partial fractions is of immense use in mathematics. Solving differential equations and doing integration by using partial fractions are the other stricking features of *Vedic Mathematics.* The Vedic numerical code, formation of decimals, recurring decimals, sum and difference of squares, elementary squaring, cubing, etc. finding square-roots and cube-roots, employment of Pythagoras' theorem, Apollonius theorem, etc. and the treatment of conic sections form the basis of our arithmetic and geometry. Thus, the complex problems of arithmetic, geometry and calculus can be solved by the Vedic formulae in a short time and in short space.

Chemistry

The knowledge of Vedic people in chemistry is evident from the processes of smelting,[152] tanning of leather and hides.[153] The chemical process of combustion is understood from the knowledge of smelting. The use of slings, strings, reins and whips by the Vedic people also go in favour of their knowledge in making these things by chemical processes.[154] The food, drink and clothing of Vedic Āryans also represent their knowledge in chemistry. They were preparing drinks and food like *soma,*[155] *surā*[156] and curds by the process of fermentation. The word

152. U. Gupta, op. cit., p. 135.
153. *Ṛgveda,* VIII.5.38.
154. Ibid., I.121.9; VI.46.14; VI.47.26; VI.53.9; VI.75.11.
155. *Ṛgveda,* IX.
156. Ibid., I.116.7; X.131.4, 5; cf. *Atharvaveda,* IV.34.6; X.6.5; *Taittirīya-Saṁhita,* I.3.3.2; *Śatapatha Brāhmana,* XII.7.3.8.

vastra[157] and *vāsas*[158] are employed in the Veda for dress and clothing. Clothes made of silk and wool were also used by the Vedic people. The word *avi*[159] means wool and *tārpya*[160] stands for silk garment. Later, Saṁhitās, Brāhmaṇas and Sūtras also mention silk garments.[161] Vedic people also knew the art of dyeing. This is evident from the garments of different colours like red, purple, brown,[162] etc. Macdonell and Keith view that the word *varṇa* (colour) is common in the *Ṛgveda*[163] and later.[164] A large number of colours are mentioned in Vedic literature, but there is no clear mention of the method/methods by which these colours were distinguished by the Vedic Āryans. The colours like *kṛṣṇa* (black), *śukla* (white), *śveta* (white), *śyenī* (black), *śyāma* (dark-grey), *nīla* (dark-blue), *hāritā* or *harit* (yellow), *pīta* as well as *pāṇḍu* (yellow), *babhru* (brown), *kapila* (monkey-coloured), *piṅgala* (tawny), *mahārājana* (saffron), *rudhira* and *lohita* (red), *aruṇa* (ruddy) and *aruṇa-piśaṅga* (reddish-brown) are traced in the Vedic literature.[165] The *Bṛhadāraṇyaka Upaniṣad* mentions a garment of saffron colour.[166]

In the *Atharvaveda*, there is a separate class of hymns

157. *Ṛgveda*, I.26.1; 134.4; III.39.2; V.29.15.
158. Ibid., I.34.1; I.115.4; I.162.16; VIII.3.24; X.26.6; X.102.2; *Taittirīya-Saṁhitā*, VI.1.9.7; VI.11.I.2; *Vājasaneyī-Saṁhitā*, II.32; XX..40; *Aitareya Brāhmaṇa*, I.3.
159. *Atharvaveda*, V.8.4; *Ṛgveda*, VIII.34.3; 66.8.
160. *Atharvaveda*, XVIII.4.31.
161. A.A. Macdonell, and A.B. Keith, *Vedic Index of Names and Subjects*, vol. I, Delhi: MLBD, 1995, rpt., p. 308.
162. U. Gupta, op. cit., p. 135.
163. *Ṛgveda*, I.73.7; I.96.5; I.123.2; IV.5.13; IX.97.15; IX.104.4; IX.105.1; X.3.3, etc.
164. *Atharvaveda*, I.22.1, 2; I.23.2; XI.8.16; *Vājasaneyī-Saṁhitā*, IV.2.26, etc.
165. *Vedic Index of Names and Subjects*, vol. II, Delhi: MLBD, 1995, rpt., pp. 246-47.
166. *Bṛhadāraṇyaka Upaniṣad*, II.3.6.

classified under the heading *āyuṣyāni* for the prolongation of life and presentation of youth and health. According to the opinion of Ray,[167] the science of chemistry was born in India from the Atharvanic alchemical notion of *āyuṣyāni* and came to be known later as *rasāyana*.

In the most primitive society, metallurgy was in use. The antiquity of copper (*ayas*) and iron (*kṛṣṇāyas*) was quite evident from the studies of ancient science. Lallanji[168] examined the Vedic evidence for the use of iron. According to his study, first use of iron is to be connected with painted grey ware at Hastinapur, etc. in India. The earliest use of iron is found in the Gangetic Valley and associated with the Āryans.

Typical features of metallurgy are discovered from the use of copper and bronze in anceint India. Bhardwaj[169] has discussed the problem of advent of copper in India. He has examined the composition of copper and copper-based alloys in Haṛappan sites and concluded that copper and bronze were in common use in ancient India along with some other metals. The word *śyāmam* denotes copper.

In the Vedic literature, there is mention of *ikṣu* (the plant of sugar cane). This word is unique to the Vedic literature only. Lallanji,[170] while drawing the antiquity of sugar-making in ancient India, says that the *ikṣu*-plant was presumably indigenous to India.

The knowledge of glass and glass-manufacturing is also evident from the Vedic literature. Most probably, glass (*kāca*)

---

167. P.C. Ray, *History of Hindu Chemistry*, London, 1907, pp. 37-38.
168. Lallanji Gopal, "Antiquity of Iron in India," *JAHRS* 28 (1-2), 1962-63, pp. 39-54.
169. H.C. Bhardwaj, "Problem of Advent of Copper in India", *IJHS* 5(2), November 1970, pp. 229-37.
170. Lallanji Gopal, "Sugar-making in Ancient India", *JESHO* 7, 1964, pp. 57-62.

came to be in application first in India in the first quarter of first millenium BCE.[171] *Śatapatha Brāhmaṇa*[172] mentions *kāca*. It describes that 101 *kācas* are studded into a *maṇi* on the tail of a horse. According to L. Gopal,[173] *kāca* is a general term for a variety of materials used for ornamental purposes. Eggeling[174] views that the word *kāca* in the *Śatapatha Brāhmaṇa* denotes the beads made of glass (pearls). A comprehensive account of Vedic metallurgy is detailed as under.

Metallurgy

Vedic people knew the art of designing vessels, tools and armours including the arrow heads from metals. Such things were made by metal-smiths.[175] The *Ṛgveda*[176] refers to the process of smelting of metal as already mentioned above. The metallic objects used by the Vedic people include the metallic tip of the arrow[177] made of iron,[178] kettles,[179] some cups,[180] bowls or pans of iron[181] and a heater or oven.[182]

---

171. G. Vijay, "Some Aspects of Glass-manufacturing in Ancient India", *IJHS* 5(2), November 1970, pp. 281-308.
172. *Śatapatha Brāhmaṇa*, XIII.2.6.8.
173. R.N. Dandekar, (ed.), *Vedic Bibliography*, vol. III, BORI, Poona, 1973, p. 738.
174. Ibid.
175. S. Piggot, *Prehistoric India*, Penguin, 1961, p. 269.
176. *Ṛgveda*, IV.2.17; IX.112.2.
177. Ibid., VI.75.15.
178. Macdonell and Keith, *Vedic Index*, vol. II, p. 32; R.T.H. Griffith (tr.), *The Hymns of the Ṛgveda*, 2 vols., 2nd edn., E.J. Lazarus and Co., Benares, 1896-97.
179. *Ṛgveda*, V.30.15.
180. Ibid., IX.1.2.
181. *Atharvaveda*, VII.10.22; *Maitrāyaṇī-Saṁhitā*, IV.2.13.
182. *Vājasaneyī-Saṁhitā*, XXX.14; *Taittirīya Brāhmaṇa*, III.4.10.1.

The word *ayas* in the *Ṛgveda* commonly denotes the name of metal in addition to gold. Gupta[183] observes that metals other than gold and silver are classified into two categories, viz. the *śyāma ayas* or iron and the *lohita ayas* or copper or bronze in the passages of the *Yajurveda* and the *Atharvaveda.*[184] In the *Yajurveda,* there is, on the other hand, a list of six metals, namely, gold, iron, copper, lead, tin and bronze.[185] As Professor Apte[186] views, the metal-smith of the Vedic period smelted ores in the furnace using the wing of a bird as a bellow to fan the flames. The picture of a smithy can be guessed from the Ṛgvedic hymn[187] IX, 112.2. It is worthy to record here that the most alarming fire-cult of the Vedas bears ample testimony for the process of combustion involved in smelting and metal-working.

Physics

Physics or the science of matter and energy unfolded with the evolution of philosophy of the origin of existent from non-existent. According to the opinion of Lange,[188] meterialism is not only as old as philosophy but the latter itself started its career as the former. Ostensibly, materialism is the odest known philosophy. Advancing this notion further, Russell[189] identifies this earliest philosophy with science. Matter, Energy

---

183. U. Gupta, op. cit., p. 133.
184. *Atharvaveda,* XI.3.7; IX.5.4. *Maitrāyaṇī-Saṁhitā,* IV.2.9.
185. *Vājasaneyī-Saṁhita,* XVIII.13; Cf. *Vedic Index,* vol. I, p. 411.
186. V.M. Apte, *Religion and Philosophy, the Vedic Age,* ed. R.C. Majumdar, and A.D. Pusalkar, George Allen and Unwin, London, 1952, p. 397; V.G. Childe, *What Happened in History,* Penguin, 1964.
187. *Ṛgveda,* IX.112.2.
188. F.A. Lauge, *The History of Materialism,* tr. E.C. Thomas, Routledge and Kegan Paul, London, 1957.
189. B. Russell, *A History of Western Philosophy,* George, Allen and Unwin, London, 1954, p. 21.

and Life are closely linked with one another. All ideas and practices of mankind have had a long history of evolution stretching far back to the emergence of man as a new species. Man is the supreme of all creations. He has the ability of thinking, experiencing and reasoning. In this context, one can say that materialism is out and out of a human experience in his surrounding. Evidently, philosophy is born as a man's attempt to have rational explanation of the universe around him and of himself as a part of the universe out of which he had originated and where he has to live, act and think.

The quest for the origin of the universe by the Vedic poets arrives at some abstract theories built upon mythological accounts. The Vedic theory of the origin of the universe is best explained by Puruṣa-Sūkta, the idea of *hiraṇyagarbha* and the philosophy of *sat* from *asat*. According to the well-known, Puruṣa-Sūkta of the *R̥gveda*,[190] everything sprang from the body of a giant (*puruṣa*). In the cosmological speculation of the *R̥gveda*, the sun (*hiraṇyagarbha*) has been regarded as an important agent of creation.[191] Besides, there are two other cosmogonic hymns in the *R̥gveda*,[192] which explain the origin of the Universe as a kind of evolution of the existent (*sat*) from the non-existent (*asat*).

The central idea of various theories of the creation as depicted in the Vedic and post-Vedic literature appears to be:

(i) the existence of water in the beginning, and

(ii) the formation of a cosmic nucleus (Prajāpati), who created the material world, i.e. ether, air, fire, water and the earth and then life. This cosmic nucleus is often

---

190. *R̥gveda*, X.90.

191. Ibid., X.121.

192. Ibid., X.72; X.129.

named as *hiraṇyagarbha* or Golden Egg, which is considered as the source of all matter and energy. All discrete substances of the Universe were aggregated here in the Golden Egg with enormous energies. The primeval body of this cosmic nucleus was disintegrated by the *supreme spirit* (the desire for creation). This happened with a great explosion producing sound of a very high pitch. *Chāndogya Upaniṣad*[193] also says that the universe came to exist after dismemberment of the cosmic egg. This explosion that brought about the creation is nothing but the Indra-Vṛtra collision mentioned in the Veda. According to modern scientific theory, the creation started from the "Big-Bang," the great explosion. This is the "Big-Bang" theory of the creation of the universe. So, Vedic speculations are based upon scientific reasoning.

Further, references of cosmic dust as the building material of the Universe occur in certain hymns of the *Ṛgveda*[194] which are addressed to Viśvakarmā who has designed this universe by blasting and smelting.[195]

The symbolic representation of the nucleus from which the universe was created and which undoubtedly has its origin in the Vedas was adopted by many nations. If we interpret the epithet *haima* or *hiraṇya* (golden) as "bright and reddish yellow" and the words "water" as "water-vapour," i.e. in its gaseous state, we can mark that the story of the Golden Egg adheres to the notion of a "hot, incandescent nebula" which is the starting point of modern cosmological theories. The epithet *haima* or *hiraṇya* (golden) is latent in all the Purāṇas.[196]

---

193. *Chāndogya Upaniṣad*, VI.32.3.

194. *Ṛgveda*, X.81; X.82.

195. *Ṛgveda*, X.72.2 (Griffith's tr.), p. 496.

196. S.M. Ali, *The Geography of the Purāṇas*, New Delhi: People's Publishing House, 3rd edn., 1983, p. 192.

The laws of gravitation found a place in the earliest theory of the creation of the universe formulated by Kant, the great Prussian philosopher (1755). According to Kant, initially, there was cold motionless cloud of matter that became in due course a vast nebula, spinning so rapidly that rings of matter were successively thrown off its equator by centrifugal action, while the residual central mass remained as the sun. Each ring was supposed to have condensed as a planet, which by a small-scale repetition of the same process threw off satellites; ultimately in this way, the entire solar system was formed. Though Kant's hypothesis is dynamically unsound, still it is important in the sense that the sepculation hint at the bottom of the existence of Cosmic nucleus (the Golden Egg) that contained the matter and energy (heat). Moreover, Kant's hypothesis is the forerunner of the very similar and justly famous nebular hypothesis of Laplace (1796) on which modern speculations on the theory of the creation of the universe rest.[197]

The philosophy of the Purāṇas revolves around the three main principles of existence, i.e. creation, preservation and dissolution, and which in turn give the notion of the cosmic cycle, i.e. the incidental dissolution of the material world at the end of definite periods (*kalpa*s of the Purāṇas) and its recreation thereafter. This is quite similar to Einstein's theory of mass transforming to energy and vice versa. The matter can be annihilated to become energy by the famous mass-energy relation of Einstein, which is $E = mc^2$ where, m is the mass, E is the energy equivalent of mass and c is the speed of light. This mass-energy transformation principle is the outcome of Einstein's special theory of Relativity.[198]

According to the Vedic bards, the entire universe is composed of the earth (*pṛthvī*), the air (*vāyu*), the water (*āp*),

---

197. Ibid.

198. S. Biswal, *Basic Physics*, vol. II, Delhi: Emkay Publications, 2000, p. 215.

the fire (*agni*) and the *antarikṣa* (the intermediate space).[199] The whole space above the earth is regarded as the sky.[200] The Cosmic order *ṛta* governs the entire universe. According to Murthy,[201] *ṛta* is the Law of the universe or the great cosmic order by which the whole of the manifest universe is working. This, in other words, appears to be the Law of Gravitation in simple terms. Varuṇa is regarded as the Lord of this Law.[202] Many years after our scientists became successful in recognizing the cycle caused due to the law of universal gravitation.

The concept of Varuṇa in the *Ṛgveda*[203] is essentially the universal force that has set an order. This cosmic order can only be the Law of Gravitation. The relative motion of celestial bodies with respect to one another suggests the General Theory of Relativity. Evidently, the paths of celestial bodies have been known as geodesics as a consequence of space-time continuum. Thus, the universal order forming the path of the sun and the moon is the gravitational attraction between them. The deity Varuṇa has been projected as controller of the universe. According to Griffiths, the Sun, the Earth, the Moon, the air, the water and the wind all are held in their positions and remain in equilibrium by gravitation.[204] The earth is described then as being present in the middle of the oceans (sedimentary rocks) and as one having magical movements. She is the one enveloped by the sky or space and causing the force of gravitational field. Varuṇa's power of controlling the waters' flow and ordering the motion of the sun, moon and

199. A.A. Macdonell, *Vedic Mythology*, Delhi: MLBD, rpt., 1981, pp. 8-9.

200. *Ṛgveda*, VIII.10.90.

201. S.R.N. Murthy, *Vedic View of the Earth*, New Delhi: D.K. Printworld (P) Ltd. 1997, p. 81

202. R.T.H. Griffiths, *The Hymns of the Ṛgveda*, New Delhi: MLBD, 1996. Cf. *Ṛgveda*, I.25.8; I.25.9.

203. *Ṛgveda*, V.85.1-6; VII.86, 5-6; VII.87.1; VIII.41.7.

204. *Ṛgveda*, X.85.1 (Griffiths' tr.).

the stars suggests that it is nothing but the force of gravitation known to modern science. Hence, the force of gravitation existing between massive bodies as proposed and formulated by Newton was known to the Vedic sages.

The change in the concept of the disc-like earth to spherical earth took place in Europe about fifth-sixth century BCE during the period of pythagoras. Even then, it was not discovered how the spherical earth could exist in space unsupported until Newton explained it by his "Theory of Gravitation" in CE 1686. But, the concept of global earth was known to the Ṛgvedic seers who carried prolonged observations on the movement of celestial bodies. The concept of global earth has been buried in the vast literature starting from the *Vedāṅga Jyotiṣa* of Lagadha to the time of Varāhamihira. The five elements of the global earth, i.e. the sky, air, fire, water and clay as proposed by Aristotle appear to be direct derivatives of the *Taittirīya Upaniṣad*.[205]

Copernicus in CE 1543 established the Heliocentric theory of the solar system in his famous book *De Revolutionibus*. Then Kepler gave the laws of motion of planets in his book *The New Astronomy* in CE 1609. Galileo supported the views of Copernicus and showed the cause for the motion of the earth and other celestial bodies. This was clearly understood and expressed by Einstein in his General Theory of Relativity later in 1920 and 1950. The mathematical reasoning of the General Theory of Relativity has been observed by Eddington[206] who says:

> The universe is composed of atoms which contain smaller basic particles. These fundamental particles of the atoms are the real essence of the material world, the constituents of the physical universe.

---

205. S.R.N. Murthy, op.cit., p. 248.

206. C.A. Ronau, *The Astronomers*, London, 1964.

Further, Ronan[207] concludes that both Eddington and Einstein had much in common with Pythagoras and Plato, who also believed that the clue to the universe is laid in the numbers. The origin of the theory of numbers is due to Vedic sages[208] and it is a result of understanding the laws of the universe through mathematical logic.

The principle of natural philosophy and the realities of the universe have been shaped basing upon the prolonged observations carried out by the Vedic sages around the earth. The *Ṛgveda*[209] suggests the parabolic shape of the space and mentions gravity (the form of the geomagnetic field). According to Macdonell,[210] Varuṇa is the chief of the Lords of natural order. His activity displays itself pre-eminently, on the control of the most regular phenomena of nature. This is evidently law of gravitation gleaned from the *ṛk* of the Ṛgvedic hymn.[211] The sun strengthens the Universal Law, i.e. of gravitation. This is evident from the *Ṛgveda*[212] also. The Vedic concept of the attraction of celestial bodies, though brought out by Bhāskara II about the twelfth *c.* CE, did not pave the way for the formulation of the theory of gravitational attraction in India. That was left to Kepler, Galileo, Copernicus and Newton in Europe.

Murthy[213] has identified a number of geological agencies in the *Ṛgveda*. According to him, Indra of the *Ṛgveda* stands for the natural geophysical phenomenon. Due to the

---

207. Ibid.

208. S.S. Satyaprakash, *Founders of Science in Ancient India*, 2 vols., Delhi, 1990, p. 675.

209. *Ṛgveda*, VI.17.3, 9, 12.

210. A.A. Macdonell, *A Vedic Reader for Students*, p. 1.97 Oxford Press.

211. *Ṛgveda* I.24.14-15.

212. *Ṛgveda* VI.50.14-15.

213. S.R.N. Murthy, op. cit., pp. 54-55.

interrelationship of Indra and other geological agencies, concepts like *Indrāgni, Indrāmarutaḥ,* etc. came into existence. The other geological agencies are the Vedic deities like Agni, Varuṇa, Maruts, etc. Indra represents the geomagnetic field which can bring out earthquakes. Agni stands for geothermal field (heat energy), Varuṇa for Universal Law of Gravitation and Maruts for the wind energy and so on. These are various forces which govern the universe, i.e. they are electric, magnetic, gravitational and nuclear forces. The concept of the last one is quite evident from the idea of atoms as the constituents of the material world. The core of the atom is the nucleus which bind the nucleons (neutrons and protons) together with nuclear forces. The Vedic Āryans finally observed that all such forces had equal identity. Then, they observed that all forces are the different aspects of one and the same fundamental force. This ultimate reality is arrived at and is identified with the *Brahman*. Ostensibly, this single, all-unified force is called *Brahman* in Indian philosophy. Many years after, modern scientists also thought of unifying all these forces which govern the universe. They are now continuing their quest for the realization of the ultimate one that rules over the world. Their recent findings are also approaching the ultimate truth positively.

More generally, the concept of Indra in the Vedas is attributed to the rains, which, in turn, suggests the Vedic vision of early Indian meteorology. Since, the concept of Indra also indicates the geomagnetic field causing the earthquakes, the deity is associated with seismology.

The divine fire Agni symbolizes the geothermal field. Next to Indra, the concept of Agni (energy) is quite significant in the *Ṛgveda*. The very first hymn of Vyāsa's edition of the *Ṛgveda* is a song to the divine fire. According to Macdonell.[214]

---

214. A.A. Macdonell, op. cit.

> Agni is the personification of the sacrifical fire and is of importance next only to Indra. At least 200 hymns of the *Ṛgveda* eulogize this deity Agni. He pervades all space in all directions. He is generated out of the friction of two twigs by force. So, he is addressed as the son of strength. The sun is noted to be a form of Agni. He is also supposed to reside in the embryo of waters. He is further described as having originated in the heavens and brought to earth by Mātariśvan. Thus, Agni has a triple origin — on earth, in waters and in the sky. The cosmic and creative powers of Agni have been well depicted in the *Ṛgveda.*

Agni gives form to all things in nature.[215] It is the energy that creates matter and life. It is the energy in the embryo which forms life-giving cells. Once a life is created, it is that energy which gives the sensation of sight, hearing and thermal condition of a material body. Agni is the supernatural power that exists in everything, either living or non-living. It also creates mental vibrations in every living organism, which, in turn, enable it to perceive the happenings of self and surroundings.

Following *Taittirīya Upaniṣad,* Achyuta Krishnananda Tirtha[216] expresses that *ākāśa* bears the qualities of sound; Vāyu, that of touch; Agni, that of form; *āpas,* that of taste; and Pṛthvī, that of smell. In this sense, Agni gives form to all things in nature. The best forms are the *ratna*s. So, Agni is called *ratnadhātamā* in the first hymn of the *Ṛgveda.* This clearly indicates that Agni is the creator of the best gemstones which are found inside the earth's crust. Due to the power of Agni, such exceptional minerals are formed inside the earth. Undergoing various, physico-chemical changes like temperature and pressure, gemstones are formed.

---

215. K.T. Achyuta, *Vanamālā Commentary on the Taittirīyopaniṣadbhāṣya,* Srirangam, 1913, p. 267.

216. Ibid.

Thus, Agni (fire) plays a significant role among other *bhūtas* (space, air, water and earth). Ostensibly, the terrestrial fire, the oceanic fire and the fire in the sun, all appear to be different aspects of one entity that is Agni. According to Griffiths,[217] *R̥gveda* mentions that the light of the sun and that of Agni are one and the same.

Following Sāyaṇācārya's commentary on the *R̥gveda* (I.50.4), Raghava Rao[218] says that Sāyaṇa gives us concrete idea about the velocity of light in half-*nimeṣa*. Sunlight travels 2,202 *yojanas* in half-*nimeṣa*. One *nimeṣa* is equal to $^{16}/_{75}$th of a second. Hence, the velocity of light can be calculated as follows:

In ½ *nimeṣa*, i.e. $^{8}/_{75}$ second, light travels 2,202 *yojanas*.

1 *yojana* = 4 *krośas*

1 *krośa* = 2000 *daṇḍas* or fathoms

1 *daṇḍa* = 2 yards

1 *yojana* = 2 × 2000 × 4 yards

$$= \frac{16000}{1760} \text{ miles } (\because 1 \text{ mile} = 1760 \text{ yards})$$

$$= \frac{100}{11} \text{ miles}$$

$$2202 \; yojanas = \frac{2202 \times 100}{11} \text{ miles}$$

Therefore, in $^{8}/_{75}$ second, light travels $\frac{220200}{11}$ miles

and in 1 second, light travels

$$\frac{220200}{11} \times \frac{75}{8} \text{ miles}$$

$$= 1,\ 87,\ 670 \text{ miles}$$

217. R.T.H. Griffiths, *The Hymns of the R̥gveda*, MLBD, Delhi, 1986, vv. 1, 50.48 I, 7.9.s

218. G.V. Raghava Rao, *Scripture of the Heavens*, Vizag, A.P. 1949, p. 135.

Thus, the velocity light comes as 1,87,670 miles/second, the modern value being 1,86,000 miles/second. In about CE 1887, Michelson and Morley conducted expreiments to determine the absolute velocity of the earth through the hypothetical "ether" medium which helped in determining the velocity of light.

Meteorology

Meteorology is the science of studying motions and phenomena of atmosphere which, in turn, provide ample scope to forecast the weather. Hence, meteorological studies unveil the atmospheric character, specifically of a region. In spite of enormous advancement of science and technology in modern times, it has been observed that the theory of meteorology has not yet been satisfactorily worked out by the physicists.[219] In this context, it becomes imperative to excavate the old treasures of science of Vedic Āryans for clearly understanding the phenomena occurring in the atmosphere. The Vedic meteorologists had accurate observations and predictions regarding the weather conditions on the earth. The Vedic bards visualized the secret laws of nature beyond space and time. Though the Vedic people were living in nature and exploiting the natural resources to the maximum for their existence, they were fully aware of safeguarding their environment. They endeavoured for natural harmony all through heaven (celestial sphere) and earth (terrestrial sphere). It will be interesting to discuss the factors that the Vedic seers had considered for controlling the weather conditions.

The Vedic people were one with the nature. They observed the natural happenings in their minutest forms. The deities, they worshipped, were nothing but the manifestations of the natural phenomena. The deity Pṛthvī represents the earth,

219. R.P. Feynman, R.B. Leighton, and M. Sands, *Lectures on Physics*, Narosa, New Delhi, 1986, pp. 3, 7-8.

Vāyu represents air or atmosphere, Marut represents divine wind, Agni represents the celestial fire, Varuṇa represents the total hydrosphere, Āpaḥ represents water, Indra represents the geomagnetic field, Rudra represents the abrupt change in the natural phenomena, and so on. Under these considerations, the entire universe can be thought of being composed of mainly five elements like earth, water, air, fire and the space. The *Ṛgveda* refers to three divisions[220] of the universe, viz. earth, air or atmosphere and heaven.[221] The earth and the heaven are connected by the intermediate space of the *antarikṣa,* the region of mists and cloud. This *antarikṣa* actually consists of air and the void (vacuum). The air or the atmosphere spreads from the earth's surface up to 300 km. This earth's atmosphere is in the form of a spherical globe enveloping the earth from all sides. Major components of the atmosphere are Nitrogen (78 per cent), Oxygen (21 per cent) and Argon (1 per cent) by volume. Other minor constituents which are present in very small quantities are carbondioxide (0.03 per cent), Neon (0.001 per cent), Helium (5.3×10^{-4} per cent), Krypton (1×10^{-4} per cent), Hydrogen (5×10^{-5} per cent), Xenon (8×10^{-6} per cent) and Ozone (1×10^{-6} per cent). This atmosphere can be divided into three parts, namely troposphere, stratosphere and tropopause. The troposphere is the lower part of the atmosphere. In this region, there exists a temperature gradient of 0.56°C per 100 m. Temperature decreases as we go away from the earth's surface. Almost all the water vapour contents of atmosphere are contained in this region. Cloud formation also takes place in this region. Stratosphere is the upper part of the atmosphere and the pressure here is very low. There is very small variation of temperature with distance in this

---

220. *Ṛgveda,* VIII.10.90.

221. Ibid. Also, cf. A.A. Macdonell, op. cit., p. 8.

region. Tropopause is a very small layer of atmosphere that separates troposphere and stratosphere.[222]

Actually, the whole atmosphere of the earth is governed by air, fire and water. Hence, the meteorological phenomenon on the planet earth is formed mainly of air, fire and water and their variables. For instance, the origin of winds, storms and hurricanes, etc. may be assigned to the air; the cyclones and the phenomena of hotness and dryness in the atmosphere may be assigned to the variables of the fire; the clouds, lightning, thunder or precipitation may be assigned to water-variables.

Besides, the other physical force, which play vital roles in the materialization of meteorological phenomena, on the earth, are metamorphosed as the Vedic deities like Agni, Indra, Marut, Vāyu and Varuṇa, etc. There are 33 hymns in the *R̥gveda* eulogizing the Maruts, only 4 hymns attributed to Vāyu, 7 hymns to Maruts associated with Indra and one each with Agni and Pūṣan. There are several hymns to Vāyu in association with others.[223] The R̥gvedic bards worshipped the atmospheric winds as divine Marut or divine Vāyu. The dynamic activities, of these divinities are exhibited in the process of natural weathering, denudation and transportation. Holmes[224] has vividly described such Kinematics in physical geology. Maruts provide lightning with flash[225] and hence help in its occurrence. They also cause the thunder (*aśani*) by inducing electric charge into *āpaḥ* (water).[226] Due to the process of

222. S. Biswal, *Basic Physics*, vol. I, Delhi: Emkay Publications, 2000, p. 157.
223. A.A. Macdonell, *A Vedic Reader for Students*, Oxford Press, 1976.
224. A. Holmes, *Principles of Physical Geology*, English Language Book Society, 1964, pp. 743-81.
225. *R̥gveda*, V.54.13.
226. Ibid., also, cf *Taittirīya Brāhmaṇa*, 1.1.3.12.

induction, the (-ve) electric charge induces its (+ve) charge and then attraction takes place between the two. Consequently, they are neutralized with a flash (evolution of energy) causing thunder.[227] Thus, the Maruts cause lightning, thunderbolt and also water-cycle.[228] They also stimulate clouds to yield rain.[229] In the Vedic terms, the *antarikṣa/dyau* represents the midsphere where all the meteorological phenomena are brought about. According to the Vedic seers, the midsphere serves as the main centre of operation of air, fire and water and their variables. These basic elements of weather-formation are often called divinities for creating the meteorological phenomena on the planet earth.[230]

In the hymns to Maruts, the sages have also described the devastating aspects of the winds. Combined effect of Agni, Rudra, Indra, Varuṇa and Marut bring about heavy downpour of rains. The destructive activity of the winds can be seen affecting the surface of the earth. Rocks can be broken into pieces, large-scale earthy material can be transported to distant places by the wind and the torrential waters of streams and rivers can be caused.

Holmes[231] has well described the origin and devastating effects of hurricanes, cyclones, tornadoes, etc. which were also well known to our early sages. The motion of winds from hot regions to the cold regions affected by a special force called the coriolis force has been well understood by the students of geophysics. The formation of NE (north-east) and SW (south-west) trade winds and their utility in the sea voyages of our

227. *Kapisthala-Saṁhitā*, 6.7.

228. *Atharvaveda*, IV.15.5.

229. Ibid., IV.15.7; IV.15.8.

230. R.P. Arya, *Vedic Science of Weather*, 1993, p. 14.

231. A. Holmes, op. cit., pp. 743-81.

ancient sages are also known.[232] The subjects of geology also include the wind erosion, the development of different kinds of deserts and the transportation of dust, sand, etc. to far-off places.

The Vedic literature refers to Vāyu resting[233] and shining[234] in the mid-space (*antarikṣa*). It also says that the mid-sphere is the centre of water-vapours.[235] Taking the territorial division of gaseous and plasmatic matters/masses into consideration, we can differentiate between *dyuloka* (celestial sphere) and *antarikṣa-loka* (mid-sphere). But, in the general sense, the objects resting in the celestial sphere are called as *daivī* or *divya,* i.e. they are the objects abiding in the mid-sphere (*antarikṣastha vastu*). The *Aitareya Brāhmaṇa* also mentions *dyau antarikṣe pratiṣṭhitaḥ,* which means the celestial sphere resides in the midsphere.

Following the Vedas, *Viṣṇu Purāṇa* mentions eight Vasus, (*aṣṭavasu*) namely, *āpaḥ* (water vapours), *dhruva* (unmoving centre of the universe, i.e. pole star), *soma* (moon), *anala* (terrestrial fire), *anila* (air), *dharma,* i.e. *dhāraṇā śakti* of Pṛthvī (gravitational pull of earth), *pratyūṣa* (twilights) and *prabhāsa* (sunlight).[236] Since the earth holds *vasus,* it is called Vasundharā. The combined effect of eight Vasus is the cause of the atmospheric phenomena on the planet earth. In fact, the Vasus like *āpaḥ, anila, anala, prabhāsa,* etc. are the chief controlling factors of meteorological phenomena on the earth. Weather conditions are out and out influenced by the actions of the Vasus.

---

232. S.R.N. Murthy, *Vedic View of the Earth,* New Delhi: D.K. Printworld (P) Ltd., 1997, p. 71.
233. *Jaiminīya Brāhmaṇa,* 2.166.
234. Ibid., 1.292.
235. *Nirukta,* 7.27.
236. *Viṣṇu Purāṇa,* 15.110.

WATER

Atharvaveda[237] uses the term *āpaḥ* for the water vapours that are transferred from oceans into the mid-sphere. According to the observations of the *Atharvan* seers, water evaporates from the earth and rises up. It receives electrical charges in the mid-sphere and hence is called *āpaḥ*.[238] The deity Varuṇa is the subordinate deity of the presiding deity, the Sūrya, who enhances the process of evaporation of waters from the water reservoirs of the earth. Such water vapours cycle back to the earth in the form of liquid water.[239] *Taittirīya Āraṇyaka*[240] describes the four phases through which these water vapours must undergo to complete the water-cycle. Actually, the moisture/vapour undergoes the change of phase as cloud, electrical charging, lightning and thunder and precipitation. The *Atharvaveda*[241] refers to the celestial river (*nadī*) which transforms into terrestrial one (*sindhu*) after falling from heaven (mid-sphere) in the form of raindrops. Yāska also seems to etymolize the word *sindhu* in the context of terrestrial waters. According to him, "The terrestrial rivers are called *nadī*, since they produce sound while flowing down."[242] The *Ṛgveda*[243] mentions the process of rain-making by way of offering oblations in the *yajñīya* fire.

Cloud-formation

The Vedic sages have compared the physical process involved in the cloud formation and precipitation with the biological

---

237. *Atharvaveda*, IV. 27.4.
238. Ibid., III.13.2.
239. Ibid., IV.27.4.
240. *Taittirīya Āraṇyaka*, 1.24.1.
241. *Atharvaveda*, III.13.1.
242. *Nirukta*, 2.25.
243. *Ṛgveda*, I.23.18.

process of conception and delivery. The conception of rain embryos has been referred in the *Ṛgveda*.[244] Sāyaṇa has aptly interpreted this concept. Varāhamihira, a leading astrologer of ancient India, describes the phenomenon of the formation of clouds by the term *garbha-dhāraṇa* (conception) and the rainfall/precipitation by the term *prasava* (delivery). The *Ṛgveda*[245] describes that the celestial fire (Agni) stirs water-vapours from the surface of the earth and transports the same to the mid-sphere. Here, the celestial fire represents the sun. Due to sunlight, the water from the surface of the earth evaporates and goes up to the mid-space. This evaporation becomes quicker with the help of air or wind-speed. Evidently, the *Atharvaveda*[246] describes that the sun, with the help of air, evaporates the terrestrial waters into the celestial ones and makes them fall on the earth in the form of rain. Śaunaka has also observed the same thing.[247] The *Atharvan* seers further explain that the water-vapours in the mid-sphere possess the electrical charge (Indra).[248] Evidently, the clouds formed of these vapours become electrically charged. The Vedic deity Soma (the moon) has great influence on these water-vapours. According to the *Atharvaveda*, these water-vapours are held in the air under the influence of the sun, or the moon.[249] Hence, the clouds are formed with the impression of the Moon in their background and thus are termed as Somapṛṣṭhā.[250] Later meteorologists named these clouds as *pakṣaja*, i.e. the clouds formed in different phases of the Moon.

---

244. Ibid., I.6.4.
245. Ibid., I.164.47.
246. *Atharvaveda*, IV.12.2.
247. *Bṛhaddevatā*, 1.68.
248. *Atharvaveda*, III.13.2.
249. Ibid., III.13.5.
250. Ibid., III.21.10.

Besides the effects of the Sun and the Moon, there are some factors due to the rotation of the earth which govern the formation of the clouds. These factors mainly include geographic conditions and geostropic motion. The geocentric factors are responsible in the cloud-formation by the sea-bearing winds which are mostly seasonal. We trace such natural phenomenon in the *Ṛgveda*[251] which proves the microscopic observations of the natural happenings by the Vedic meteorologists. The *Atharvaveda*[252] also mentions this fact. According to the Vedic scholar Ravi Prakash Arya,[253] this can be illustrated as follows:

> Let all the directions fill with the sea-bearing winds which make the rain-embryos (*abhra*s) float all around. Let the directions overcast with rain-embryos and the sea-bearing winds irrigate the earth with waters.

The Vedic seers were familiar with the artificial means of declouding, since they applied them to ward off rains. They investigated several natural symptoms for cloud formation and also visualized indications for the impairment of seeding.[254]

Lightning and Thunder

Electrical charges are produced in the clouds after their formation. The Vedic sages named this as *vidyut*. In modern meteorological explanations, it is understood that the electrical charges are produced due to the violent collisions between the huge cloud-pieces.[255] The Vedic meteorologists had also knowledge of such a phenomenon. In one of the hymns of the

---

251. *Ṛgveda*, I.35.4.
252. *Atharvaveda*, IV.12.1.
253. R.P. Arya, *Vedic Meteorology*, Delhi: Parimal Publications, 1st edn., 1995, p. 35.
254. Ibid., p. 40; Also, cf. *Bṛhat-Saṁhitā*, 21.25-26.
255. Aeolus, *Meteorology*, Eng., U. Press Ltd., 1952, p. 71.

Atharvaveda.[256] We trace this reference. This hymn can be enunciated as under:

> Because you are sent forth (evaporated) by Varuṇa (radiation heating from the sun) and you have condensed so well, Indra (electrical charge) possesses you. You are, therefore, called *āpaḥ* (charged clouds).[257]

The Vedic term *pravāta*s refers to floating clouds and *pravātonapāt* means the daughter of floating clouds (*napāt of pravāta*s). On this connection, *Vājasaneyī-Saṁhitā* says —

> I salute you O'! electrical charge. You take birth in the floating clouds.[258]

In the terms of the *Atharvaveda,*[259] *hetu/āgneya* means negative charges of electricity whereas *vapu/somīya* refers to positive charges.

The Vedic deity Indra symolizes *vidyut.* Indra has also been taken as the rain-god, i.e. the actual physical force operating in the mid-sphere for the promotion of rain.[260] In the Vedic vision, Indra is often assisted by *marut*s. When Indra kills Vṛtra (cloud), *marut*s sport around him.[261] In fact, the ionization of air particles (*marut*s) leads to the production of spark (lightning) as the oppositely charged clouds are enormously attracted towards each other causing a huge collision.[262] Thus, lightning and thunder occur simultaneously. The Vedic term *stanayitnu* has been used for the thunderstorm.

---

256. *Atharvaveda,* III.13.2.
257. R.P. Arya, op. cit., p. 42.
258. *Vājasaneyī-Saṁhitā,* 36.21.
259. *Atharvaveda,* III.13.3
260. *Bṛhaddevatā,* 1.68.
261. *Śatapatha Brāhmaṇa,* 2.5.3.20.
262. *Ṛgveda,* V.54.3.

The theory of induction of positive charge by the negative charge is gleaned from the etymological explanations of the word *apsaras* as given by the ancient Vedic scholar Yāska. He conceives this word as *apsaras apasāriṇī, apsu, sāriṇī,*[263] i.e. *apsaras* is that which gets induced in the *āpaḥ*. Evidently, this means that negative ions of air particles are neutralized by the positive charges (*apasaras*). Obviously, Indra represents the negative charge and *apsaras* symbolizes the positive charge of electricity. Due to the contact of the negative and positive charges, lightning is produced. The *Ṛgveda*[264] describes that the lightning is created due to collision between the two charges. This phenomenon of lightning and thunder has been clearly explained in the *Taittirīya Brāhmaṇa*.[265] According to this:

> When Agni is expanded into two forms, negative and positive, its nucleus is shattered or, say, it is neutralized and so thunderbolt comes into being.[266]

The *Kāṭhaka-Saṁhitā*[267] also bears similar enumerations. The Vedic reader R.P. Arya translates this as under:

> The ionization of air particles helps produce the discharge between the opposite charges and so nucleus of Agni is shattered. This discharge causes the origin of thunderbolt.[268]

The thunder sound produced during the collision of two oppositely charged clouds is termed as Rudra in the Vedic literature. Because of simultaneous production of lightning and thunder, it is described as the form of Agni or *rudro 'agniḥ*.[269]

---

263. R.P. Arya, op. cit., p. 45.
264. *Ṛgveda*, V. 54.3.
265. *Taittirīya Brāhmaṇa*, 1.13.12.
266. R.P. Arya, op. cit., p. 45.
267. *Kāṭhaka-Saṁhitā*, 6.7.
268. R.P. Arya, op. cit., p. 45. Also, *Ṛgveda*, V.83.1-10.
269. *Kāṭhaka Saṁhitā*, 8.8; 24.6; 42.6. Also, *Ṛgveda*, V.83,1-10.

The Rains

The Ṛgvedic *sūkta* 83 describes the rains in detail. Here, the deity Parjanya is prayed for good shower for the growth of abundant crops.[270] There are beautiful descriptions of rain-clouds covering the sky, roaring sound of the thunderbolt, flashing of lightning and the echo of the thunder sound.[271] The Vedic poet has also described how the pouring of the rains helps the lives to exist on the surface of the earth. The seeds germinate,[272] the plants shoot up[273] and food springs abundantly for all living creatures.[274] The rain-waters are called as goddesses who help the cattle to quench their thirst.[275] This rain-water is also described as *amṛt* having full of healing powers.[276]

AIR

Air (*vāyu*) plays a significant role in creating the meteorological phenomena on the earth. The Vedic bards called air as *prāṇa,* because of its life-giving activity. This air spreads over 300 km from the surface of the earth. The entire region of air is called the atmosphere which lies in-between the earth and the sky. The air prompts the process of evaporation and hence helps in the formation of water-cycle. Without the help of air, the weather conditions cannot be brought about. Various

---

270. R.T.H. Griffiths, *The Hymns of the Ṛgveda,* Delhi: MLBD, 1986.
271. *Ṛgveda,* V.83.3-4.
272. Ibid., V. 83.1.
273. Ibid., V.83.4.
274. Ibid.
275. Ibid., I.23.18.
276. Ibid., I.23.19.

forms of this air are known as winds, storms and hurricanes. Our ancient seers identified different kinds of winds blowing through different layers. These winds are (i) *āvaha* (ii) *pravaha* (iii) *saṁvaha* (iv) *udvaha* (v) *vivaha* (vi) *parivaha* and (vii) *prāvaha*.[277]

Āvaha is the lowest layer of wind on the surface of the earth. According to the *Sūrya Siddhānta*,[278] *āvaha* or provector wind impels the planets towards their ellipses. The other layers spread over and above this lowest layer one after the other as per the list given above. In the Vedic Saṁhitās, the term *reśma* is employed for the winds of strong intensity.[279] *Vaiśeṣika-Sūtra*[280] mentions the basic physical quantities as *pṛthvī*, *āpaḥ* and *vāyu* to mean solid, liquid and gas. The wave aspect is felt with the *ākāśa* (sky) which represents the plasma state of matter.[281]

The *Ṛgveda* refers to the *vāyu* alone in its four hymns, whereas there are 33 hymns praying to the Maruts. Besides, many other hymns are traced eulogizing this deity *vāyu* in association with the other Vedic deities. *Vāyu* represents the god of wind. *Vāyu* is associated with the Vedic deities like Indra, Agni and Pūṣan. *Vāyu* is described as great, mighty, young and unageing, fierce, terrible and playful. *Vāyu* makes thunder noise and causes mountains to quake. *Vāyu* shed rains covering the sun causing darkness. Evidently, the Ṛgvedic sages worshipped the atmospheric winds as divine *vāyu* or Marut which, according to them, are the powerful agents for the meteorological phenomena on the earth.[282]

---

277. *Atharvaveda*, VI.102.3; Also, R.P. Arya, op. cit., p. 58.

278. R.P. Arya, op. cit., p. 58.

279. Ibid.

280. *Vaiśeṣika-Sūtra*, 2.1.1-4.

281. N.G. Dongre, *Physics in Ancient India*, New Delhi: New Age International Publishers Limited, 1994, pp. 18-19.

282. *Ṛgveda*, I.37.6-12; I.39.3-5; I.85.5,10; I.88.2,3; V.52.6,9; V.54.3, 8, 9; V.55.5, 7; V.56.4; V.57.4; V.60.2, V.66.7,9; VII.63.1; VIII.60.5; X.168.1.

According to the Beaufort scale[283] of wind force, the wind having a speed of less than a mile per hour (mph) is termed as the calm air. The gales have speeds ranging from 22 mph to 63 mph. A wind having a speed of 64 to 75 mph is called storm and the wind with the speed of over 75 mph is called a hurricane.

FIRE

The concept of *agni* has been associated with fire in the *Ṛgveda*. The anthropomorphism of the physical appearance of the divinity *agni* is connected chiefly with the sacrificial fire.[284] *Agni* is described as glowing like the sun with a lustre resembling that of the dawn and the lightning of the rain-cloud. The flames of *agni* are narrated as roaring like ocean waves and sounding like thunder. As *agni* (fire) is generated out of the friction of two twigs by force, he is addressed as the son of strength. *Agni* is supposed to reside in the embryo of waters. *Agni* has triple origin — on earth, in waters and in the sky. *Agni* has been interpreted as the form-maker as he creates various forms in nature. *Agni* is the life-maker. Due to solar radiation, water-cycle is caused, carbohydrates are formed in plants, germination of seeds is effected, life-cells are created in the mother's womb and all living and non-living organisms exist in this universe with the influence of *agni* (fire). The *Ṛgveda*[285] also holds that the light of the sun and that of *agni* are one and the same. The entire visible universe has sprung from *agni*. He is the creator of the solid, liquid and the gaseous matter. The destroying aspect of *agni* is attributed to Rudra. Both the geological and meteorological phenomena on the earth happen due to the force of divine fire.

---

283. S.R.N. Murthy, *Vedic View of the Earth*, New Delhi: D.K. Printworld (P) Ltd., 1997, p. 77.

284. Ibid., p. 58.

285. *Ṛgveda*, I.50.4; I.7.9.

3

Seismology

THE Greek word seismos means shaking. Seismology is the science of studying and predicting earthquakes. The theory of predicting earthquakes is the subject of seismology. This science is as old as the *Ṛgveda*. The problems of earthquakes were analysed by the Ṛgvedic sages who were the earliest students of earthquake studies in the world. There are umpteen *sūkta*s in the *Ṛgveda* praising Indra, Agni, Varuṇa and Vāyu while describing them as shakers of the earth. Bhat[1] has narrated the story of the shaking of the earth in the early times. According to this, the earth was being shaken severely by the winged mountains which flew up and came dowm heavily. Not able to withstand hits such the earth approached the creator "Brahmā" to save her from this kind of torture. Hearing the words of mother earth, Brahmā ordered Indra to cut-off the wings of flying mountains for removing the humiliation of mother earth. Indra acted accordingly and the earth is noted to have been rendered relatively stable. Indra also said to the earth that wind, fire, himself and Varuṇa will shake the earth in the four parts of the day and night put together respectively in order to reveal the good and bad effects of action to the world.

Causes

The Vedic sages had also investigated the causes of this shaking

---

1. M. Ramakrishna Bhat, *Varāhamihira's Bṛhat-Saṁhitā*, Delhi: MLBD, 2 vols., 1986, p. 1106.

of the earth.[2] According to some sages, the earthquake is caused due to the presence of huge animals in the ocean. Other sages like Garga opine that the earthquakes are caused by the elephants supporting the earth in eight directions. These elephants are tired of the weight of the earth. Vaṣiṣṭha holds that the earthquakes are caused by the atmospheric wind colliding with another and falling to the earth with a booming sound. The seer Vṛddha Garga observes that the earthquakes are caused by some unseen power. Parāśara points out that the earthquakes are brought about by the eclipses of the luminaries, unnatural phenomena occuring in the planets and special movements of the heavenly bodies.

Raman[3] has analysed the observations of the sage Parāśara of the time of the beginning of Kaliyuga (3102 BCE). He has opined that the shaking of a planet is caused due to the change of the course of a planet from its normal path. This happens because of the attractive force of other planets. The sage Garga says that the shaking of the earth is brought about by volcanic eruptions. Out of these two views, the former one seems to be more reasonable on the basis of astrological proofs.[4] According to Aristotle,[5] earthquake sometimes happens during the time of eclipse of the moon. The views of the sages differ from one another. Following these views, Varāhamihira has given the following explanations about the causes of the earthquakes.

There are seven constellations in the stellar circle presided over by the wind-god (Vāyu). These constellations are

---

2. S.R.N. Murthy, *Vedic View of the Earth*, New Delhi: D.K. Printworld (P) Ltd., 1997, p. 262; Also, cf. *Varāhamihira's Bṛhat-Saṁhitā*, op. cit.
3. B.V. Raman, *Astrology in Predicting Weather and Earthquakes*, Bangalore, 1993, p. 87.
4. S.R.N. Murthy, op. cit., p. 263.
5. Ibid.

Uttarāphālgunī, Hastā, Citrā, Swāti, Punarvasu, Mṛgaśirā and Aśvini. Before the happenings of the earthquakes, the symptoms of this circle as observed are the following: there will appear smoke covering all the directions; a strong wind will blow throwing the dust of the earth breaking down trees; and the sun will not shine brightly.

The fire circle (Agni Maṇḍala) consisting of the seven asterisms, namely Puṣyā, Kṛttikā, Viśākhā, Bharaṇī, Maghā, Pūrvābhadrā and Pūrvāphālgunī, exhibits the following symptoms before the occurrence of the earthquake: there will be falling stars and meteors filling the sky and it will glow due to the fire in the horizon. The fire aggravated by the wind will rage over the land.

The Indra circle is constituted with the seven asterisms, namely Abhijit, Śravaṇā, Dhaniṣṭhā, Rohiṇī, Jyeṣṭhā, Uttarabhadrā and Anurādhā. This Indra circle projects the following symptoms before the occurrence of the earthquake; there will be large cloud-pieces looking like moving mountains; producing loud thunder-sound and flashes of lightning; and resembling in colour of buffaloes' horn. There will appear swarms of bees and serpents. There will be heavy rains pouring down cats and dogs.

Varuṇa circle reveals some other symptoms before the happening of the earthquake. In this circle, there are also seven asterisms known as Revatī, Pūrvāṣāḍhā, Ārdrā, Āsleśā, Mūḷā, Uttarabhadrāpadā and Śatabhiṣā. This circle exhibits the following symptoms one week before the occurrence of the earthquake: there will be high clouds looking like blue lily, bees and collyrium in colour, rumbling pleasantly, and shining with falshes of lightning. Such clouds will pour down slender lines of water resembling sharp sprouts.

It is also noticed that the earthquake appears after bearing fruit in six months and a portentous thunder in two months.

According to the sage Garga, the other portents like eclipses and fall of meteors are also the observed symptoms of an approaching earthquake. Varāhamihira has observed that the fruition of an earthquake of Wind circle takes two months, the Fire circle takes three fortnights, Indra's circle takes seven days and Varuṇa's circle takes immediate effect.

Effects

Now we will focus on various effects of the earthquakes caused by Vāyu Maṇḍala, Agni Maṇḍala, Indra Maṇḍala and Varuṇa Maṇḍala.

Destruction of crops, water, forests and herbs, outbreak of swellings, asthma, lunacy, fever and phlegmatic conditions are some observable effects caused by an earthquake of the Wind circle (Vāyu Maṇḍala). The trading class, courtesans, warriors, physicians, women poets, musicians, traders of commodities, artisans, etc. face constraints to work properly after the earthquake. People of some specific regions are also the worst affected. Such masses and the region include the Saurāṣṭras, Kurus, Magadha country, Daśārṇa region and the Matsyas.[6]

The earthquake casued by the Fire circle (Agni Maṇḍala) brings about the following effects: there will be destruction of clouds; drying up of the lakes and tanks; breaking out of fever, scab, herpes, erysipelas and jaundice; etc. It will create troubles for the men of great valour, hot tempered persons, the Aśmakas, Aṅgas, Bāhlikas, Taṅgaṇas, Kaliṅgas, Vaṅgas Drāviḍas and hillmen of various tribes.

The earthquake caused by Indra's circle will ruin the people of high families and upper castes, famous persons, kings and heads of corporations. It will also produce dysentery, swelling of the throat, facial diseases and severe vomiting. It will cause

6. Ibid., p. 51.

trouble to the people of Kāśī, Yugandhara, the Pauravas, Kirātas, Kiras, Abhisaras, Halas, Madras, Arbudas, Saurāṣṭra and Mālavā countries. However, it will cause good rain.

The earthquake caused by Varuṇa's circle will kill those who depend upon the seas and the rivers; and will bring about excessive rains. Poeple will also bury the hatchet. It will destroy the Gonardas, Kukuras, Kirātas and the peopel of Videha.

In addition to the above, the earthquake of the Fire circle and wind period or vice versa will bring about calamities or death of celebrated monarchs and will torture people by the dread of famine, mortality and drought. On the other hand, the earthquake occurring in the Varuṇa circle and Indra period or vice versa will bring abundant food crops, prosperity, rain and joy and happiness in the world. The cows will yield milk in abundance and the kings will have good understanding between them.

Following Varāhamihira's *Bṛhat-Saṁhitā,* Bhat[7] explains that the earthquake caused by the Wind circle shakes the earth to an extent of 200 *yojanas*, that of the Fire circle spreads over 110 *yojanas*; one of the Varuṇa Maṇḍala extends over 180 *yojanas* and one of the Indra Maṇḍala shakes the earth over 160 *yojanas*.

Symptoms

Some of the symptoms of the earthquake to occur have been illustrated in *Samāsa-Saṁhitā*[8] of Varāhamihira. In the light of this text, Bhat[9] and then Murthy[10] have analysed the symptoms as under.

Many unnatural happenings are observed before an earthquake to take palce. These include meteors, dust

7. M. Ramakrishna Bhat, op. cit.
8. Ibid.
9. Ibid.
10. S.R.N. Murthy, op. cit., p. 53.

portentous thunder, fires in all directions, furious winds, eclipses of the luminaries, rain without clouds, unnatural phenomena in the case of any star or group of stars or in the sky as a whole, excessive rain or stormy rain, smoke without fire, flames without sparks, entry of wild animals into a village, sight of rainbow at night, broken halos round the sun or the moon, contrary flow of rivers, and sounds of musical instruments in the heaven. Any other unnatural happenings can be predicted on the basis of the *maṇḍala*s mentioned above.

Modern Method of Forecasting an Earthquake

In spite of enormous advancements in the field of seismology, it still remains a difficult task of forecasting exactly the earthquake to occur. All that is done today is the post-mortem analysis of the earthquakes. Murthy[11] has examined the issue of the earthquakes from different angles. After the Assam earthquake of 1897, real scientific insight was given to the study of the earthquakes. From then onwards, the discipline of seismology took a different shape. R.D. Oldham[12] made a thorough study of the Assam earthquake in the Geological Survey of India. Such a study made the scientists to believe that the earthquakes occur due to differential movements along fault planes. Now, the causes of the earthquakes are attributed to the theory of plate tectonics. This theory predicts that the earthquakes occur along the plate margins where a considerable amount of strain is accumulated which gets released suddenly due to unknown reasons. A model of Olivin-Spinel phase transformation has been proposed by Green[13] for forecasting the deep focus earthquakes. But, no

11. S.R.N. Murthy, *Glimpses of Hindu Astrology and Some Aspects of Indology*, Sadguru Publications, Delhi, 1993, p. 308.

12. R.D. Oldham, *Memoir in Geological Survey of India*, 29, Calcutta, 1899.

13. H.W. Green "Solving the paradox of the Deep Earthquakes," in *Scientific American*, September, 1994.

concrete solution of the problem of predicting the quakes has been arrived at yet. In this context, it is worth attempting to examine the theory of earthquakes put forth by the Vedic seers as well as Varāhamihira for their veracity. Ostensibly, it is now a crying need to formulate an integrated theory for predicting earthquakes.

Classification

There are three types of earthquakes as per the depth of focus or origin. These are shallow quakes, intermediate ones and the deep focus earthquakes. The depth of the shallow quakes does not exceed 60 km, the depth of the intermediate ones ranges from 70 km to 300 km, and the depth of the deep focus earthquakes is 300 km or more.[14] Different causes have been assigned to the occurrence of these earthquakes. The shallow quakes may be caused due to falling of portions of the earth from top owing to landslides and may also happen due to the pressure exerted by water reservoir areas. Reservoir effects and shallow level faults may bring about the intermediate focus earthquakes. The deep focus earthquakes may be caused due to a sudden shift in the centre of the earth mass. It is difficult to forecast the first two categories of quakes whereas there is a method designed by the Vedic sages to predict the deep focus earthquakes.

Vedic Theroy of Predicting Deep Shock Earthquakes

Varāhamihira's *Bṛhat-Saṁhitā* includes a chapter Bhūkampa-lakṣaṇādhyāya describing the method of forecasting the earthquakes of the third kind mentioned above. The *maṇḍala*s of Indra, Agni, Varuṇa and Vāyu may create disturbances which are geological, magnetic, electrical, geothermal, hydrospherical and atmospheric ones. The thumb rule given

---

14. C.F. Ritcher, *Elementary Seismology*, New Delhi: Eurasia Publishing House, 1958.

by Varāhamihira is not so effective in predicting the time and place of occurrence of the earthquakes.[15]

The theory is based upon the process of finding the total angular momentum of the solar system during the first half of the twentieth century. As the total angular momentum of the solar system remains constant without external influences, its path in space must be smooth. But, the orbits of all the planets in the solar system are not perfectly circular. These are slightly elliptical. Because of this, the planets accumulate a certain amount of strain over a long period of time, the sudden release of which shifts the mass centre causing earthquakes.

From the mass, linear velocity and radius of any planet, the angular momentum of it can be calculated using the relation

$$H = mrv$$

where, m is the mass, r is the radius and v is the linear velocity of a planet. For the earth, these values[16] are

$$m_e = 5.975 \times 10^{27} \text{ gm}$$

$$r_e = 145.5 \times 10^{6} \text{ km}$$

$$v_e = w_e \times r_e = (7.292115851 \times 10^{-5} \times 145.5 \times 10^{6}) \text{km/s}$$

where, w_e = angular velocity of the earth

$$= 7.292115851 \times 10^{-5} \text{ radians/sec.}$$

The total angular momentums of the planets as calculated by Boris Levin[17] are

15. S.R.N. Murthy, op. cit., p. 264.

16. B. Gutenberg (ed.), *Internal Constitution of the Earth,* Dover, 1951, p. 439.

17. Levin Boris, *The Origin of the Earth and Planets,* ed. J. Gibbons and tr. from the Russian by A. Shkarovsky, Moscow: Foreign Language Publishing House, p. 91; Also, cf. S.R.N. Murthy, op. cit., p. 265.

Mercury	→	0.03
Venus	→	0.69
Earth	→	1.00
Mars	→	0.13
Jupiter	→	723.00
Saturn	→	294.00
Uranus	→	64.00
Neptune	→	95.00
Pluto	→	1.00

The angular momentum of the sun is about 20, which is even less than 2 per cent of the total angular momentum of the entire solar system. The remaining 98 per cent of the total angular momentum of the solar system is concentrated with the planets. It is thus clear that the superior planets have greater angular momentum in the solar system in order to keep the system in equilibrium. Murthy[18] has shown that the abrupt change in the direction of the path of the total angular momentum of the solar system indicates the occurrence of the earthquake. In like manner, the Vedic geological forces forward the exact cause of the earthquakes to happen. Evidently, a deep focus earthquake is expected whenever there is abrupt change in the total angular momentum of the solar system, i.e. there is shifting of the dynamic centre of the system. So, it is necessary to calculate and locate the positions of the planets and the sun in the solar system. From such a study, the position of the dynamic centre of the system can be ascertained. Any abrupt change in the dynamic centre of the solar system brings about a deep focus earthquake. This can be accomplished by the advanced calculation of the planetary positions.

18. S.R.N. Murthy, "Correlation of Deep Shock Earthquakes with the Dynamic Centre of the Solar System", *Jour. Geo. Soc. Ind.*, vol. 36, pp. 535-38.

The time of occurrence and the place of occurrence are the two significant aspects in forecasting the earthquakes to take place. It is possible to determine the timing of earthquakes. But, it still remains a difficult task in predicting the exact locations of the earthquakes. However, one can discover the causes of the earthquake in terms of the Vedic geological agencies like Indra, Agni, Vāyu, Varuṇa, etc.

The prediction of time of occurrence of an earthquake is based on the calculation of change in angular momentum of the solar system. This is a subject of Newtonian Mechanics. According to some scientists, such a theory of predictive seismology violates the principle of uncertainty. Hawking[19] remarks, "One certainly can not predict future events exactly if one cannot even measure the present state of the universe precisely!" But, this may be a situation in particle physics. It cannot intervene with many astrological and astronomical focal points which go a long way in predicting a lot of things accurately about the future-earth. These predictions are based on the prolonged observations of the motions of the planetary bodies. Such a practice has its root in the Vedic thoughts and pursuits and finds its successful applications even today. The most striking fact is that the Vedic speculations march far ahead of the uncertainty principle propounded by Heisenberg.

---

19. S.W. Hawking, *A Brief History of Time,* New York: Bantam, 1994, p. 198.

4

Botany

Vedic Flora : A Study

THE *Ṛgveda* or the *Veda of verses* is the most ancient and the most important text of Vedism. It is available in the form of a collection of 1028 hymns (*sūktas*), divided into ten "circles" (*maṇḍalas*). The main feature of the *Ṛgveda* is the depiction of the glory of the gods and goddesses. The deities worshipped by the Vedic people are mainly Agni (the fire), Indra, Varuṇa, Viṣṇu, Rudra, Savitā, Marut, Sūrya (the Sun), Vāyu (the air), Soma, Dyāvāpṛthvī (the world), Mitra, Pūṣaṇ, Uṣā (morning), Parjanya, Aśvin and Yama. Evidently, most of these deities relate to the natural environment in which we live. Since the Vedas are the sacred texts of the Āryan culture, it is quite obvious that the Āryans were worshipping the components of natural creations as gods and goddesses. It is ture that the physical world outlined in the Vedic hymns and *sūtras* play an important role in shaping the habits, customs, manners and culture of the Vedic people.

The Vedas depict the cosmology, cosmogony, astronomy, astrology, philosophy, science, society, history, geography, tradition, culture, language and literature, etc. According to the Vedas, the universe is divided into three parts, each sometimes duplicated and even triplicated. They are the earth, the *antarikṣa* and the sky.[1] Space is conceived, in fact, like an ocean, divided into two, three or four seas. For the sun, the

1. B.L. Ray, *Studies in Sanskrit, Indology and Culture,* New Delhi: Classical Publishing Company, 1998, p. 11.

common Vedic notion is that it has a bright and a dark face. The *nakṣatras* or lunar mansions appear perhaps in the most recent parts of the *Ṛgveda*. It is seen that the astronomical phenomena are latent in the Vedic hymns in mythical forms. Further the four Vedas, viz. *Ṛg*, *Yaju*, *Sāma* and *Atharva* deal with some cities, towns, countries, states, rivers, mountains, lakes, forests, trees, birds, animals, the earth, the air, the water, the fire, the climate, the herbs, the plants, the flowers, the fruits, the vegetables, the weeds, etc. Moreover, some place names are available from the Vedic hymns. All the above items together focus on the Vedic culture and civilization prevailing at that time. This also shows the vast knowledge of the Vedic seers about their surrounding nature and natural resources. The world of plants, herbs, flowers and fruits exhibits the social life, custom and tradition of the Vedic people. The other living organisms like animals, birds and insects add to the above knowledge more concretely. In the present study, an attempt has been made to survey the Vedic flora and plant world in order to uncover the various aspects of Vedic civilization and culture. The *Ṛgveda* mentions a large number of trees, plants, grains, flowers and grasses in connection with the performance of sacrifices.

Plants

The *Ṛgveda* includes a plant named *araṭu*[2] from the wood of which the axle of a chariot was sometimes made. The botanical name of this species is *Colosanthes indica*. Other varieties are: *ajaśṛṅgi*,[3] *adhyāṇḍā*,[4] *apāmārga* (*Achyranthes aspera*),[5] *amalā* (*Emblica*

2. *Ṛgveda*, VIII.46.27. Also, *Atharvaveda*, XX.131.17.
3. *Atharvaveda*, IV.37. This plant is equated with *viṣāṇin* (*Odina Pinnata*). Its other name is *arāṭakī* (*AV*, IV.37.6).
4. *Śatapatha Brāhmaṇa*, XIII.8.1.16.
5. *Atharvaveda*, IV.17.6; IV.18.7; IV.19.4; VII.65.2. This plant is described in the *Atharvaveda* (IV.17.2) as "revertive" (*punaḥ-sara*), because it has reverted leaves.

officinalis),[6] *amūlā* (*Methonica superba*),[7] *arāṭaki*,[8] *arundhatī*,[9] *arka* (*Calotropis gigantea*),[10] *alāpu* (*Lagenaria vulgaris*),[11] *avakā* (*Blyxa octandra*),[12] *aśvavāra* or *aśvavāla* (*Saccharum spontancum*),[13] *ādāra*,[14] *ābayu* (mustard plant),[15] *uśānā* (a plant),[16] *eraṇḍa* (*Ricinus communis*),[17] *aukṣagandhi*,[18] *karīra* (*Copparis aphylla*),[19] *kumuda* (*Nymphaca esculenta*),[20] *kuṣṭha* (*Costus speciosus* or *Arabicus*),[21]

---

6. *Jaiminīya Upaniṣad Brāhmaṇa*, I.38.6.
7. *Atharvaveda*, V.31.4. This plant has no root. Its botanical name is *Methonica superba*, which was used for poisoning arrows.
8. *Atharvaveda*, IV.37.6.
9. Ibid., IV.12.1; V.5.5.9; VI.59.1.2; VIII.7.6; XIX.38.1. This plant possesses healing properties in case of wounds, as a fabrifuge, and as inducing cows to give milk. Being a climber, it attaches itself to trees like the *plakṣa*, *aśvattha*, *nyagrodha* and *parṇa* (*AV*, V.5.5).
10. *Atharvaveda*, VI.72.1.
11. Ibid., VIII.10.29-30.
12. Ibid., VIII.7.9; VIII.37.8-10. The *gandharva*s are said to eat this plant (*AV*, IV.37.8). Its later name is *śaivāla*, and it is identical with the *śīpāla*.
13. *Maitrāyaṇī Saṁhitā*, III.7.9. This is a species of reed.
14. *Śatapatha Brāhmaṇa*, IV.5.10.4. This plant was prescribed as substitute for *soma*. It is identified with *pūtīka*.
15. *Atharvaveda*, VI.16.1.
16. *Śatapatha Brāhmaṇa*, III.4.3.13; IV.2.5.15. *Soma* was prepared from this plant.
17. *Sāṅkhāyana Āraṇyaka*, XII.8.
18. *Atharvaveda*, IV.37.3. The name of this plant denotes some sort of fragrant plant.
19. *Taittirīya-Saṁhitā*, II.4.9.2.
20. *Atharvaveda*, IV.34.5. It is identified with the white water-lily.
21. Ibid., I.65. It grew especially on the mountains, along with the *soma*, on the high peaks of the Himalayas, where the eagles nest. Like *soma* it is said to have grown in the third heaven under the famous *aśvattha* tree.

jaṅgiḍa (*Terminalia arjuneya*),[22] *jāmbila* (citron),[23] *tājadbhaṅga*,[24] *tilvaka* (*Symplocos racemosa*),[25] *taudi*,[26] *trāyamāṇa*,[27] *narācī*,[28] *nalada* or *naladi* (nard),[29] *nyastikā* (*Andropogon aciculatus*),[30] *pāṭā* (*Clypea hernandifolia*),[31] *pilā*,[32] *pūṭika* (*Guilandina Bonduc* or *Basella cordifolia*),[33] *pṛṣṇiparṇī* (*Hermionitis cordifolia*),[34] *praprotha*,[35] *pramagandha*,[36] *pramandanī*,[37] *prasū* (young shoot),[38] *baja* (mustard

---

22. Ibid., II.4; XIX.34.35. It is a healing plant. It was used as an amulet against the diseases like fevers and rheumatic pains.
23. *Maitrāyaṇī Saṁhitā*, III.15.3.
24. *Atharvaveda*, VIII.8.3. It has been identified with the castor-oil plant in the *Kauśika-Sūtra*.
25. *Śatapatha Brāhmaṇa*, XIII.8.1.16. A tree near which it is inauspicious to construct a grave.
26. *Atharvaveda*, X.4.14.
27. Ibid., VIII.2.6.
28. Ibid., V.31.4. It is a poisonous plant.
29. Ibid., VI.102.3. This plant is mentioned as used for garland making.
30. Ibid., VI.139.1.
31. Ibid., II.27.4. It is a medicinal plant.
32. Ibid., IV.37.3. This is the name of some fragrant plant.
33. *Kāṭhaka-Saṁhitā*, XXXIV.3. This plant is usually identified with the *Guilandina bondue*. It is used as a substitute for the *soma* plant.
34. *Atharvaveda*, II.25.1. This plant has been used as a protection against evil beings inducing abortion.
35. *Pañcaviṁśa Brāhmaṇa*, VIII.4.1. This plant is used as a substitute for *soma*.
36. *Ṛgveda*, III.53.14.
37. *Kauśika-Sūtra*, VIII.17. This word devotes a sweet-scented plant.
38. *Ṛgveda*, I.95.10.

plant),[39] *bimba* (*Momordica monadelpha*),[40] *bhāṅga* (hemp),[41] *mañjiṣṭhā* (madder),[42] *madāvatī* (intoxicating),[43] *madugha* (honey plant),[44] *viṣāṇakā*,[45] *vihalha*,[46] *virudh* (plant),[47] *śana* (hemp),[48] *saphaka*,[49] *śipāla* (*Blyxa octandra*),[50] *sarṣapa* (mustard),[51] *saha*,[52] *sahadeva*,[53] *sahadevī*,[54] *sahamāna*,[55] *silāci*,[56] and *silāñjalā*,[57] etc.

Besides the above, the names of some water-plants and weeds are also mentioned in the Vedic literature.

WATER-PLANTS AND WEEDS

Some plants like lotus, lily, etc. grow in water. Similarly, different kinds of weeds germinate in the water medium. Some

---

39. *Atharvaveda*, VIII.6.3.6.7.24. This plant was used against a demon of disease.
40. *Jaiminīya Upaniṣad Brāhmaṇa*, III.5.6.
41. *Atharvaveda*, XI.6.15.
42. *Aitareya*, III.2.4; (*Āraṇyaka*) *Sāṅkhāyana*, VIII.7 (*Āraṇyaka*).
43. *Atharvaveda*, VI.16.2.
44. Ibid., I.34.4. *Ṛgveda*, VI.70.1.5.
45. *Atharvaveda*, VI.44.3.
46. Ibid., VI.16.2.
47. *Ṛgveda*, I.67.9. This plant has practically the same sense as *oṣadhi*.
48. *Atharvaveda*, II.4.5. This plant grows in the forest.
49. *Atharvaveda*, IV.34.5. It is so called because its leaves are shaped like hoofs (*śapha*).
50. *Ṛgveda*, X.68.5.
51. *Chāndogya Upaniṣad*, III.14.3.
52. *Atharvaveda*, XI.6.15.
53. *Ṛgveda*, I.100.17.
54. *Atharvaveda*, VI.59.2.
55. Ibid., II.25.2; IV.17.2; VIII.2.6; VIII.7.5.
56. *Atharvaveda*, V.5.1; V.5.8.
57. Ibid., VI.16.4. This plant is perhaps a "grain creeper."

weeds are found floating in water and some grow on the soil inside water. Among the water plants, *āṇḍika* (lotus),[58] *kiyāmbu,*[59] *kumuda* (lily),[60] *puṇḍarīka* (lotus blossom)[61] and *puṣkara* (lotus flower)[62] are the prominent names traced in the Vedic literature. The name *āla*[63] denotes weed. *Bisa*[64] is identified with lotus fibre and *śalūka*[65] with lotus shoot.

HERBS AND GRASSES

The word *tṛṇa*[66] is found in the Vedic literature. It is identified with grass. It was used as straw to roof a house or hut.[67] The other varieties of grasses referred to in the Vedic texts are *dūrvā (Panicum dactylon),*[68] *iṣīkā* (reed grass),[69] *ulapa,*[70] *kāśa (saccharum spontancum),*[71] *kuśa (Poa cynosuroides),*[72] *darbha,*[73]

58. *Atharvaveda,* IV.34.5; V.17.16. This is one edible plant, apparently with fruit or leaves of egg-shape akin to the lotus.
59. *Ṛgveda,* X.16.13; *Atharvaveda,* XVIII.3.6. According to the funeral hymn in the *Ṛgveda* (as mentioned above), on the place where the body of the dead was burnt, these plants grow.
60. *Atharvaveda,* IV.34.5. This plant is idenified with lily that grows in water.
61. *Ṛgveda,* X.142.8. This plant denotes the blossom of the lotus.
62. Ibid., VI.16.13; VII.33.11. This word denotes the blue lotus flower.
63. *Atharvaveda,*VI.16.3.
64. Ibid., IV.34.5.
65. Ibid.
66. *Ṛgveda,* I.161.1; 162.8; X.102.10. *Atharvaveda,* II.30.1; VI.54.1.
67. *Aitareya Brāhmaṇa,* III.22; VIII.24.
68. *Ṛgveda,* X.16.13; 134.5; 142.8.
69. *Atharvaveda,*VII.56.4; XII.2.54.
70. *Ṛgveda,* X.142.3.
71. Ibid., X.100.10.
72. *Śatapatha Brāhmaṇa,* II.5.2.15; III.1.2.16; V.3.2.7.
73. *Ṛgveda,* I.191.3.

balbaja,[74] *viraṇa* or *viriṇa*,[75] *śāda*,[76] *sugandhitejana*,[77] *sairya*,[78] *stamba*,[79] etc. Moreover, some grass-related words are spotted. These are *naḍa* (reed),[80] *naḍvalā* (reed bed), *piñjula* (bundle of grass),[81] *śara* (reed),[82] *śaṣpa* (young grass)[83] and *śumbala* (straw).[84] *Sasa*[85] is a kind of herb mentioned in the *Ṛgveda*. The word is also applied to the *soma* plant[86] and the sacrificial straw.[87] *Prasū* in the *Ṛgveda*[88] denotes the young shoots of grass or herbs used at sacrifices.

GRAINS AND CREEPERS

The Vedic texts mention a number of grains and grain-creepers

---

74. *Atharvaveda*, XIV.2.22.23; *Taittirīya-Saṁhitā*, II.2.8.2; *Kāṭhaka-Saṁhitā*, X.10; *Maitrāyaṇī-Saṁhitā*, II.2.5.
75. *Śatapatha Brāhmaṇa*, XIII.8.1.15.
76. *Ṛgveda*, IX.15.6; *Vājasaneyī-Saṁhitā*, XXV.1
77. *Taittirīya-Saṁhitā*, VI.2.8.4; *Kāṭhaka-Saṁhitā*, XXV.6; *Aitareya Brāhmaṇa*, I.28.28; *Śatapatha Brāhmaṇa*, III.5.2.27; *Pañcaviṁśa Brāhmaṇa*, XXIV.13.5.
78. *Ṛgveda*, I.191.3.
79. *Atharvaveda*, VIII.6.14.
80. *Ṛgveda*, VIII.1.33.
81. *Vājasaneyī-Saṁhitā*, XXX.16; *Taittirīya Brāhmaṇa*, III.4.12.1.
82. *Ṛgveda*, I.191.3; *Atharvaveda*, IV.7.4.
83. *Vājasaneyī-Saṁhitā*, XIX.13, 81; XXI.29; *Aitareya Brāhmaṇa*, VIII.5.3; VIII.8.4; *Śatapatha Brāhmaṇa*, XII.7.2.8; XII.9.1.2. The word denotes "young or sprouting grass."
84. *Śatapatha Brāhmaṇa*, XII.5.2.3. The word has been identified with straw and dried cotton fibre.
85. *Ṛgveda*, I.51.3; X.79.3.
86. Ibid., III.5.6; IV.5.7.
87. Ibid., V.21.4.
88. *Ṛgveda*, I.95.10; III.5.8; VII.9.3; VII.35.7; VIII.6.20. The word denotes young shoots of grass or herbs used at the sacrifice.

which add to the knowledge of our environment. Some of the grains are used as food grains by the Vedic people. Nowadays, such species are also available in nature and some are also cultivated by the people. The word *aṇu*[89] symbolizes the grain in general. The list of grains mentioned in the Vedic literature includes *kulmāṣa* (beans),[90] *garmut* (wild bean),[91] *godhūma* (wheat),[92] *tandula* (rice grains),[93] *tila* (sesamum),[94] *dhāna* (grains of corn),[95] *dhānya* (grain),[96] *pūlpa* or *pūlya* (shrivelled grain),[97] *priyaṅgu* (*Panicum italicum*),[98] *masūra* (*Ervum hirsulum*),[99] *yava* (barley),[100] *vrīhī* (rice),[101] *śāli* (rice),[102] *śaṣya* (corn),[103] *plāśuka* (fast growing rice),[104] etc. After harvesting the paddy-plants, we

---

89. *Vājasaneyī-Saṁhitā*, XVIII.12.
90. *Chāndogya Upaniṣad*, I.10.2, 7.
91. *Taittirīya-Saṁhitā*, II.4.4.1-2.
92. *Maitrāyaṇī-Saṁhitā*, I.2.8; *Vājasaneyī-Saṁhitā*, XVIII.12; XIX.22; XIX.89; XXI.29.
93. *Atharvaveda*, X.9.26; XI.1.18; XII.3.18, 29-30.
94. Ibid., IV.7.3;Ibid., II.8.3; VI.140.2; XVIII.3.69.
95. *Ṛgveda*, I.16.2; III.35.3; III.52.5.
96. Ibid., VI.13.4.
97. *Atharvaveda*, XIV.2.63.
98. *Taittirīya-Saṁhitā*, II.2.11.4; *Taittirīya Brāhmaṇa*, III.8.14.6.
99. *Vājasaneyī-Saṁhitā*, XVIII.12.
100. *Ṛgveda*, I.23.15; I.66.3; I.117.21; I.135.8; I.176.2; II.5.6; II.14.11; V.85.3; VII.3.4; VIII.2.3; VIII.22.6; VIII.63.9; VIII.78.10.
101. Ibid., V.53.13. The word is identified with *dhānya bīja* (rice seeds).
102. A.A. Macdonell, and A.B. Keith, *Vedic Index of Names and Subjects*, vol. II, Delhi: MLBD, rpt. 1995, p. 376.
103. *Atharvaveda*, VII.11.1; VIII.10.24.
104. *Śatapatha Brāhmaṇa*, V.3.3.2.

get *palāla* (straw)[105] and the paddy-grains. By the way of processing the rice and the husk (*tuṣa*)[106] are separated. *Taila* (oil)[107] obtained from the seeds of sesamum is also referred in the Vedic hymns.

Among the creepers, the prominent names are *alasālā*,[108] *nīlāgalasāla* or *nīlākalasālā*,[109] *vratati*,[110] etc. Besides, many names of fruits, flowers and seeds are also found in the Vedic literature.

FLOWERS, FRUITS AND SEEDS

The word *puṣpa*[111] meaning flower is mentioned in the Vedic literature. Among flowers, lotus (*puṣkara*),[112] lily (*kumuda*),[113] *aśmagandhā*[114] or *aśvagandhā* (*Physalis flexuous*), etc. are the common names. *Āmalaka*[115] denotes a fruit. Another fruit mentioned is the *urvārū* or *urvāruka*,[116] which means cucumber. The flowers and fruits of *palāśa*[117] and *śālmali*[118] are traced in

---

105. *Atharvaveda*, VIII. 6.2. The meaning of the word is "straw" in which sense it occurs in the *Kauśika-Sūtra* (XXX.27).
106. Ibid., IX.6.16; XI.1.12, 29; XI.3.5; XII.3.19. It is the husk of grain and very often used for a fire.
107. Ibid., I.7.2.
108. Ibid., VI.16.4.
109. Ibid.
110. *Ṛgveda*, VIII.40.6. *Nirukta*, I.14; VI.28.
111. *Atharvaveda*, VIII.7.12.
112. *Ṛgveda*, VI.16.13; VII.33.11.
113. *Atharvaveda*, IV.34.5.
114. *Śataptha Brāhmaṇa*, XIII.8.1.16.
115. *Chāndogya Upaniṣad*, VII.3.1.
116. *Ṛgveda*, VII.59; *Atharvaveda*, XIV.1.17.
117. *Kauṣītakī Brāhmaṇa*, X.2; *Śatapatha Brāhmaṇa*, I.5.4.5; V.2.1.17.
118. *Ṛgveda*, VII.50.3.

the Vedic texts. In general *bīja* (seed)[119] is mentioned in this literature; the operation of sowing seed (*vap*) being several times referred to in the *Ṛgveda*[120] and later.[121] In a metaphorical sense the term is used in the Upaniṣads of the classes of beings according to origin, of which the *Chāndogya Upaniṣad*[122] enumerates three, the *Aitareya*[123] four. The former list includes *aṇḍa-ja* (egg-born), *jīva-ja* (born alive) and *udbhij-ja* (produced from sprouts) while the latter adds *sveda-ja* (sweat-born), i.e., generated by hot moisture.

TREES

The names of many big and small trees are found in the four Vedas, Brāhmaṇas, Āraṇyakas and Upaniṣads. Vedic *sūtra*s also mention some varieties of them. The word *vṛkṣa*[124] in the Vedas generally stands for the tree. *Druma*[125] is also another word used for the tree. Two words *vayā*[126] and *śākhā*[127] have been employed to mean the branch of the tree. *Valka*[128] stands for the bark and *valśa*[129] for the twig of the tree. The words *dāru*,[130] *kṛmuka*[131] and *kruṁuka*[132] stand for the wood. *Vakala*[133] is

119. Ibid., X.94.13; X.101.3.

120. Ibid.

121. *Atharvaveda*, X.6.33.

122. *Chāndogya Upaniṣad*, VI.3.1.

123. *Aitareya Upaniṣad*, III.3.

124. *Ṛgveda*, I.164.20, 22; II.14.2; II.39.1; IV.20.5; V.78.6.

125. *Ṣaḍviṁśa Brāhmaṇa*, V.11; *Nirukta*, IV.19; V.26; IX.23.

126. *Ṛgveda*, II.5.4; V.1.1; VI.7.6; VI.13.1; VIII.13.6; VIII.13.17.

127. Ibid., I.8.8; VII.43.1; X.94.3.

128. *Taittirīya-Saṁhitā*, II.5.3.5; III.7.4.2; *Taittirīya Brāhmaṇa*, I.4.7.6.

129. *Taittirīya-Saṁhitā*, VII.3.9.1; *Ṛgveda*, III.8.11; *Atharvaveda*, VI.30.20.

130. *Ṛgveda*,VI.3.4; X.145.4; *Atharvaveda*, X.4.3.

131. *Kāṭhaka-Saṁhitā*, I.180; *Śatapatha Brāhmaṇa*, VI.6.2.11.

132. *Taittirīya-Saṁhitā*, V.1.9.3.

133. *Taittirīya Brāhmaṇa*, III.7.4.2.

used for the bast. The big trees like *aśvattha* (*Ficus religiosa*),[134] *nyagrodha* (*Ficus indica*),[135] *bilva* (*Aigle marmelos*),[136] *udumbara* (*Ficus glomerata*),[137] *karkandhu* (*Zizyphus jujuba*),[138] *kākambira*,[139] *kārṣmarya* (*Gmelina arborca*),[140] *kiṁśuka* (*Butea frondosa*),[141] *khadira* (*Acacia catechu*),[142] *kharjūra* (*Phanix silvestris*),[143] *talāśa* (*Flacourtia cataphracta*),[144] *palāśa* (*Butea frondosa*),[145] *pippala* (berry),[146] *badara* (jujube),[147] *rohitaka* (*Andersonia rohitaka*),[148] *pūtudru* (Deodar),[149] *prakṣa* (*Ficus infectoria*),[150] *plakṣa* (*Ficus infectoria*),[151] *śamī*,[152] *śālmali* (*Salmalia malabarica*),[153] *śiṁśapā* (*Dalbergia śiśu*),[154] *haridru* (*Pinus*

134. *Ṛgveda*, I.135.8; X.97.5; *Atharvaveda*, III.6.1; IV.37.4.

135. *Ṛgveda*, I.24.7; *Atharvaveda*, IV.37.4; V.5.5.

136. *Atharvaveda*, XX.136.13.

137. Ibid., XIX.31.1. The wood of this tree like that of other kinds of fig tree — *aśvattha*, *nyagrodha* and *plakṣa* — was considered suitable for use in sacrifices (*Taittirīya-Saṁhitā*, III.4.8.4).

138. *Kāṭhaka-Saṁhitā*, XII.10; *Maitrāyaṇī-Saṁhitā*, III.11.2; *Vājasaneyī-Saṁhitā*, XIX.23.91.

139. *Ṛgveda*, VI.48.17.

140. *Taittirīya-Saṁhitā*, V.2.7.3-4; VI.2.1.5.

141. *Ṛgveda*, X.85.20.

142. Ibid., III.53.19; *Atharvaveda*, III.6.1; V.5.5; VIII.8.3.

143. *Taittirīya-Saṁhitā*, II.4.9.2. of *Yajurveda*.

144. *Atharvaveda*, VI.15.3.

145. *Kauṣītakī Brāhmaṇa*, X.2; *Śatapatha Brāhmaṇa*, I.5.4.5.

146. *Ṛgveda*, I.164.20.

147. *Kāṭhaka-Saṁhitā* of *Yajurveda*, XII.10.

148. *Maitrāyaṇī-Saṁhitā*, III.9.3.

149. *Atharvadeda*, VIII.2.28.

150. *Taittirīya-Saṁhitā*, VI.3.10.2.

151. *Atharvaveda*, V.5.5.

152. Ibid., VI.11.1; VI.30.2.3.

153. *Ṛgveda*, VII.50.3.

154. *Ṛgveda*, III.53.19.

deodora),[155] *sphūrjaka* (*Diospyros embryopteris*),[156] etc. are mentioned in our ancient literature. Out of the above trees, some are grown wildly and some are planted by the people for their use in the treatment of diseases. Vedic people also knew the medicinal value of all these trees, plants, herbs, creepers, grains, flowers, fruits, shoots and seeds. As they lived in the forests depending on the natural resources, they gradually practised cultivating those varieties of plants helpful for their living. Thus, *kṛṣi*[157] was the main occupation of the Vedic people. In the *Atharvaveda Pṛthī Vainya* is credited with the origination of ploughing,[158] and even in the *Ṛgveda* the Aśvins are spoken of as concerned with the sowing of grain by means of the plough.[159]

Thus, the nature and the natural resources like the earth, air, water, fire, mountains, forests, lakes, rivers, seas, oceans, etc. have been described in the Vedas and Vedic texts as gods and goddesses. Vedic groups worshipped them with the notion that the deities have been manifested in nature in different forms to help them in their lives. The entire plant-world noted above go a long way in solving their problems of living and earning bread and butter. Vedic people were using medicinal plants and herbs in the cure of diseases. Nowadays, such a cure is known as Āyurvedic treatment, which was actually developed during Vedic period.

---

155. *Śatapatha Brāhmaṇa*, XIII.8.1.16.
156. Ibid., XIII.8.1.16.
157. *Ṛgveda*, I.23.15; X.34.13.
158. *Atharvaveda*, VIII.10.24.
159. *Ṛgveda*, I.117.21.

5

Zoology

Vedic Fauna : A Focus

THE Vedas, Saṁhitās, Āraṇyakas (forest texts), Upaniṣads, Brāhmaṇas, Kalpasūtras and the Vedāṅgas are full of descriptions of our nature and natural beauty. The four Vedas, namely *Ṛg, Sāma, Yaju* and *Atharva* deal with some countries, states, cities, towns, seas, oceans, rivers, lakes, mountains, forests, trees, birds, animals, insects, the earth, air, water, fire, climate as well as some place names. Being the primary sources of human civilization and knowledge, the Vedas and the Vedic texts are the anthologies of our rich natural resources. This, in turn, provides environmental aspects of the Vedas. The geographical account given in the Vedic texts adds to the knowledge of our environment more concretely and coherently.

Specifically, the flora and fauna of the Vedic literature, too, have permeated the national religious life in a very intimate way. Birds and animals were employed as the vehicles of Vedic deities. The elephant played a very important role in religious processions, and the lotus was frequently used in the worship of the deities as well as in religious symbolism. Since the Vedic people were depending on agriculture and cattle assets for their living, both plant and animal worlds played a very significant role in influencing their social life and culture. The role of the plant kingdom has been discussed in the previous chapter and the objective of the present chapter is to throw light on the animals and birds mentioned in the Vedic literature. Like the flora and plant kingdom, the exploration of the Vedic fauna will no doubt help us in gathering knowledge about the then people and society of Vedic period.

The Animals

Among all the animals, the cows were very much intimate to the Vedic people. In fact, the cow has all along been a very popular animal with the Indo-Āryans. Other animals mentioned in the Vedic literature are goats, sheep, horses, elephants, asses, cats, etc. These were the domestic animals. Wild animals like tigers, wolves, Jackals, etc. are included in the Vedas. The serpent was a much dreadful reptile. It was most probably due to the fear of this reptile that the Āryan people were compelled to perform certain sacrifices, such as the *śravaṇā* to propitiate snakes.[1] Besides these, the birds, the aquatic creatures and the insects of certain species are included in the Vedic literature. Right from the times of the *Ṛgveda,* the frog attracted the attention of the Āryan poets.[2] Existence of four-footed and two-footed animals in the Vedic environment are also gleaned from the words *catuṣpada* (quadruped)[3] and *dvipada* (biped)[4] mentioned in the *Ṛgveda* and other Vedic texts. *Catuṣpada,* as an adjective applying to *paśavaḥ* (animals) is also found.[5]

1. B.L. Ray, *Studies in Sanskrit Indology and Culture,* New Delhi: Classical Publishing Company, 1998, p. 17.
2. B.L. Ray, "Ṛgvedic Flora and Fauna", in *VIJ,* vols. XXXI-XXXII, pts. i-iv, June–December, 1993-94, p. 70.
3. *Ṛgveda,* I.49.3; I.94.5; I.119.1; III.62.14; *Atharvaveda,* IV.11.5; X.8.21; *Vājasaneyī-Saṁhitā,* VIII.30; IX.31; XIV.8; XIV.25; *Aitareya Brāhmaṇa,* VI.2; VIII.20.
4. *Ṛgveda,* X.117.8; *Atharvaveda,* VI.107.1.
5. *Aitareya Brāhmaṇa,* II.18; VI.2; *Śatapatha Brāhmaṇa,* III.7.3.2; VI.8.2.17.

The other species of animals traced in the Vedic literatures are: *uṣṭi* (camel),[6] *ṛkṣa* (bear),[7] *ṛṣya* (stag),[8] *eta* (deer),[9] *kapi* (monkey),[10] *kaśikā* (weasel),[11] *gardabha* (ass),[12] *gavaya* (species of ox),[13] *chāga* (goat),[14] *tsaru* (crawling animal),[15] *dāna* (a chariot horse),[16] *piśa* (deer),[17] *praṣṭi* (side horse),[18] *basta* (goat),[19] *maṇḍūka* (frog),[20] *madhyamavaḥ* (horse),[21] *mahiṣa* (buffalo),[22] *akra* (horse),[23] *aja* (goat),[24] *atya* (racer),[25] *aśva* (horse),[26] *āśu* (steed),[27] *ibha*

6. *Ṛgveda*, X.106.2.
7. Ibid., V.56.3.
8. Ibid., VIII.4.10.
9. Ibid., I.165.2; I.169.6-7; V.54.5; X.77.2.
10. Ibid., X.86.5.
11. Ibid., I.126.5.
12. Ibid., III.53.23.
13. Ibid., IV.21.8.
14. Ibid., I.162.3.
15. Ibid., VII.50.1.
16. Ibid., V.27.5; VII.18.23; VIII.46.24.
17. Ibid., I.64.8.
18. Ibid., I.39.6; VII.27.8.
19. Ibid., I.161.13.
20. Ibid., VII.103.1; X.166.5.
21. Ibid., II.29.4.
22. Ibid., VIII.58.15; IX.92.6; X.123.4.
23. Ibid., I.143.7; I.189.7; III.1.12; IV.6.3; X.72.2.
24. Ibid., X.16.4.
25. Ibid., II.34.3; IX.109.10; X.68.11.
26. *Atharvaveda*, V.17.15.
27. *Ṛgveda*, II.16.3; II.31.2; II.38.3.

(elephant),[28] *udra* (otter),[29] *ula* (jackal),[30] *uṣṭra* (camel),[31] *eḍaka* (ram),[32] *eṇi* (deer),[33] *kaśyapa* (tortoise),[34] *kiṁpuruṣa* (ape),[35] *kurkura* (dog),[36] *kuluṅga* (gazelle),[37] *kūrma* (tortoise),[38] *kṛkalāsa* (chameleon),[39] *khaṅga* (rhinoceros),[40] *khara* (ass),[41] *gaja* (elephant),[42] *godhā* (crocodile),[43] *jatū* (bat),[44] *jahakā* (pole-cat),[45]

---

28. Ibid., I.84.17; IV.4.1; IX.57.3; *Taittirīya-Saṁhitā,* I.2.14.1; *Vājasaneyī-Saṁhitā,* XIII.9.
29. *Taittirīya-Saṁhitā,* V.5.20.1; *Maitrāyaṇī-Saṁhitā,* III.14.18; *Vājasaneyī-Saṁhitā,* XXIV.37.
30. *Atharvaveda,* XII.1.49.
31. *Ṛgveda,* X.106.2; *Atharvaveda,* XX.127.2; XX.132.13; *Vājasaneyī-Saṁhitā,* XIII.50.
32. *Śatapatha Brāhmaṇa,* XII.4.1.4; *Jaiminiya Brāhmaṇa,* I.51.4.
33. *Atharvaveda,* V.14.11. It is the feminine of *eta* (*ṚV,* I.165.2).
34. *Atharvaveda,* IV.20.7.
35. *Aitareya Brāhmaṇa,* II.8; *Śatapatha Brāhmaṇa,* I.2.3.9; VII.5.2.32; *Vājasaneyī-Saṁhitā,* XXX.16; *Taittirīya Brāhmaṇa,* III.4.12.1.
36. *Atharvaveda,* VII.95.2.
37. *Taittirīya-Saṁhitā,* V.5.11.1; *Maitrāyaṇī-Saṁhitā,* III.14.9; III.14.13; *Vājasaneyī-Saṁhitā,* XXIV.27; XXIV.32.
38. *Atharvaveda,* IX.4.16.
39. *Taittirīya-Saṁhitā,* V.5.19.1; *Maitrāyaṇī-Saṁhitā,* III.14.21; *Vājasaneyī-Saṁhitā,* XXIV.40; *Bṛhadāraṇyaka Upaniṣad,* I.5.22; *Jaiminīya Brāhmaṇa,* I.221. Also, *Journal of the American Oriental Society,* 18, 29.
40. *Maitrāyaṇī-Saṁhitā,* III.14.21.
41. *Aitareya Āraṇyaka,* III.2.4.
42. *Journal of the American Oriental Society,* 13, 265, 269.
43. *Ṛgveda,* X.28.10.11.
44. *Atharvaveda,* IX.2.22.
45. *Taittirīya-Saṁhitā,* V.5.18.1.

durvarāha (wild boar),[46] *dvīpin* (panther),[47] *dhūmra* (camel),[48] *nakula* (ichneumon),[49] *nākra* (crocodile),[50] *nāga* (elephant),[51] *nyaṅku* (gazelle),[52] *pāṅktra* (field rat),[53] *puruṣa mṛga* (deer),[54] *puruṣa hastin* (ape),[55] *pūrvavaḥ* (horse),[56] *pṛṣata* (antelope),[57] *pṛṣatī* (antelope),[58] *petva* (ram),[59] *makara* (crocodile),[60] *maya* (horse),[61] *mayu* (ape),[62] *markaṭa* (ape),[63] *marya* (stallion),[64] *mahāja* (great goat),[65] *mahāsuhaya* (great horse),[66] *mācala* (dog),[67] *mūṣika*

---

46. *Śatapatha Brāhmaṇa,* XII.4.1.4.
47. *Atharvaveda,* IV.8.7; VI.38.2; XIX.49.4.
48. *Taittirīya-Saṁhitā,* I.8.21.1.
49. *Atharvaveda,* VI.139.5.
50. *Taittirīya-Saṁhitā,* V.5.13.1.
51. *Śatapatha Brāhmaṇa,* XI.2.7.12.
52. *Taittirīya-Saṁhitā,* V.5.17.1; *Maitrāyaṇī-Saṁhitā,* III.14.9.
53. *Vājasaneyī-Saṁhitā,* XXIV.26; *Maitrāyaṇī-Saṁhitā,* III.14.7.
54. *Aitareya Brāhmaṇa,* III.33.5.
55. *Vājasaneyī-Saṁhitā,* XXIV.29; *Maitrāyaṇī-Saṁhitā,* III.14, 8, of *Yajurveda.*
56. *Taittirīya Brāhmaṇa,* I.1.5.6; *Śatapatha Brāhmaṇa,* II.1.4.17; *Kāṭhaka Saṁhitā,* XIII.3.
57. *Taittirīya-Saṁhitā* of *Yajurveda,* V.5.17.1.
58. *Ṛgveda,* VIII.64.10-11.
59. *Atharvaveda,* IV.4.8.
60. Ibid., VIII.6.12.
61. *Vājasaneyī-Saṁhitā,* XXII.19.
62. *Taittirīya-Saṁhitā,* V.5.12.1.
63. Ibid., V.5.11.1.
64. *Ṛgveda,* III.31.7; III.33.10; IV.20.5.
65. *Śatapatha Brāhmaṇa,* III.4.1.2.
66. *Bṛhadāraṇyaka Upaniṣad,* VI.2.13.
67. *Jaiminīya Brāhmaṇa,* II.440.

(mouse),[68] *mṛga* (deer),[69] *menā* (female animal),[70] *rāsabha* (ass),[71] *ruru* (deer),[72] *rohit* (red mare),[73] *rohita* (red horse),[74] *lopāśa* (jackal),[75] *vaḍavā* (mare),[76] *vadhu* (female animal),[77] *varāha* (boar),[78] *vāraṇa* (elephant),[79] *vṛka* (wolf),[80] *vṛddhavāsinī* (female jackal),[81] *vṛścika* (scorpion),[82] *vṛṣadaṁśa* (cat),[83] *śalabha* (locust),[84] *śalyaka* (porcupine),[85] *śaśa* (hare),[86] *śitpuṭa* (cat),[87] *śukladanta* (elephant),[88] *śvān* (dog),[89] *śvāpad* (predator),[90] *śvāvidh*

---

68. *Ṛgveda,* I.105.8; X.33.3; *Nirukta,* IV.5.
69. *Aitareya Brāhmaṇa,* III.33.5.
70. *Ṛgveda,* I.51.13.
71. Ibid., I.34.9; I.116.2; I.162.21; III.53.5; VIII.85.7.
72. *Taittirīya-Saṁhitā,* V.5.19.1 of *Yajurveda;* Also, *Ṛgveda,* VI.75.15.
73. *Ṛgveda,* I.14.12; I.100.16; V.56.5.
74. Ibid., I.94.10; I.134.9; II.10.2.
75. Ibid., X.28.4.
76. *Taittirīya-Saṁhitā,* VII.1.1.2; *Taittirīya Brāhmaṇa,* I.8.6.3; III.8.22.3.
77. *Ṛgveda,* VIII.19.36.
78. Ibid., I.61.7; VIII.77.10; IX.97.7; X.28.4.
79. Ibid., VIII.33.8; X.40.4.
80. Ibid., I.42.2; I.105.7; I.116.14; II.29.6; VI.51.14; VII.38.7.
81. *Nirukta,* V.21.
82. *Ṛgveda,* I.191.16; *Atharvaveda,* X.4, X.9.15; XII.1.46.
83. *Taittirīya-Saṁhitā,* V.5.21.1 of *Yajurveda.*
84. *Atharvaveda,* IX.5.9.
85. *Vājasaneyī-Saṁhitā,* XXIV.35.
86. *Ṛgveda,* X.28.2.
87. *Taittirīya-Saṁhitā,* V.5.17.1.
88. *Aitareya Brāhmaṇa,* VIII.23.3.
89. *Ṛgveda,* I.161.13.
90. *Atharvaveda,* VIII.5.11; XIX.39.4.

(porcupine),[91] *sapti* (swift steed)[92], *śārameya* (dog),[93] *siṁha* (lion),[94] *sūkara* (wild boar),[95] *śṛgāla* (jackal),[96] *svaja* (viper),[97] *svedaja* (vermin),[98] *haya* (horse),[99] *hariṇa* (gazelle),[100] *hastin* (elephant),[101] *starī* (barren cow),[102] etc.

Meṣa denotes "ram" in the *Ṛgveda,*[103] and later,[104] while *meṣī* means "sheep."[105] Both the words are also used to denote the wool of the sheep, specially as employed for the *soma* filter. There are some specific terms used in the Vedic texts to mean the species of cattle family.

THE CATTLE

The livestock cow, ox, bull, calf, etc. come under the cattle category. Sometimes horses, goats and sheep are included in this group. Generally, the domestic animals, which are brought

---

91. Ibid., V.13.9.
92. *Ṛgveda,* I.85.1, 6; I.162.1; II.34.7; III.22.1.
93. Ibid., VII.55.2. This word denotes Indra's mythical dog. This is applied to a dog on earth in the *Ṛgveda,* as also to the dogs of Yama (*ṚV,* X.14.10).
94. Ibid., I.64.8; I.95.5; III.2.11; III.9.4; III.26.5; IV.16.14.
95. Ibid., VII.55.4.
96. *Śatapatha Brāhmaṇa,* XII.5.2.5.
97. *Atharvaveda,* III.27.4; V.14.10.
98. *Aitareya Upaniṣad,* III.3.3.
99. *Ṛgveda,* V.46.1; VII.74.4.
100. Ibid., I.163.1; V.78.2.
101. Ibid., I.64.7; IV.16.14.
102. Ibid., I.101.3; I.116.22; I.117.20.
103. Ibid., I.43.6; I.116.16; VIII.2.40; X.27.17.
104. *Atharvaveda,* VI.49.2.
105. *Ṛgveda,* I.43.6.

up under the same roof, are termed as cattle. Vedic seers have distinguished them from each other taking into consideration their functions and physical features. Under the heading cattle, the Vedic words traced are *go* (ox, cow),[106] *usrā* or *usriyā* (cow),[107] *dughā* (cow),[108] *vatsa* (calf),[109] *vaśitā* (cow),[110] *starī* (barren cow),[111] *dhenā* (milch cow),[112] *dhenu* (milch cow),[113] *dhenuṣṭarī* (barren cow),[114] *nivānyavatsā* or *nivānyā* (cow with a strange calf),[115] *mahokṣa* (great ox),[116] *vāha* (ox),[117] *vaśā* (barren cow),[118] *anaḍvāḥ* (draught ox),[119] *vehat* (cow that miscarries),[120] *sūtavaśā* (cow barren after calving),[121] *vatsatara* or *vatsatarī* (young calf),[122] *vṛṣabha* (bull),[123] *vaṁsaga* (bull),[124] *usrika* (bull),[125]

---

106. Ibid., I.83.1.
107. Ibid., VI.12.4 and V.58.6.
108. Ibid., VIII.50.3; X.67.1.
109. Ibid., VIII.6.1; VIII.8.8; VIII.9.1; VIII.11.7.
110. *Atharvaveda,* V.20.2.
111. *Ṛgveda,* I.101.3; I.116.22; I.117.20.
112. Ibid., III.34.3.
113. Ibid., I.32.9.
114. *Kāṭhaka-Saṁhitā,* XIII.6; *Maitrāyaṇī-Saṁhitā,* II.5.4.
115. *Śatapatha Brāhmaṇa,* XII.5.1.4.
116. Ibid., III.4.1.2.
117. *Ṛgveda,* IV.57.4; IV.57.8 *Atharvaveda,* VI.102.1.
118. *Ṛgveda,* II.7.5; VI.63.9; X.91.14.
119. Ibid., X.59.10; X.85.10; III.53.18; *Atharvaveda,* III.11.5; IV.11.1.
120. *Atharvaveda,* XII.4.37.
121. *Taittirīya-Saṁhitā,* II.1.5.4; VI.1.3.6 of *Yajurveda.*
122. *Taittirīya-Saṁhitā,* I.8.17.1; I.18.1.
123. *Ṛgveda,* I.94.10; I.160.3; VI.46.4.
124. Ibid., I.7.8; I.55.1; I.58.4; V.36.1.
125. Ibid., I.190.5.

ṛṣabha (bull),[126] *maryaka* (bull),[127] *maharṣabha* (great bull),[128] *mahānirașṭa* (great castrated ox),[129] etc. The young cow is called *gṛṣṭi.*[130] According to the colour, white and red cows are mentioned. They are *karki*[131] and *rohiṇī*[132] respectively. Taking age of the ox, three types are found. These are *turyavāḥ* (four-year-old ox),[133] *trivatsa* (three-year-old ox)[134] and *tryavī* (eighteen-months-old ox).[135] Again the word *yūtha*[136] denotes the herd of the cows.

The Birds

The Vedic literature refers to the words, *pakṣin,*[137] *patatrin,*[138] *vi,*[139] *śakun,*[140] *śakuni,*[141] *śakunta,*[142] and *śakuntaka,*[143] which denote birds. *Śakunti,*[144] is taken as the bird of omen. A bird is

---

126. *Śatapatha Brāhmaṇa,* XIII.5.4.15.
127. *Ṛgveda,* V.2.5.
128. *Atharvaveda,* IV.15.1.
129. *Taittirīya-Saṁhitā,* I.8.9.1.
130. *Ṛgveda,* IV.18.10.
131. *Atharvaveda,* IV.38.6-7.
132. *Ṛgveda,* VIII.93.13; VIII.101.13.
133. *Taittirīya-Saṁhitā,* IV.3.3.2; *Maitrāyaṇī-Saṁhitā,* III.11.11; III.13.17; *Vājasaneyī-Saṁhitā,* XIV.10; XVIII.26.
134. *Pañcaviṁśa Brāhmaṇa,* XVI.13; XVIII.9; XXI.14.
135. *Ṛgveda,* III.55.14.
136. Ibid., I.10.2; I.81.7; III.55.17; IV.2.18.
137. *Ṛgveda,* I.48.5; I.182.5; X.127.5.
138. *Atharvaveda,* VIII.7.24; X.10.14.
139. *Ṛgveda,* II.29.5; II.38.7; VI.64.6.
140. Ibid., IV.26.6; IX.85.11.
141. Ibid., II.42.2.
142. *Atharvadeda,* XI.6.8.
143. Ṛgveda, II.43.1; I.191.1.
144. Ibid., II.42.3; II.43.1.

generally accepted as a winged creature. The Vedic world of birds includes: *ulūka* (owl),[145] *kapota* (pigeon),[146] *gṛdhra* (vulture),[147] *cakravāka* (*Anas casarca*),[148] *takvaṇ* (swift flying bird),[149] *ropaṇāka* (thrush),[150] *varttikā* (quail),[151] *vāyasa* (crow),[152] *śāri*,[153] *śyena*[154] (eagle), *haṁsa* (gander),[155] *hāridrava* (water wagtail),[156] *kalaviṅka* (sparrow),[157] *aliklava* (carrion bird),[158] *kukkuṭa* (cock),[159] *kuṭaru* (cock),[160] *kuṣitaka* (sea crow),[161] *kṛkavāku* (cock),[162] *kruñc* (curlew),[163] *khargalā* (owl),[164] *darvidā* (woodpecker),[165] *dātyauha* (gallinule),[166] *darvāghāta* (wood

---

145. Ibid., I.165.4.
146. Ibid., I.30.4; and *Atharvaveda*, XX.135.12.
147. *Ṛgveda*, I.118.4; II.39.1.
148. Ibid., II.39.3.
149. Ibid., I.66.2.
150. Ibid., I.50.12.
151. Ibid., I.112.18; I.116.4; I.117.16; I.118.8; X.39.13.
152. Ibid., I.164.32.
153. *Tattirīya-Saṁhitā*, V.5.12.1; *Maitrāyaṇī-Saṁhitā*, III.14.14; *Vājasaneyī-Saṁhitā*, XXIV.33.
154. *Ṛgveda*, I.32.14; I.33.2; I.118.11.
155. Ibid., I.65.5; I.163.10; II.34.5.
156. Ibid., I.50.12; VIII.35.7.
157. *Taittirīya-Saṁhitā*, II.5.1.2.
158. *Atharvaveda*, XI.2.2; XI.9.9.
159. *Vājasaneyī-Saṁhitā*, I.16.
160. Ibid., XXIV.23.
161. *Taittirīya-Saṁhitā*, V.5.13.1.
162. *Atharvaveda*, V.31.2.
163. *Maitrāyaṇi-Saṁhitā*, III.11.6.
164. *Ṛgveda*, VII.104.17.
165. *Taittirīya-Saṁhitā*, V.5.13.1 of *Yajurveda*.
166. Ibid., V.5.17.1.

pecker),[167] *dhvāṅkṣa* (crow),[168] *pārāvata* (turtle dove),[169] *pika* (cuckoo),[170] *plava* (pelican),[171] *balākā* (crane), *bhāsa* (bird of prey),[172] *madgu* (diver),[173] *mahāsuparṇa* (great eagle),[174] *laba* (quail),[175] *saghan* (eagle)[176] and *haṁsasāci*,[177] etc.

Mayūra (peacock)[178] occurs in the *Ṛgveda* in the compounds describing Indra's horses. The pea-hen (*mayūrī*)[179] is mentioned in the *Ṛgveda* and the *Atharvaveda*.

The Insects

Micro-organisms like ants, bees, flies, spiders, etc. are mentioned in the Vedic texts. The names of these insects are: *āraṅgara* (bee),[180] *indragopa* (cochineal insect),[181] *upajihvikā* or *upajikā* or *upadīkā* (ant),[182] *ūrṇanābhi* or *ūrṇavābhi* (spider),[183]

---

167. Ibid., V.5.15.1.
168. *Atharvaveda*, XI.9.9; XII.4.8.
169. *Ṛgveda*, V.52.11; VIII.100.6; *Atharvaveda*, XX.135.14.
170. *Taittirīya-Saṁhitā* (of *Yajurveda*), V.5.15.1.
171. Ibid., V.5.16.1.
172. *Adbhuta Brāhmaṇa*, VI.8.
173. *Taittirīya-Saṁhitā* (of *Yajurveda*), V.5.20.1.
174. *Śatapatha Brāhmaṇa*, XII.2.3.7.
175. *Maitrāyaṇī-Saṁhitā*, III.14.5.
176. *Taittirīya-Saṁhitā*, III.2.1.1; *Taittirīya Brāhmaṇa*, II.8.6.1.
177. *Taittirīya-Saṁhitā*, V.5.20.1.
178. *Ṛgveda*, III.45.1; VIII.1.25.
179. Ibid., I.191.14; *Atharvaveda*, VII.56.7.
180. *Ṛgveda*, X.106.10.
181. *Bṛhadāraṇyaka Upaniṣad*, II.3.6.
182. *Ṛgveda*, VIII.102.21; *Atharvaveda*, II.3.4; *Taittirīya Brāhmaṇa*, I.1.3.4.
183. *Taittirīya Brāhmaṇa* I.1.2.5; *Kāṭhaka-Saṁhitā*, VIII.1.

kaṅkaṭa (scorpion),[184] *kaṅkaparvan* (scorpion),[185] *kṛkalāsa* (chameleon),[186] *khadyota* (firefly),[187] *jabhya* (grain insect),[188] *tarda* (grain insect),[189] *tṛṇajalāyuka* (caterpillar),[190] *tṛṇaskanda* (grasshopper),[191] *daṁśa* (fly),[192] *pataṅga* (winged insect),[193] *pipīla* (ant),[194] *pipīlikā* (ant),[195] *bhṛṅgā* (bee),[196] *makṣa* (fly),[197] *makṣā* or *makṣikā* (fly),[198] *maṭacī* (locust),[199] *madhukara* (bee),[200] *maśaka* (mosquito),[201] *saragh* (bee),[202] *saraḥ* (bee),[203] *sūcīka*,[204] etc. The *Ṛgveda* describes *sūcikā* as a stinging insect. As per the narrations of the Vedic texts, most of these insects are the Victims at the *Aśvamedha* sacrifice (horse sacrifice).

---

184. *Ṛgveda*, I.191.1.
185. *Atharvaveda*, VII.56.1.
186. *Taittirīya-Saṁhitā*, V.5.19.1 of *Yajurveda*.
187. *Chāndogya Upaniṣad*, VI.7.3.5.
188. *Atharvaveda*, VI.50.2.
189. Ibid., VI.50.1-2.
190. *Bṛhadāraṇyaka Upaniṣad*, IV.2.4.
191. *Ṛgveda*, I.172.3.
192. *Chāndogya Upaniṣad*, VI.9.3; VI.10.2.
193. *Atharvaveda*, VI.50.7.
194. *Ṛgveda*, X.16.6.
195. *Atharvaveda*, VII.56.7.
196. Ibid., IX.2.22.
197. *Ṛgveda*, IV.45.4; VII.32.2.
198. Ibid., I.162.9; *Atharvaveda*, XI.1.2; XI.9.10.
199. *Chāndogya Upaniṣad*, I.10.1.
200. *Taittirīya-Saṁhitā*, I.5.6.5; IV.2.9.6.
201. *Atharvaveda*, VII.56.3.
202. *Śatapatha Brāhmaṇa*, III.4.3.14.
203. *Ṛgveda*, I.112.21.
204. Ibid., I.191.7.

Reptiles

THE SERPENTS

Different types of snakes and crawling animals are mentioned in the Vedic literature. The serpent has been described as a much dreadful reptile. The word *sarīsṛpa* meaning reptile is traced in the *Ṛgveda*.[205] The Vedic names of serpents are: *aghāśva*,[206] *ajagara*[207] (boa constrictor), *asita*[208] (black snake), *āligi*,[209] *āśiviṣa*,[210] *kaṇikrada* or *karikrata*,[211] *kalmāṣagriva*,[212] *kasarṇīla*,[213] *jīrṇī*,[214] *tiraścarāji*,[215] *taimāta*,[216] *daśonāsī* or *naśonāsī*,[217] *nāga*[218] (cobra), *pṛdāku*,[219] *bhujyu* (adder),[220] *bhoga* (coil),[221] *mahānāga*,[222] *rajju*

---

205. *Ṛgveda*, X.162.3.
206. *Atharvaveda*, X.4.10.
207. Ibid., XI.2.25; XX.129.17.
208. Ibid., III.27.1; V.13.5-6; VI.56.2.
209. Ibid., V.13.7.
210. *Aitareya Brāhmaṇa*, VI.1.
211. *Atharvaveda*, X.4.13.
212. Ibid., III.27.5.
213. Ibid., X.4.5.
214. Ibid., II.24.5.
215. *Taittirīya-Saṁhitā*, V.5.10.2; *Atharvaveda*, III.27.2; VI.56.2.
216. Ibid., V.13.6; V.18.4.
217. Ibid., X.4.17.
218. *Śatapatha Brāhmaṇa*, XI.2.7.12.
219. *Atharvaveda*, I.27.1; III.27.3; VI.38.1.
220. *Ṛgveda*, I.112., I.112.20.
221. Ibid., V.29.6; VI.75.14.
222. *Śatapatha Brāhmaṇa*, XI.2.7.12.

datvatī,[223] *ratharvī*,[224] *lohitāhi* (red snake),[225] *vāhasa* (boa constrictor),[226] *viligi*,[227] *śerabha* or *śerabhaka*,[228] *śevr̥dha* or *śevr̥dhaka*,[229] *śvitra*,[230] *satinakaṅkta*,[231] *sarpa*,[232] *svaja* (viper),[233] etc.

The word *ahi*[234] is also used to mean "serpent" instead of *sarpa*, but it appears in the later Vedic texts. Many of the above-listed have been identified with their zoological names, still some are yet to be identified.

THE WORMS

Besides the names of animals, birds, cattle and serpents, the Vedic literature mentions some species of worms. These are of two varieties like *dr̥ṣṭa* and *adr̥ṣṭa*[235] or visible and invisible. Generally, the word used for the worms is *kīṭa*.[236] The worms mentioned in the Vedic literature are : *alāṇḍu* or *algaṇḍu*,[237]

---

223. *R̥gveda*, I.162.8; *Atharvaveda*, III.11.8; VI.121.2.
224. Ibid., X.4.5.
225. *Tatittirīya-Saṁhitā* (of *Yajurveda*), V.5.14.1.
226. Ibid., V.5.13.1.
227. *Atharvaveda*, V.13.7.
228. Ibid., II.24.1.
229. Ibid.
230. *Pañcaviṁśa Brāhmaṇa*, XII.11.11.
231. *R̥gveda*, I.191.1.
232. Ibid., X.16.6.
233. *Atharvaveda*, III.27.4; V.14.10; VI.56.2; X.4.10, 15, 17.
234. Ibid., X.4.23; XI.3.47.
235. *R̥gveda*, I.191.4; *Atharvaveda*, VI.52.2-3.
236. Ibid., IX.4.16.
237. Ibid., II.31.2.

avaskava,[238] *ejatka,*[239] *kapanā,*[240] *kaṣkaṣa,*[241] *kurūru,*[242] *kṛmi,*[243] *nīlaṅgu,*[244] *yavāṣa* or *yevāṣa,*[245] *vaghā,*[246] *vṛkṣasarpi,*[247] *śaluna,*[248] *śavarta,*[249] *sipavitnuka,*[250] *śvavarta,*[251] *stega,*[252] etc.

Both the Vedas *Ṛg*[253] and *Atharva*[254] mention the word *adṛṣṭa* (the unseen) for designating a species of vermin. In the *Atharvaveda,* the epithets "seen" and "unseen" are applied to the worm (*kṛmi*), their use being no doubt due to the widespread theory of diseases caused by the worms, whether discernible by examination or not. Especially in the *Atharvaveda,* worms play a considerable part. They are regarded as poisonous, and are spoken of as found in the mountains, in forests, in waters, in plants, and in the human body. In accordance with widespread primitive ideas, they are considered to be the causes, of diseases in men and animals. The *Atharvaveda* contians three hymns[255] as charms directed

238. Ibid., II.31.4.
239. Ibid., V.23.7.
240. *Ṛgveda,* V.54.6.
241. *Atharvaveda,* V.23.7.
242. Ibid., II.31.2; IX.2.22.
243. Ibid., II.31.32; V.23.7
244. *Taittirīya-Saṁhitā* (of *Yajurveda*), V.5.11.1.
245. *Atharvaveda,* V.23.7-8.
246. Ibid., VI.50.3; IX.2.22.
247. Ibid., IX.2.22.
248. Ibid., II.31.2.
249. Ibid., IX.4.16.
250. Ibid., V.20.7.
251. Ibid., IX.4.16.
252. *Ṛgveda,* II.31.9; *Atharvaveda,* XVIII.1.39; *Taittirīya-Saṁhitā* (of *Yajurveda*), V.7.11.1.
253. *Ṛgveda,* I.191.4.
254. *Atharvaveda,* VI.52.2; VI.52.3.
255. Ibid., II.31.32; V.23.7.

against them. The first of these hymns is of a general character, the second is meant to destroy worms in cattle, and the third is intended to cure children of worms. When found in men, worms are said to have their place in the head and ribs,[256] and to creep into the eyes, nose, and teeth.[257] They are described as dark brown, but white in the fore part of the body, with black ears, and as having three heads.[258] They are known in different names as mentioned above.

Thus, innumerable species of animals, birds, cattle, serpents, insects and worms are found in the Vedic literature starting from the Vedas to the *sūtras*. Such an account provides a clear picture of the fauna of the Vedic period. All these organism including human beings maintain enviornmental equilibrium, some are being *khādya* (food) and some are *khādaka* (food-eater). This is only possible with the presence of natural resources like forests, rivers, lakes, mountains, streams, seas, oceans, etc. Remarkably, it is also observed that there is no reference to the animal "tiger" in the Vedas,[259] though these species are still available in our forests and zoos, and are popular among the Indians.

As the Vedic people were composed mainly of agricultural and pastoral communities, the domestication of animals and cultivation of plants provided them ample opportunities of knowing and observing many animals, birds and plants. This brief survey of the fauna of the Vedic period shows that the Vedic people had gained much about their surroundings during the course of their settlement and formation of their society.

---

256. Ibid., II.31.4.

257. Ibid., V.23.3.

258. Ibid., V.23.4.

259. A.A. Macdonell, and A.B. Keith, *Vedic Index of Names and Subjects*, vols. I and II, Delhi: MLBD, rpt., 1995. Also, U. Gupta, *Materialism in the Vedas*, New Delhi: Classical Publishing Company, 1987, p. 138.

6

Medicine

Introduction

THE earliest roots of Indian culture have attracted the minds of the scholars, the investigators, the scientiests and the common mass at large in order to explore the healing tradition and practices which prevailed during the period of the Vedas. Examining the earliest textual evidence of medicine, it is understood that the Indian medical heritage goes back to the Vedic age. It is all too easy to fall into the trap of talking about "Vedic Medicine" as though this was an integrated medical system. But there are, of course, no medical texts existent in the Vedic period,[1] nor do we have any evidence that such texts were ever written separately by the Vedic seers. The best we can do in this regard is to comb meticulously through the surviving Vedic literature and to reconstruct, from such texts, a picture of medical thought and practice prevailing during the period of the Vedic literature.

Reading and rereading the Veda again and again create new ideas and insights. The Veda is a vast and fascinating subject that constantly beckons one to plunge ever deeper into its texts in an attempt to unlock the wonderful mysteries of the archaic mind. The enigmatic and clever hymns of the *Ṛgveda* and *Atharvaveda* provide us many facts connected with physiology, anatomy, embryology, toxicology in particular and biology in general. Vedic toxicology is one important part

1. K.G. Zysk, *Medicine in the Veda,* Delhi: MLBD, 1996, Foreword.

of this healing tradition. Several hymns of the *Atharvaveda* and a few of the *R̥gveda* concern themselves with poisoning usually caused by animals and with the remedial measures to cure it. The most remarkable fact is that India's long and renowned tradition of toxicology has been derived from the basic knowledge of poisons and poisonous animals found in the Veda. With the advancement of time, the Indian healing arts depicted in the Vedic hymns gave birth to the Āyurvedic system of healing.

Pharmacopoeia forms the distinctive part of the Vedic medicine. Vedic knowledge of the local flora and its rich description of the plant world show the botanical wisdom of the Vedic seers. The hymns of the *Atharvaveda* largely deal with the medicinal plants and herbs and thus adhere to a tradition of healing plant goddesses. On the other hand, the hymns of the *R̥gveda* reveal less of a familiarity with indigenous plant life, and as observed these hymns relate principally to a tradition of a male plant divinity. A homologization of these two botanical traditions is reflected in the mythological connections between the principal plant deities mentioned in each text, and occurs in mythical parts of the Atharvavedic medical hymns. Here are found myths of both the healing plant god Kuṣṭha, and the healing plant goddess Arundhatī. *Kuṣṭha* was generally identified with the aromatic costus, native of Kashmir. It was used to cure fever (*takmān*). It was known to have been an important export from India in the spice trade. The healing plant goddess Arundhatī was used in the treatment of fractures and wounds, and is identified among others with *lākṣā*, the Sanskrit term for the resinous "lac." *Kuṣṭha* is linked with the R̥gvedic plant *soma* and the Atharvavedic plant Arundhatī mythologically. *Soma* is significant in sacrificial rites, whereas Arundhatī is related to the medical cults. Both *soma* and *kuṣṭha* grow high in the Hemavant Mountains, the birth place of eagles, the third heaven from earth and the seat of the gods.

Kuṣṭha is called Soma's brother in the mythological epithets. Likewise a number of the epithets associated with *Kuṣṭha* are identical to those given to Arundhatī. They are both perennial, life-giving, and harmless. Kuṣṭha's mythological link with Soma and his name-association with Arundhatī imply a conscious effort to homologize a Ṛgvedic botanical tradition dominated by a male plant divinity with a medical-botanical tradition of plant goddess particular to the *Atharvaveda*.[2] Thus, the medicinal values of the plant-world as experienced by the Vedic people are closely associated with their botanical knowledge. The mythological traditions of plant divinities depicted in the *Ṛgveda* and *Atharvaveda* reveal interesting aspects of the homologization of religious ideas and help identify elements of indigenous beliefs in ancient India.

The Vedic healer's knowledge of the local flora tends to link him to an agrarian-oriented group of poeple; and his use of magical rituals, amulets, and incantations reflects fundamental folk beliefs. Vedic literature has traditionally been in the form of folklore, often transmitted orally from generation to generation. In many Indo-European cultures, folk literature preserves the peoples' medical knowledge in the form of folk medicine and home remedies. Learned and well-experienced Vedic people have produced the healing hymns of the *Atharvaveda*, which project one of the earliest forms of folk healing of Indo-European antiquity, and present an excellent instance of the ancient folk literature.[3]

The priests of the Vedic period have significant

2. K.G. Zysk, *Asceticism and healing in ancient India*, Oxford University Press, 1991, pp. 17-19.
3. K.G. Zysk, "Reflections on an Indo-European system of medicine," in *Perspectives on Indo-European Language, Culture and Religion. Studies in honor of Edgar Polomē*, vol. 2, McLean, Virgina Institute for the Study of Man, 1992, pp. 321-36.

contributions towards the ancient healing traditions. Their functions in the performances of Vedic rites and sacrifices were thought to bring them into direct contact with the greater cosmic forces. The Vedic healers also required knowledge of the means to control the natural forces in order to cure the diseases. The priests gained such type of knowledge from the sacrificial cults and had access to the spirit world with control over them. Evidently, there were two types of priests — the medical priests and the sacrificial priests. The medical priest probably enjoyed relative freedom in the social structure and was not confined to a particular social group, as he served the needs of all people irrespective of their social standing. The sacrificial priest, on the other hand, fearing contamination from impure elements of the society, was restricted to the social milieu of the first order. Gradually the healer-group established their stand in the ancient society and this led eventually to a radical shift in medical thinking. Ostensibly, a new approach to medicine was developed and which came to be regarded as classical Āyurveda.

The ancient healing tradition is based on magico-religious beliefs and practices. The classical medical treatises of Caraka and Suśruta deal with the methods of treatment pertaining to Āyurveda. From the medical books of Caraka and Suśruta, it is cleraly evident that the Vedic form of medicine never completely disappeared, but was probably superseded over time by a system of medicine based on empiricio-rational principles and practices. Vedic healing practices relied on close observation of phenomena in order to develop its unique form of mythical and religious classifications and associations. The foundation of Vedic medicine was a belief in a multitude of benevolent and malevolent deities or spirits that populated the cosmos and caused good and bad effects in the human realm. Controlling and taming these entities were the ultimate goals of this healing system.

Āyurvedic method of treatment is fully dependent on the basic understanding of the interrelationship between humans and their environment. There should be perfect harmony between humans and the nature surrounding them. Disease occurs when the harmony breaks. Restoration of the equilibrium between the two was the goal of this medical system. In course of time, the Vedic tradition of healing was shifted to the classical form with the development of the process of observing and defining the ailments.

The tradition of religious healing is also reflected in the Buddhist culture and literature. The Buddhists acquired a radically different view of the world and humankind's place in it, fostered by their intense meditative discipline. In fact, early Buddhist literature reveals that their understanding of the relationship between humans and nature was not very different from that which contributed to Āyurvedic medical thought. Medicine became part of Buddhism by providing the means to maintain a healthy bodily state characterized by an equilibrium — both within the body and between the body and its surroundings. Portions of the repository of medical lore were codified in the early monastic rules, thereby giving rise to a Buddhist monastic medical tradition.

During the early part of the Christian era, Brāhmanism assimilated the storehouse of medical knowledge into the socio-religious and intellectual tradition and by the application of an orthodox veneer rendered it a Brāhmanic science. Over the nine centuries of this transitional phase of Indian medicine, the medical system represented in the early Vedic literature gradually diminished in significance until medicine became part of Brāhmanism, whose intellectuals consciously revived the ancient medical wisdom in order to legitimize a largely heterodox body of knowledge and make it orthodox.[4]

---

4. K.G. Zysk, *Medicine in the Veda*, Delhi: MLBD, 1996, p. XV.

Characteristics of Vedic Medicine

The earliest Indian textual evidence of medicine is randomly inserted in the corpora of its principal religious literature, primarily in the *Atharvaveda* and to a much lesser extent in the *Ṛgveda*. Actually, the *Atharvaveda* deals with the real medical doctrines of secular nature. The *Ṛgveda*, on the other hand, provides for the most part mythological stories illustrating the healings performed by various gods of the Vedic pantheon. The medical references are found scattered in the Ṛgvedic hymns and such episodes provide us an idea about the medical philosophy and practice of the Vedic people. This fact is clearly exposed in the report of the investigations carried out by R. Müller[5] on the medicine of the *Ṛgveda*.

Any medical treatment is based on the study of the anatomy and physiology of the patient. Anatomical knowledge in ancient India was derived principally from the sacrifice of the horse and of man. In case of the horse, the anatomical knowledge is traced in *Ṛgveda* I.162.18. This is gradually transmitted through the exegetical Brāhmaṇa-texts. Still there were difficulties in identifying some of the internal parts of the body. However, the native authorities tried to explain the organs by their observations on a locality. Such identifications provided the principal sources of anatomical knowledge until the time of the classical treatises (Saṁhitās) of Āyurvedic medicine, when the visual inspection of the body by a type of dissection was introduced, perhaps from the West, into the traditional system of medical education. This, in turn, contributed a totally new dimension to the human body.[6]

---

5. R. Müller, "Die Medizin in Ṛgveda," *Asia Major*, 6, 1930, pp. 315-76, 386-87.
6. K.G. Zysk, "The Evolution of Anatomical Knowledge in Ancient India, with special reference to cross-cultural influences," *JAOS*, 106.4.

With the knowledge of the ancient Indian medical tradition, it is observed that the Vedic healing tradition fully rests on the magico-religious system. In such a system, the causes of diseases are not attributed to physiological functions, but rather to external beings or forces of a demonic nature who enter the body of their victim and produce sickness. The removal of such malevolent entities usually involved an elaborate ritual.

The empirical medicine evident during this Vedic period, on the other hand, involved both observation and experience in order to determine the cause of disease and to effect an appropriate treatment.

During the period of the Vedas, there was the belief that evil spirits, demons and other malevolent forces invaded the body and caused their victims to exhibit a state of disease. These demons were often personified and deified, giving rise to an entire pantheon of gods of disease. One, who commits sin against the gods, suffers. The suffering may also come from witchcraft and sorcery. Accroding to the notion of the Vedic Indians, bone injuries or wounds are caused accidentally or as a result of warfare. Vedic people thought that the external diseases and afflictions were caused by noxious insects and vermin, which were demonic in nature.

Vedic tradition of healing actually, lacks the idea of health. Any disease or injury caused by the demons is a negative approach to the sufferings of a patient.

It was the general concept of the various cultures of the world that an individual was considered to be healthy if his lifetime was long, and if he showed complete recovery from illness. It was also noticed that the intake of nutritious food keeps a body healthy. In this connection, the comments of Rahul Peter Das are noteworthy. In an elaborate review, he has broached the topics of magic, religion and science in the medical context. His observations could serve as a point of departure for a complete examination and reappraisal of these terms in the light of modern scholarship in the history of medicine, the history of religions, and anthropology.[7]

Vedic tradition of healing was based on the rituals. In order to cure a patient from sufferings caused by the disease-demon, an elaborate healing ritual was performed. The principal figure in the rite was the healer (*bhiṣaja*) who recites *mantra*s and practises *tantra*s to make the patient free from the disease-demon. He is a shaker (*vipra*) and at the same time a chanter (*kavi*). The contents of the hymns suggest that he possessed a special knowledge of the preparation and use of medicines, including medicinal herbs or simples, and often water. The consecration of these remedies formed a significant part of his sacred utterances. In certain instances, the healer waved or stroked plants over the patient in the course of his ritual performance. The healer, like the professional carpenter who fixed something broken, was also known to be one who repaired the fracture, suggesting that one of his professional activities was the setting of bones.[8]

Process of Healing

The healing procedure was entirely dependent upon religious rites adhering to the recitation of Vedic *mantra*s or hymns. An analysis of these verses illustrates certain apotropaic devices which included the use of sympathetic magic, of rhetorical questions of onomatopoeic sounds, of the identifying name, of the esoteric word or phrase which, when properly uttered focused the demon's attention on the healer, leading to its loss of grip and power. Disease-demons were often transferred from the patient to enemies or less desirable people, dispelled into the ground or carried away by birds to places where

7. *Indo-Iranian Journal* 23.3, 1984, pp. 232-44.

8. *Ṛgveda,* IX.112.1.

they could no longer be a menace to the community. Amulets or talismans (*maṇi*, literally "jewel"), usually of vegetal origin, were ritually bound to drive out demons and to act as prophylactic measures in preventing further attacks. Fragrant plant substances were burnt to help expel the patient's demon, to protect him, and to make his environment pure and generally favourable for healing. Early morning (dawn), noon, and early evening (twilight) seem to have been the most auspicious times of the day to carry out healing rituals. Some rites were performed when certain stars were in a particular part of the heavens, suggesting that astrology may have played an important role in Vedic tradition of healing.[9]

Mythology in the Vedic way of Healing

Mythology played a significant role in the Vedic tradition of healing. The charms and hymns recited by the healer are closely linked with mythology. Major disease-demons are not only deified but also often mythologized, pointing to the important and long-lasting impact they had on the people. Likewise, certain curative herbs were treated as deities. These were often personified and worshipped as gods and more commonly as goddesses. Mythological stories about plant divinities, uttered during the rite, imbued the herbs and plants employed there with supernatural powers and hence made them extremely potent. Reverence for plant-life was an integral part of the Vedic Indian's medical tradition and gave rise to an elaborate pharmacopoeia which is evident in all phases of Indian Medical history.[10]

Vedic healers, through their diagnosis and prognosis, could be able to identify and isolate the dominant and recurring symptoms, many of which were considered to be separate demonic entities. This technique illustrates the importance

9. K.G. Zysk, op. cit., p. 9.

10. Ibid.

which the recording of observable facts played in Vedic medicine. Various conditions of a patient were observed carefully, given names and recorded. Plants and herbs were also put under the same rigorous scrutiny and their important features and qualities noted. Such "empirical" mode of thought was reflected in later Indian philosophical, religious and scientific literature.

The Vedic way of treatment was systematic and classificatory in nature. The Vedic healers were familiar with more empirical procedures of healing. Vedic medicine was connected with magico-religious rites. The recitations of the proper words, the performance of the correct actions, and the employment of the right procedures made the treatments successful. One can visualize clearly the principal doctrinal remains of the Vedic phase of Indian medicine by going deep into the text of the most significant hymns pertaining to the Vedic way of healing.

VEDIC PHYSICIANS AND PRACTICE OF MEDICINE

The word *bhiṣaja* commonly occurred in the Vedic Saṁhitās to denote physician.[11] Similarly *bheṣaja* traced in the Vedic hymns means the practice of medicine.[12] The medical profession, in the early Vedic period, was not hereditary. It is evident from the hymn of the *R̥gveda* (IX.112.3) where the poet says, "I am a poet, dad is a leech." In those days, the physicians were a respected group of the community because, the Vedic gods like the Aśvins,[13] Varuṇa[14] and Rudra[15] are reverently called

11. *R̥gveda,* II.33.4; VI.50.7; IX.112.1; *Atharvaveda,* V.29.1; VI.24.2; *Taittirīya-Saṁhitā,* VI.4.9.2; *Vājasaneyī-Saṁhitā,* XVI.5; XIX.12.8; XXX.10.
12. *R̥gveda,* I.89.4; II.33.2; *Atharvaveda,* V.29.1; VI.21.2.
13. *R̥gveda,* I.116.16; I.157.6; VIII.18.8; 86.1; X.39.3.5; *Atharvaveda,* VII. 53.1.
14. *R̥gveda,* I.24.9.
15. Ibid., II.33.4, 7.

physicians. That the practice of medicine was a means of livelihood is attested by the following verse, "we have various hopes and plans and many are the ways of men, the craftsman seeks a job to do, the priest his flock, the leech the sick."[16] This profession, however, gradually came to disrepute till the rise of the classical Indian medicine, the Āyurveda. In course of time, the profession come to be disliked by the priestly class. This is clear from the inclusion of a physician in the list of victims at the *Puruṣamedha* sacrifice.[17] *Atharvaveda*[18] also mentions hundreds of medical practitioners and thousands of medicinal herbs as distinct from priest-magicians and the amulets. But, one priest-magician is said to be equal in power with hundreds of ordinary physicians and his amulet was not less in potency than that of the thousands of herbs together. As pointed out by Uma Gupta,[19] most of the medical practices of the *Atharvaveda* are merely magical in nature. It, however, contains many empirico-rational elements.[20] Hence, the exponents of the classical system of Indian medicine, the Āyurveda, either derive their science from or relate it to the *Atharvaveda*.[21]

Both the *Atharvaveda* and the *Ṛgveda* refer to many wonderful cures and surgical feats performed by the Vedic

16. Ibid., IX.112.1.

17. *Vājasaneyī-Saṁhitā*, XXX.10; *Taittirīya Brāhmaṇa*, III.4.4.1; Also, A.B. Keith, *The Religion and Philosophy of the Vedas and Upaniṣads*, Harvard Oriental Series, vols. XXXI and XXXII, Harvard University Press, Cambridge, Mass., 1925, pp. 379-80.

18. *Atharvaveda*, II.9.3.5.

19. Uma Gupta, *Materialism in the Vedas*, New Delhi: Classical Publishing Company, 1987, p. 137.

20. P. Kutumbiah, *Ancient Indian Medicine*, Orient Longmans, 1962, S.N. Dasgupta, *Āyurveda-Vijñāna*, Prabāsī, vol. XXXIV, Part I, no. 3 1934, pp. 349-57.

21. V.W. Karambelkar, *The Atharvaveda and the Āyurveda*, Nagpur, 1961.

physicians. Credit goes to the Aśvins for the healing of the lame,[22] the restoration of the eyesight to the blind,[23] the rejuvenation of the aged,[24] and the giving of an iron leg to Viṣpalā when her own leg was lost.[25] The healing powers of the medicinal plants used by a physicain are also referred to.[26]

The diseases mentioned in the Vedas are of two types — the internal diseases and the external diseases. According to Professor Dasgupta,[27] diseases were classified into three types as per their origin. These are

(i) the diseases produced by wind, water or by fire;

(ii) the diseases produced by worms or germs, and

(iii) the diseases caused due to sorcery by enemies.

Diseases

INTERNAL DISEASES

The analyses of the medical lore surrounding the internal diseases have been divided into two sections,[28] namely,

(A) those related to *yakṣmā* and/or *takmān,* and

(B) those unrelated to *yakṣmā* and/or *takmān.*

The first section examines the disease-entities which demonstrate a definite connection with one or the other of the major internal disease-demons, *yakṣmā* and *takmān.* Since many of the symptoms are shared by both, some overlapping can be expected. The second section explains the demonic diseases

22. *R̥gveda,* I.112.8; X.39.3.
23. Ibid., I.116.16.
24. Ibid., X.39.4; I.116.13.
25. Ibid., I.116.15.
26. Ibid., X.97.
27. S.N. Dasgupta, op. cit., pp. 330-31.
28. K.G. Zysk, op. cit., p. 12.

which exhibit the general characteristic of being in the body.

Diseases Related to Yakṣmā and/or Takmān

In the first category of internal diseases, *yakṣmā* (consumption, tuberculosis),[29] *jāyānya,*[30] *kṣetrīya,*[31] *rāpas,*[32] *hṛddyotā* or *hṛdroga* (chest-pain, angina pectoris?),[33] *harimān* (jaundice),[34] *balāsa* (swelling),[35] *takmān* (fevers, malaria, etc.)[36] and *kāsā* (cough)[37] are included. We will now focus on the causes and remedies of these diseases as depicted in the Vedic literature.

Yakṣmā: *Yakṣmā* is the general disease-demon traced in the *Atharvaveda-Saṁhitā.*[38] It is found both in humans and Cattle.[39] It affects each and every part of the body.[40] It causes disintegration of the limbs, fever in the limbs, heartache and pain in all parts of the body.[41] H. Zimmer opines that *yakṣmā* refers to a class of diseases whose principal characteristics are those of consumption.[42] R. Müller considers that, in the eyes of the Vedic people, *yakṣmā* was simply a demon or external

---

29. *Ṛgveda,* I.122.9; X.97.12; X.161.5; X.163.2; *Atharvaveda-Saṁhitā* (Śaunakīya recension), II.33, VI.85.1, IX.8.7, IX.12.3.
30. *Atharvaveda-Saṁhitā,* op. cit., VII.76; *Taittirīya-Saṁhitā,* II.3.5.1-2.
31. *Atharaveda-Saṁhitā,* II.8; III.7.
32. Ibid., IV.13; VI.91; and *Ṛgveda,* VII.50.
33. *Atharvaveda-Saṁhitā,* I.22. *Ṛgveda,* I.50.11.
34. V.W. Karambelkar, op. cit., p. 205.
35. *Atharvaveda-Saṁhitā,* op. cit., VI.14.127.
36. Ibid., I.25; V.22; VI.20; VII.116.
37. Ibid., VI.105.
38. *Atharvaveda-Saṁhitā,* VIII.7.15; XII.2.1.
39. Ibid.
40. *Ṛgveda,* I.122.9; X.97.12; etc. *Atharvaveda-Saṁhitā,* II.23; VI.85.1; XI.8.7; XI.12.5, etc.
41. *Atharvaveda-Saṁhitā,* V.30.8-9; XI.8.5, 13-19, 21, 22, etc.
42. K.G. Zysk, op. cit., p. 12.

force who, when entering the body, caused malady.[43] However, there exist similarities between *yakṣmā* and consumption. It is also a fact that *yakṣmā* brings about a general condition of bodily decay.

The *Atharvaveda-Saṁhitā* refers to various kinds of *yakṣmā*[44] affecting both children and adults.[45] Specifically, there is the *ajñātayakṣmā* (unknown *yakṣmā*)[46] and the *rājayakṣmā* (royal-*yakṣmā*).[47]

The causes of this disease are also described in the Vedic hymns. Vedic people had a notion that *yakṣmā* was caused by sin.[48] It was believed to be divinely sent.[49] According to the *R̥gveda,* it is the dishonest man himself who, in a sly way, presses the *soma* and causes the *yakṣmā* to enter his heart.[50] This is an example of a type of sin committed before the gods and which causes the disease.[51]

Separate charms are prescribed to cure the *yakṣmās*.[52] Along with the use of herbs, the hymn 2.33 of the *Atharvaveda-Saṁhitā* is recited to remove *yakṣmā.* The disease is dispelled downward with the help of the herbs *kuṣṭha*[53] and *cīpūdru.*[54] Arundhatī

43. Ibid., p. 13.
44. *Atharvaveda-Saṁhitā,* IX.8.10-12.
45. Ibid., XIX.36.3.
46. Ibid., VI.127.3.
47. Ibid., III.11.1.
48. Ibid., VIII.7.3.
49. Ibid., VIII.7.2.
50. K.G. Zysk, op. cit., p. 13. fn. 16.
51. *Atharvaveda-Saṁhitā,* XIII.4.8.
52. Ibid., XIX.44.2.
53. Ibid., V.4.9.
54. Ibid., VI.127.1.3.

also makes man free from *yakṣmā*.[55] The *Ṛgveda* mentions that the healer, holding the herb, stroked or waved it over the patient, causing the demon to leave the body and to fly away with birds.[56] Likewise a lead amulet dispels the *yakṣmā* downward[57] and the ointment (*añjana*) has the power to remove it from the limbs.[58] As it is divinely sent, gods also have the power to destroy it. The divinities most helpul for the eradication of *yakṣmā* included Agni,[59] Savitṛ,[60] Vāyu[61] and Āditya.[62] Water was also used in the therapy.[63] Thus, charms, gods and other plant materials were utilized to prevent attacks from the *yakṣmās*. An amulet fashioned from the *varaṇā*-tree is able to restrain *yakṣmā*.[64] The *śatavara*-amulet protects one from the *yakṣmās*;[65] and the scent of the burning *gulgulū*-plant[66] is said to disperse them.

Jāyānya: The disease-entity known as *jāyānya* is mentioned in the *Atharvaveda-Saṁhitā*.[67] In the *Taittirīya-Saṁhitā*,[68] it is noticed in the form of *jāyenya* which is closely, associated with the demonic disease, *yakṣmā*. The exact nature of the disease is in

55. Ibid., VI.59.2.
56. *Ṛgveda*, X.97.11-13.
57. *Atharvaveda-Saṁhitā*, XII.2.1, 14.
58. Ibid., XIX.44.1-2.
59. Ibid., V.29.13.
60. Ibid.
61. Ibid., IV.25.5.
62. Ibid., IX.8.22; here Āditya is said to appease the limb-disintegrating *yakṣmā*.
63. Ibid., III.12.9; XIX.2.5.
64. Ibid., VI.85.
65. Ibid., XIX.36.
66. Ibid., XIX.38.
67. Ibid., VII.76.
68. *Taittirīya-Saṁhitā*, 2.3.5, 1-2.

doubt. Filliozat and some other researchers, basing on its inclusion in a hymn which begins with the removal of the skin disorder, *apacīt*, consider it to be a term designating various types of suppurating skin ulcers.[69] The *jāyānya* traced in the *Atharvaveda-Saṁhitā* possesses the characteristic of flight, which is also shared by the *apacīts*.[70] The *Ṛgveda*[71] suggests that *yakṣmā* may also be a disease-demon that can fly. Sāyaṇa equates it with *jāyenya* of *Taittirīya-Saṁhitā*. Following Sāyaṇa, others opine that the disease is a form of *yakṣmā*, etymologically signifying perhaps a type of venereal or congenital disease.[72] This later explanation is supported by the *Taittirīya-Saṁhitā*[73] which mentions the mythological origin of the disease-demon. This text further explains that the *jāyenya*, like the *yakṣmā*, invades every part of the body from the head to the feet, including the spinal column.[74] *Jāyenya* is also considered to be a *yakṣmā*[75] and it appears to be a *yakṣmā*[76] that enters the abdomen and causes it to swell. From this description, it is clear that traditionally *jāyenya* was considered as a type of *yakṣmā* invaded the body and produced the symptomatic condition of a swollen belly.

Jāyānya is cured by the performance of an offering in the house of the patient. The healer, through his knowledge of its origin, establishes his power over the demon.[77] A medicine is

69. K.G. Zysk, op. cit. p. 18 and fn. 1.
70. *Atharvaveda-Saṁhitā,* VII.76(80).2(4); VI.83.1.3; P.1-59.4.
71. *Ṛgveda,* X.97.13.
72. K.G. Zysk, op. cit., p. 18 and fn. 3.
73. *Taittirīya-Saṁhitā,* 2.3.5.2.
74. Ibid., vv., 1, 2.
75. Ibid., 19.44.2.
76. Ibid., 19.40.9.
77. Ibid., 19.44.3.

also mentioned in this text for curing the disease.[78] This medicine may be ointment (*añjana*) which is able to cure *jāyānya* along with other *yakṣmās*.[79]

Kṣetrīya: The *Atharvaveda-Saṁhitā*[80] contains charms used for healing the internal disease-demon *kṣetrīya.* Etymologically, the word is derived from *kṣetra* meaning "field," "land" or "soil." This word also occurs in the *Kāṭhaka-Saṁhitā*[81] and the *Taittirīya Brāhmaṇa.*[82] According to the *Aṣṭādhyāyī,* the disease *kṣetrīya* is curable in another womb.[83] Here, *kṣetra* has the medical meaning "healthy womb."[84] Sāyaṇa and the native tradition consider it to be an anomalous word signifying a disease beginning with consumption, skin-disease and epilepsy, derived from the limbs of the father or mother, etc. contaminated by the defilements (causing) consumption, skin-disease, etc. and curable in the body of a grandson or son, etc.[85] Ostensibly, the word clearly denotes a type of hereditary disease. Western interpreters, however, decline to follow it. Weber considered it to be either crop-damage or a type of disease which afflicted new-born children.[86] Particularly, the *Kāśikāvṛtti* associates the disease with *kuṣṭha,* a class of skin-diseases which includes leprosy.

The medical meaning of *kṣetra* is "healthy womb." The term *Kṣetrīya* was looked upon as a demon or evil by the Vedic

78. Ibid., 19.44.2.
79. *Atharvaveda-Saṁhitā,* XIX.44.1-2.
80. Ibid., II.8; III.7.
81. *Kāṭhaka-Saṁhitā,* 15.1.
82. *Taittirīya Brāhmaṇa,* 2.5.6.1-3.
83. *Aṣṭhādhyāyī,* 5.2.92; *kṣetriyac parakṣetre cikitsyaḥ.*
84. P. Kutumbiah, *Ancient Indian Medicine,* Orient Longman Ltd., Bombay, rpt. 1974, p. 184.
85. Sāyaṇa to *Atharvaveda-Saṁhitā,* II.8.1.
86. Weber, *Indo-Iranian Journal,* XIII, pp. 149, 156; XVII, p. 208.

people.[87] This disease-demon is associated with seizure (*grāhī*)[88] with the curse (*śapatha*), sorceresses (*yātudhānī*) and evil spirits (*arāyī*), female demons (*abhikr̥tvarī*) and demons belonging to the magical realm (*saṁdeśyā*).[89] The *sadānvā*-demons mentioned in the *Atharvaveda-Saṁhitā* are said to be part of the *kṣetrīyas*.[90] This demon is specifically mentioned in relation to *yakṣmā*.[91] He is said to dwell internally.[92]

The use of a *kṣetrīya*-destroying plant can cure the disease. This plant is called *apāmārga*.[93] Barley and sesame were also employed in the treatment of the disease and, together with the plant, may have been originally fashioned into an amulet.[94]

Rāpas: The word *rāpas* is mentioned in the charms of the *R̥gveda*[95] and *Vājasaneyī-Saṁhitā*.[96] In the *Nirukta*, Yāska equated *rāpas* with *pāpa* (evil).[97] The term has thus been traditionally interpreted by the commentators. Particularly, Sāyaṇa[98] has commented on this term in respect of the hymns of the *R̥gveda* and the *Atharvaveda*. More recently, R. Müller has suggested that it is a general expression for fragility and sickness;[99] while R. Emmerick understood it to be a "local morbid symptom,"

---

87. *Atharvaveda-Saṁhitā*, II.10.1-6.
88. Ibid., II.10.6.
89. Ibid., II.8.2.5.
90. Ibid., II.14.5.
91. Ibid., II.10.5-6.
92. Ibid., III.7.2.
93. Ibid., II.8; IV.18.7.
94. Ibid., II.8.2-5.
95. *R̥gveda*, VII.50.
96. *Vājasaneyī-Saṁhitā*, 4.13, 6.91.
97. *Nirukta*, 4.2.
98. *R̥gveda*, X.137.2, *Atharvaveda-Saṁhitā*, I.22.2.
99. "Medizin in R̥gveda," *Asia Major*, 6 (1930), p. 345.

corresponding to the classical Indian medical use of *roga.*[100]

The association of *rāpas* with *yakṣmā*[101] and *harimān*[102] is gleaned from the hymns of the *Atharvaveda.* The disease-demon is occasionally equated with *viṣā* (neuter) or poison.[103] Likewise, it is said to have a divine origin[104] and is allied with various evils and demonically caused problems.[105] This disease often attacked the foot as observed by the Vedic seers.[106] The *Ṛgveda* describes a sick person who seems to have been suffering from a crooked or deformed limb.[107] The disease seems to have developed after contact with polluted water.[108]

This disease can be cured by using watery medicines,[109] wind for resuscitation[110] and the plant barley[111] ad *kuṣṭha.*[112] There is also the suggestion that cauterization with fire was used to eradicate the disease.[113] In the *Ṛgveda,* various deities are said to effect the removal of *rāpas.*[114]

Hṛddyotā (Chest-Pain): The *Ṛgveda* and the *Atharvaveda* refer

---

100. *Atharvaveda-Saṁhitā,* IV.13.4.
101. Ibid., IV.13.5.
102. Ibid., I.22.2.
103. Ibid., VI.57.3; VI.91.1.2.
104. Ibid., VI.58.1-3.
105. *Ṛgveda,* I.34.11.
106. Ibid., VII.50.1-3.
107. Ibid., VIII.20.26.
108. Ibid., VII.50.3.
109. Ibid., VII.50.4; VIII.20.23-25.
110. Ibid., VIII.18.9; X.137.2-3.
111. *Atharvaveda-Saṁhitā,* VI.91.1.
112. Ibid., V.4.10.
113. Ibid., VII.50.2.
114. Ibid., I.34.11; 157.4 and VIII.18.3.

to *hṛddyotā*[115] and *hṛdroga*[116] respectively. Filliozat has fairly convincingly show that *hṛddyotā* or *hṛdroga* means heart-affliction. It refers to a burning pain in the chest. It is synonymous with *hṛdayāmayā,* an affliction associated with *balāsa.*[117] It is also connected with the *yakṣmā*s and *balāsa.*[118] It is said to be an ailment sent to foes[119] and a disease or symptom characteristic of internal diseases.[120] It is associated with a wide range of demons, in particular internal disease-demons, including *rāpas.*[121] These internal disease-demons affect the limbs.[122] R. Müller has shown that the *hṛddyotā* or *hṛdroga* is linked with the god Agni which lies at the root of all Vedic diseases.[123]

The principal remedy for *hṛddyotā* was water.[124] A hymn of the *Atharvaveda*[125] demonstrates the use of associative magic for the removal of the symptoms. The purpose of the healing rite as illustrated by this charm (I.22) was to eliminate the undesired bodily condition and to replace it with the desired one.

Harimān (Jaundice): The *Atharvaveda-Saṁhitā*[126] mentions *harimān* as an internal disease-entity. *Harimān* means

---

115. *Ṛgveda,* I.50.11.
116. *Atharvaveda-Saṁhitā,* I.22.
117. *Atharvaveda-Saṁhitā,* VI.14.1.
118. Ibid., V.30.9; VI.127.2.
119. Ibid., V.20.12.
120. Ibid., VI.24.1.
121. Ibid., I.22.2.
122. Ibid., IX.8.9.
123. R. Müller, *Asia Major,* 9 (1930), pp. 359-61.
124. *Atharvaveda-Saṁhitā,* VI.24.1.
125. Ibid., I.22.
126. Ibid.

"yellowness" and quite naturally suggests jaundice, which is rather a symptom than an actual malady.[127] Karambelkar, however, asserts that it is a proper disease.[128] The disease-demons responsible to cause this disease also include *rāpas*[129] which spread in the limbs.[130] Both *hṛdroga* and *harimān* exemplify the essential fiery nature or association with the god Agni which is root-cause of all Vedic ailments.

The remedy for *harimān* was ointment (*añjana*).[131] There was also magical treatment of this disease.[132] In every way, the healer endeavours to surround the victim with redness.[133] His aim was to overwhelm and to drive away the undesired colour with the desired one. In the final verse, the healer exercises the demon, i.e. jaundice, with the use of birds which are naturally yellow and thus suitable hosts for jaundice.[134] He requests them to remove the yellowness and to carry it completely away to a place, perhaps near the sun, where it could no longer affect anyone. This charm (vv. 1-3 of *AV* I.22) represents one of the best examples of associative or sympathetic magic among the healing hymns of the *Ṛg* and *Atharva* Vedas.

Balāsa (Swelling): The disease-demon *balāsa* is mentioned in the *Atharvaveda-Saṁhitā*.[135] This disease appears as a type of symptomatic swelling commonly associated with internal diseases. The commentators Sāyaṇa and Mahīdhara have

---

127. Filliozat, *La doctrine*, p. 89.
128. Karambelkar, *The Atharvaveda and the Āyurveda*, p. 205.
129. *Atharvaveda-Saṁhitā*, I.22.2.
130. Ibid., IX.8.9.
131. Ibid., IV.9.3; XIX.44.2.
132. Ibid., I.22.
133. Ibid., I.22.1-3.
134. Henry, *La magie*, p. 182.
135. *Atharvaveda-Saṁhitā*, VI.14.127.

understood the word to mean consumption or tuberculosis; and this was followed by H. Zimmer.[136] Grohmann considered it to be a type of aqueous sore or swelling commonly found on a fever-patient.[137] Ludwig has rendered it as "dropsy."[138] According to Karambelkar, *balāsa* is related to *kilasa* (leukoderma) in form. It was a skin-disease.[139]

The Atharvavedic hymns imply that *balāsa* was a type of internal disease. It affects the limbs, particularly the joints. It afflicts the heart.[140] One of the causes appears to have been excessive emotion, for it is said to arise out of desire, abhorrence, and from the heart.[141]

The swelling part was removed from the body of the patient by operation. The healer requested the disease-demon to dry up, become like ash, and fly away.[142] The chief remedy for him was the *cīpudru*-plant,[143] which may have been called specifically the *balāsa*-destroying plant.[144] Ointment (*añjana*) was also applied on the swelling portion of the body for healing. The *jaṅgiḍā*-amulet was used to protect the patient from further attacks from *balāsa*.[145]

Takmān (fevers): A few hymns of the *Atharvaveda*[146] describe the disease-demon causing fevers. Such charms were used

136. *Vājasaneyī-Saṁhitā,* 12.97.
137. K.G. Zysk, op. cit., p. 32.
138. Ibid.
139. *The Atharvaveda and the Āyurveda,* p. 219.
140. *Atharvaveda-Saṁhitā,* VI.14.1
141. Ibid., IX.8.8.
142. Ibid., VI.14.2.3; IX.8.10.
143. Ibid., VI.127.2.
144. Ibid., VIII.7.10.
145. Ibid., XIX.34.10.
146. Ibid., I.25; V.22; VI.20 and VII.116 (121).

against the internal disease-demon *takmān*. The procedure of curing the disease has also been mentioned in the hymns of the *Atharvaveda*.[147] According to V. Grohmann, *takmān* bears a very close resemblance to malaria fever.[148] Many of the symptoms and characteristics of this disease relate to malaria. This was first described in the Hippocratic works and in the writings of Celsus.[149] Likewise, the references to its most severely-felt occurrence during the rain season allude to the *anopheles* mosquitoes which breed abundantly during this time of the year and act as vectors of the disease. Zysk points out that all of the symptoms, however, do not correspond precisely to the tropical disease malaria and suggests that all similar types of disease characterized by high fever and chills must be doubted as malaria.[150] He, further, adds that the dominant febrile malady indicated by *takmān* is, nevertheless, malaria; in which case, this would be the earliest recorded testimony of the occurrence of the disease.

The Vedic Indians considered *takmān* to be a divinity,[151] who, in the form of the thunder and lightning accompanied the monsoon rains and attacked his victim. Then, it brought about the morbid bodily condition characterized by intermittent and recurring fevers, chills along with other symptoms.

An elaborate ritual was followed for the removal of the demonic force that caused the disease. First the healer had to appease the demon. He did this by paying homage to him.[152] He then had to gain access to his world. This was accomplished

147. Ibid., V.4; VI.95 and XIX.39.

148. K.G. Zysk, op. cit., p. 34 and fn. 2.

149. Ibid.

150. K.G. Zysk, op. cit., p. 34.

151. *Atharvaveda-Saṁhitā*, VI.20.2.

152. Ibid., I.25.1-4; VI.20.1-3.

by knowing the secret key, the demon's esoteric name, *hruḍu.*[153] Once he had appeased him and had entered his realm, he could then dispel him. He sent him, like other internal demons of disease, back to where he originated, and also downward, deep into the ground, where he would be harmless to living things.[154] The healer expelled the demon and employed him to attack enemies and other undesirables.[155] It is most interesting to note that the healer dispatched *takmān* to the frogs which were very much active during the rains.[156] The use of a frog is also found in the *Kauśika-Sūtra.*[157] The use of frogs is also marked in the healing rites in Europe. Grohmann has noted an interesting Bohemian practice in which a frog is used to cure the chills of fever.[158]

The two basic remedies or medicines which the healer employed were *añjana* (ointment)[159] and the plant *kuṣṭha.* As a prophylactic measure, the *jaṅgiḍā*-amulet was worn to render the fever powerless.[160]

Kuṣṭha was considered to be the principal medicine for one suffering from fever.[161] It was known to be a divine, aromatic plant[162] with all-pervading strength,[163] the medicine

153. Ibid., I.25. 2-3.
154. Ibid., V.22.2-4.
155. Ibid., V.22.6.7.12.
156. *Ṛgveda,* VII.103.
157. *Kauśika-Sūtra,* 32.17.
158. K.G. Zysk, op. cit., p. 39.
159. *Atharvaveda-Saṁhitā,* IV.9.3.8.
160. Ibid., XIX.34.10.
161. Ibid., V.4.1.2.
162. Ibid., XIX.39.1.
163. Ibid., V.22.3.

for all diseases,[164] and the choicest among herbs.[165] The hymns themselves do not tell us how or in which form the *kuṣṭha*-plant was employed. The *Kauśika-Sūtra*,[166] however, elaborates the procedure of using the plant. According to this, the plant is to be crushed, mixed with fresh butter and rubbed on the patient from his head to his feet.[167] In the tradition of later Indian medicine, its aromatic root is used, among other things, for cough and fever, and also as a pastille for fumigation.[168] Because *kuṣṭha* is termed an aromatic plant, with all-pervasive strength, one might speculate that the healer initially used the plant as a type of fumigant to help ward off and dispel the demon.

Kāsā (*Kāsa*): The *Atharvaveda*[169] mentions the morbid symptom *kāsā* (*kāsa*), a word used for "cough." It is closely associated with *takmān*. It is called the sister of *takmān*.[170] Likewise, along with *takmān*, she is looked upon as one of the harmful effects of thunder and lightning.[171] She is considered to be one of Rudra's weapons.[172] She causes headache also. Although cough does not normally accompany malaria, it does occur in the most severe kinds, in particular, "estivoautumnal malaria," and tends to indicate a very advanced stage of the disease.[173]

---

164. Ibid., XIX.39.5-9.
165. Ibid., V.4.9; XIX.39.4.
166. *Kauśika-Sūtra*, 28.13.
167. K.G. Zysk, op. cit., p. 40.
168. U.C. Dutta, and G. King et al., *The Materia Medica of the Hindus*, Calcutta, 1922, p. 181.
169. *Atharvaveda*, VI.105.
170. Ibid., V.22.10-11.
171. Ibid., I.12.3.
172. Ibid., XI.2.22.
173. T.R. Harrison et al., *Principles of Internal Medicine*, 5th edn., New York: McGraw-Hill, 1966, p. 1766.

In order to eradicate the disease, the healer took the help of an incantation and drove away the demon from the victim. The ritual practice found in the *Kauśika-Sūtra* has very little to do with the eradication of cough; rather it prescribes the performance of a rite used in the case of one suffering from *ariṣṭa*, "epilepsy."[174] Such a treatment is mentioned in the *Kauśika-Sūtra*,[175] which bears a link with the hymn of the *Atharvaveda-Saṁhitā*.[176] The healer first makes a woman; who has recently borne a child, and the patient, possessed of the evil, take one step forward (to the east, from the house); he then gives them a medicinal concoction to drink, lets them sip water and makes them worship the sun.[177]

General Treatment of Internal Diseases Related to Yakṣmā and Takmān

The *Atharvaveda-Saṁhitā* contains a charm[178] devoted to the exorcism of various types of internal disease demons characterized as either *yakṣmā* or *takmān*-types. The name of another diesease-entity is also mentioned in the *Atharvaveda-Saṁhitā*.[179] This is the female *apvā*. She is located in the stomach. According to the *R̥gveda*, she tries to confuse her victim's mind, to seize his limbs and then to depart, to burn him in the heart and to cause the unfriendly ones to suffer from blind darkness.[180] Yāska considers her to be either a disease or fear (*vyādhir vā bhayaṁ vā*).[181] Following this idea, Macdonell and

---

174. *Kauśika-Sūtra*, 31.27.
175. Ibid., 28.15-16.
176. *Atharvaveda-Saṁhitā*, V.6 (4.1).
177. *Kauśika-Sūtra*, 28.15-16.
178. *Atharvaveda-Saṁhitā*, IX.8.
179. Ibid., IX.9.
180. *R̥gveda*, X.103.12.
181. *Nirukta*, 6.12 (cf. 9.33).

Keith have suggested that *apvā* represents a type of stomach disease, perhaps dysentery, or diarrhoea, induced by fear.[182] Geldner holds that she was probably the personification of fright or panic, conceived to be an internal disease.[183] She was considered as one of the most dreaded demons causing abnormal bodily condition. The *Atharvaveda-Saṁhitā* depicts the general procedure for curing the internal diseases. The healer implores the venom of all *yakṣmā*s to be discharged with urine and requests the disease-demon to go down the body.[184] Both the *yakṣmā*s and various other types of agents of pain are driven away form the body of the patient through the anus with the onomatopoeic sound of flatulence, *kahābāha*. Because of the suggestion that the disease-entities should be expelled from the anus, one might speculate that the charm was recited during the administration of a purgative. The most auspicious time for performing such a healing rite appears to have been early morning, when the sun begins to rise.[185]

The later ritual practice is purely symbolic and rather short, offering little insight into the original rite and no indication of therapeutics. The healer first touches the patient (presumably on the head) while muttering the charm; and then with the last two verses, he worships the sun.[186]

Diseases not Related to Yakṣmā and/or Takmān

Āmīvā: The word *āmīvā* mentioned in the *Ṛgveda* and the *Atharvaveda* means "to cause pain." It is related to the verb *āmāyati* derived from the root *am* which means "to seize." *Āmīvā* is a feminine term. According to R. Emmerick, it

---

182. A.A. Macdonell and A.B. Keith, *Vedic Index*, vol. I, p. 27.

183. K.G. Zysk, op. cit., p. 46 and fn. 3.

184. *Atharvaveda-Saṁhitā*, IX.10.

185. Ibid., IX.22.

186. *Kauśika-Sūtra*, 32.18-19.

probably originally had the meaning "seizure by a god."[187] The *Ṛgveda* mentions that she is often found in connection with the nocturnal demons, the *rākṣasas*.[188] Likewise, she occurs with a host of other evil or demonic elements.[189]

Other references indicate that she was associated with the committed sins which are attached to the body[190] and perhaps also with the sins which lead one astray.[191] She is described as a domestic demon[192] and is found in relation to *ānirā,* or lack of nourishment.[193] Ostensibly, the ancient Indians had a notion that the *āmīvā* was a feminine demon who attacked her victim by seizing his body, bringing about a general state of malnutrition and sufferings that cause bodily decay. In another aspect as an evil-named flesh-eater, she indicates a demon which attacks unborn children causing abortion or still birth.[194] The symptoms developed by the *āmīvā* seem to have included sin; and most significantly, she seems to have been a domestic demon.

The *Atharvaveda-Saṁhitā* also mentions the anti-*āmīvā* calling it as *anamīvā* which is very auspicious, indications a healthy and sound bodily condition.[195] Similar references are also found in the *Ṛgveda.*[196] She is associated with the greatest (*vārṣiṣṭha*)

---

187. R. Emmerick, *Indo-Iranian Concepts of Disease and Cure,* p. 12.
188. *Ṛgveda,* I.35.9.10; III.15.1; VII.38.7.
189. Ibid., I.35. 9-10; I.189.2-3.
190. Ibid., VI.74.2.3.
191. Ibid., I.189.1.3.
192. Ibid., VI.74.2; VII.46.2.
193. Ibid., VII.71.2; VIII.48.11.
194. K.G. Zysk, op. cit., p. 49.
195. *Atharvaveda-Saṁhitā,* II.30.3.
196. *Ṛgveda,* III.59.3; VII.46.2; VII.54.1.

wealth (*raī*)[197] and is related to long life.[198] She is connected with the dawn (*uṣas*);[199] and food *īṣas*) is prayed to be devoid of *āmīvā*.[200] Anti-*āmīvā* condition is desired not only in the cows but also in the humans.

The Vedic Indians applied various methods of treatment for the eradication of *āmīvā*. The bad conditions caused by this disease were removed by applying ointment (*añjana*).[201] *Āmīvā* can also be dispelled by the plant *pūtūdru*.[202] A shell (*śaṅkha*)-amulet is stated as being able to overcome *āmīvā* and *āmati* (indigence).[203] Likewise, the *jaṅgiḍā*-amulet and an amulet of plants and material derived from a tiger's limbs (probably its claw or tooth) were worn to ward off *āmīvā*.[204] However, water-therapy is the most significant one in removing the *āmīvā*-symptoms.[205] The *Ṛgveda* refers to many divinities to dispel *āmīva*.[206] It is also known that the healer who held medical herbs in his hand was considered to be a dispeller of *āmīvā* and a destroyer of the disease-demons, i.e. the *rākṣasas*.[207] The divinities prayed to in the *Ṛgveda* to remove *āmīvā* are the

---

197. Ibid., III.16.3.
198. Ibid., X.37.7.
199. Ibid., X.35.6.
200. Ibid., III.22.4; III.62.14.
201. *Atharvaveda-Saṁhitā*, XIX.44.7.
202. Ibid., VIII.2.28.
203. Ibid., IV.10.3.
204. Ibid., XIX.34.9; VIII.7.14.
205. Ibid., III.7.5; VI.91.3.
206. *Ṛgveda*, VII.71.2; VIII.35.16-18.
207. Ibid., X.97.6.

Aśvins,[208] Agni,[209] Soma,[210] Rudra,[211] Sūrya,[212] Ādityas,[213] Uṣas,[214] Viśvedevas,[215] etc.

Viṣkandha — Sāṁsakandha (Tetanus?): The *Atharvaveda-Saṁhitā* contains charms for the cure of *viṣkandha*[216] (neuter). It is a demonic force that causes troubles to human body. An exact determination of the malady which *viṣkandha* represents is difficult. Sāyaṇa considered it to be an impediment (*vighna*), a problem which causes the body to dry up, or even the name of a great wind-type disease that brought about the dislocation of the shoulders.[217]

Viṣkandha appears to have been considered demonic in nature, for it is often found associated with other demons and evils;[218] there exist nearly one hundred and one types of then scattered all over the earth.[219] It causes a morbid bodily condition. In the *Atharvaveda-Saṁhitā,* it is mentioned in a list of four physical disabilities which create severe pain.[220] It is said to be a malady from which one suffers when wounded.[221] The commentator Sāyaṇa describes it as a

208. Ibid., VII.71.2; VIII.35.16-18.
209. Ibid., I.12.7; I.28.1.
210. Ibid., I.91.12; VIII.48.11.
211. Ibid., VII.74.2.
212. Ibid., X.37.4.
213. Ibid., VIII.18.10.
214. Ibid., X.35.6.
215. Ibid., X.63.12.
216. *Atharvaveda-Saṁhitā,* II.4; III.9; XIX.34, 35.
217. Ibid., II.4.1 and XIX.34.5.
218. Ibid., I.16.3; II.4.3.4.
219. Ibid., III.9.6.
220. Ibid., II.4.2.
221. Ibid., I.46.3.

condition of the body in which the limbs, beginning with the shoulders, are deformed.[222] Finally, it is mentioned along with *sāṁsakandha,* which, etymologically, would suggest its opposite.[223] Evidently, *viṣkandha* was conceived as a demonic force that rendered the body unhealthy.

A lead (*sīsā*) amulet[224] was used to expel the disease *viṣkandha. Añjana* (ointment) is said to protect one from its attacks.[225] The most important protector and destroyer of the demonically caused malady, however, was the *jaṅgiḍā*[226] which appears to have been a cutlivated plant[227] used as an amulet.

Ascites: There are no specific Vedic hymns or charms dealing with ascites. This disease has been included in the later medical literature under the general category of diseases of the abdomen, called *udara.*[228] We have some scattered references to an abnormal bodily condition suggesting ascites. In the *Atharvaveda-Saṁhitā,* there exist two hymns to Varuṇa which have been traditionally prescribed for use in a rite to cure dropsy (*jalodara*).[229]

In order to cure the disease, the healer performs a rite in the honour of the deity Varuṇa who has been identified by the scholars as a seizure creating the disease. The ancient Indians considered ascites as a malady sent by Varuṇa. As is evident from the Ṛgvedic and Atharvavedic hymns, the victim

---

222. *Taittirīya-Saṁhitā,* VII.3.11.1.
223. K.G. Zysk, op. cit., p. 55 and fn. 12.
224. *Atharvaveda-Saṁhitā,* I.16.3.
225. Ibid., IV.9.5.
226. Ibid., XIX.34.9.
227. Ibid., II.4.5; XIX.34.6.
228. K.G. Zysk, op. cit, p. 59 and fn. 1.
229. *Atharvaveda-Saṁhitā,* I.10; VII.83 (88).

looks like a quivering, inflated water-bag.[230] The patient is also described as experiencing thirst while being surrounded by water. According to *Aitareya Brāhmaṇa,* Varuṇa sent a disease which caused the stomach of Ikṣvāku's descendant to swell; and when the bonds of disease were released, his abdomen began to shrink, until it came to normal size.[231] In both the *Caraka*[232] and *Suśruta*[233] Saṁhitās, an *udara*-condition called either *dakodara* or *udakodara* (water-belly) is described. It is said to be caused by the drinking of cold water at the wrong time, or by the drinking of oil;[234] and the afflicted patient's abdomen enlarges, resembling a fully inflated water-bag which fluctuates under pressure. The patient is also said to suffer from thirst. These symptoms bear a rather close resemblance to those found in the Vedic literature. Basing upon these evidences, Zysk opines that ascites was a disease from which the early Indians suffered when seized by Varuṇa.[235]

The Vedas prescribe the propitiation of the god Varuṇa for curing the disease. The Āyurvedic texts[236] have prescribed, among other things, a laparotomy in order to release the water. The water must, however, be released slowly so that complications do not set in.

Insanity: Two types of insanity have been mentioned in the hymn of the *Atharvaveda*. These are *unmādita* and *unmatta.*[237] The first one implies the demented state brought on by the

---

230. *Ṛgveda,* VII.89 and *Atharvaveda-Saṁhitā,* IV.16.
231. K.G. Zysk, op. cit., p. 60.
232. *Cikitsāsthāna,* 13.45-48.
233. *Nidānasthāna,* 7.21-24.
234. *Taittirīya-Saṁhitā,* 6.4.2.3-4.
235. K.G. Zysk, op. cit., p. 61.
236. *Caraka-Saṁhitā, Cikitsāsthāna,* 14.18.
237. *Atharvaveda-Saṁhitā,* VI.111.

patient himself as a result of his infringement of certain divine mores or taboos; and the second one suggets an abnormal mental state caused by possession by demons, such as the *rākṣasas*.[238] The Vedic people considered insanity as a state when the mind leaves the body.[239] Likewise the patient exhibited the distinctive symptom of uttering nonsense.[240]

Insanity was cured by returning the mind to the body.[241] The healer did this primarily by making offerings to the gods in order to appease them, in the case of *unmādita* (madness). He also prepared medicines, perhaps to calm the patient, and to drive away the evil forces invading his body, in the case of *unmatta* (madness). The Atharvavedic charm also suggests that a victim of madness was restrained, perhaps in a sort of straightjacket, presumably so that he could not harm anyone.[242] Zysk points out that the insanity caused by gods, sages, *pitṛ*s and *gandharva*s was cured by employing magical healing rites which involve the recitation of Vedic charms. The execution of various sacrificial, religious, ascetic and propitiatory observances is carried out for the removal of insanity.

Kṛmi (worms): The *Atharvaveda-Saṁhitā* mentions charms against *kṛmi* or worms, vermin, etc. A general incantation against worms is described in a charm[243] while another charm is specifically directed to worms in children.[244] The eradication of worms in cows, however, has been described in another charm.[245] Worm-disease is historically important because it

238. Ibid., VI.111.3.

239. Ibid., VI.111.2.

240. Ibid., VI.111.1.

241. Ibid., VI.111.4.

242. Ibid., VI.111.1.

243. Ibid., II.31.

244. Ibid., V.23.

245. Ibid., II.32.

provides an unbroken continuity from the very early Vedic texts down to the classical medical treatises of Caraka and Suśruta.

The word *kṛmi* does not occur in the *Ṛgveda.* In the *Atharvaveda,* it designates any type of parasitic and crawling vermin which enters either man or animal. Sāyaṇa defines them as "all small animals which have gone inside the body."[246] There are two types *kṛmi;* those which are visible, diurnal, and those which are invisible, nocturnal.[247] They can be black, red, dark-brown eared,[248] black with white legs variegated with white underparts,[249] and some seem to possess a poison-sac.[250] In a more mythical vein, some worms are described as being spotted and whitish with three heads and three horns;[251] others are said to be vulture (-like) and wolf (-like).[252] Various names of such worms are also traced in the *Atharvaveda-Saṁhitā.* These are *kurūru, algāṇḍu, śalūna, avaskavā, vyadhvarā,*[253] *yevāṣa, kāṣkaṣa, ejatkā, śipavitnukā* and *nadanimān.*[254] The meanings of these words are not yet clearly understood. The sex of these creatures has also been distinguished by the Vedic people.[255] One type of worm has also been spotted, which is said to live on the decaying corpse.[256] This variety is known to be a maggot.[257]

246. Ibid., II.31.1.
247. Ibid., II.31.2; V.23.6.
248. Ibid., V.23.4.
249. Ibid., V.23.5.
250. Ibid., II.32.6; V.23.13.
251. Ibid., V.23.9.
252. Ibid., V.23.4.
253. Ibid., II.31.2-4.
254. Ibid., V.23.7-8.
255. Ibid., V.23.13.
256. Ibid., XI.9.10.
257. K.G. Zysk, op. cit., p. 65.

The varieties of *kṛmi*s mentioned above were known to have become most active during the early rainy season,[258] and to have resided in mountains, in forests, in plants, in domestic animals, in the waters and, most importantly, in the body.[259] The bodily *kṛmi*s were located in the entrails, in the ribs and in the head including the eyes, nostrils and teeth.[260]

In order to remove the *kṛmi*s from the body, a ritual was performed by the healer. In the rite, the healer identified himself with the serpent-killer *par excellence*, Indra with his great weapon, the *vajra* or thunderbolt.[261] Since the worms reside inside the body, a symbolical rite takes place outside the body to throw effect on them. Agastya's charm is recited to overpower and ensure the death of the demonic *Kṛmi*s.[262] There is a suggestion about the time of performing the rite. The most auspicious time is at sunrise, when the sun's rays expose the invisible *kṛmi*s and help in destroying the noxious vermin with their heat.[263]

Urine-retention and Constipation: The retention of urine and its remedy have been described in the *Atharvaveda-Saṁhitā*.[264] It was known to the Vedic Indians that the waste-matter was blocked in the bowels, in the two *gavīnī*s and in the bladder.[265] As the urine does not normally become obstructed in the

---

258. *Atharvaveda-Saṁhitā*, XII.1.46.
259. Ibid., II.31.5.
260. Ibid., II.31.4; V.23.3.
261. Ibid., II.31.1-4; V.23.1, 5, 8, 9, 13.
262. Ibid., V.23.10.
263. Ibid., V.23.6-7.
264. Ibid., I.3.
265. Ibid., I.3.6.

bowels, we are led to assume that the hymn may have also been used in case of constipation. This is also supported by the *Kauśika-Sūtra*.[266] *Udāvarta* mentioned in the later Indian medicine represents a class of diseases characterized by constipation, retention of flatus and retention of urine.[267]

The means of liberating the obstructed flow of urine involved the breaching of the urethra and the probing of the bladder-orifice[268] with what appears to have been an arrow-like reed. It has been suggested that this reed was a primitive type of catheter, called *vasti-yantra* in later Indian medicine.[269] The magical quality of the Atharvavedic charm helped the patient to discharge water. The hymn would have had the psychological effect of aiding the patient to relax his/her bladder and to let the urine flow freely.

The later ritual works in corporate elements of both magical and empirical medicine. The reading of the passages are not so clear to understand the disease and its treatment.[270]

EXTERNAL DISEASES

The Vedic literature has described the external diseases less precisely. But, such ailments are quite naturally distinguished as those afflictions which affect the exterior of the body. These include broken limbs and flesh wounds, blood-loss, perhaps due to excessive menstrual discharge and skin disorders, such as discolouration of the skin (leukoderm), rash with pustules, and loss of hair.

---

266. *Kauśika-Sūtra*, 25.10-19.

267. *Caraka-Saṁhitā*, *Cikitsāsthāna*, 26.6-25.
Suśruta-Saṁhitā, *Sūtrasthāna*, 55.

268. *Atharvaveda-Saṁhitā*, I.3.7.

269. G.N. Mukhopadhyaya, *Surgical Instruments of the Hindus*, 2 vols., Calcutta: Calcutta University, 1913-14, vol. 1, p. 137.

270. K.G. Zysk, op. cit., p. 70.

Broken Limbs and Flesh Wounds: The *Atharvaveda-Saṁhitā* includes charms to cure broken bones and wounds[271] as well as to cure flesh wounds characterized by bleeding.[272] The common external injury suffered by both men and animals was the broken bone (*asthnāḥ chinnāsya*)[273] which was caused by falling into a hole or by being struck by a rock.[274] The principal cure for such an injury is said to be the plant *rohaṇī,* made efficacious through its association with the goddess Arundhatī.[275] Similarly, the cure of the fracture (*rūta*) or wound (*ārus*) caused by a club, an arrow or a flame was described in the *Atharvaveda-Saṁhitā.*[276] The remedy prescribed to mend the injury was *lākṣa* or *silāci* which were plants having parasitic characteristics.[277] Modern interpreters refer to a resin or exudation for healing the injury. Filliozat[278] and Vishva Bandhu[279] view *lākṣa* as such a substance, which is commonly called lac, an Āyurvedic medicine. Likewise, K.N. Dave has understood it to mean lac and has even noticed in the charm the process of the production of lac from the so-called lac-insect.[280]

The charms *Atharvaveda-Saṁhitā* (II.3, VI.44 and VI.109) refer to the cure of a bodily affliction called *roga* (or *rogaṇa*). Etymologically, the word *roga* points to a breach of some part

---

271. *Atharvaveda-Saṁhitā,* IV.12 and V.5.
272. Ibid., II.3; VI.44; VI.109.
273. Ibid., IV.12.1.
274. Ibid., IV.12.7.
275. Ibid., IV.12.1.
276. Ibid., V.5.4, 6.
277. A.A. Macdonell and A.B. Keith, *Vedic Index,* vol. 2, p, 450.
278. J. Filliozat, *La doctrine,* Paris, 1949, pp. 109-11.
279. Vishva Bandhu, *Vishveshvarananda Indological Journal,* vol. IX, 1971, pp. 1-3.
280. K.N. Dave, "Lac and the lac-insect in the Atharvaveda," Nagpur: *International Academy of Indian Culture,* 1950, pp. 1-16.

of the body, i.e. a flesh-wound or affliction.[281] Which, according to the *Atharvaveda-Saṁhitā,*[282] does not affect the divinities of the heaven. The wound is characterized by *āsrava,* which represents any bodily discharge or flux.[283] Closely realted to this bloody discharge is the morbid condition known a *vātikṛta* which, etymologically, suggests perhaps gastric problems and which may look back to the very beginnings of what later could have given rise to the *tridoṣa*-doctrine of classical Āyurveda.[284]

The medicine used in the treatment of such a wound included water and herbs.[285] As mentioned in the *Atharvaveda-Saṁhitā,* termites (*upajikās*) are said to have taken up this type of water.[286] However, water is used against poison, because termites are not normally linked with the salty water of the ocean. The herbs or plants are also used to cure such a disease. Such plants include *viṣāṇakā* and *pippalī.*[287] Arundhatī is also used as the medicine for *vātikṛta.*[288] Another plant, *mūñja*-grass is said to have been used in this healing rite.[289]

Blood-Loss: The *Atharvaveda-Saṁhitā* contains a charm[290] to stop the flow of blood. The variant readings of Paippalāda recension and *Nirukta* disclose that the blood-flow was considered to be characterized by an excessively heavy menstrual

281. T. Chowdhury, *JBORS,* 17, p. 48.
282. *Atharvaveda-Saṁhitā,* VI.120.3.
283. *Kauśika-Sūtra,* 25.6.
284. J. Filliozat, op. cit., pp. 140-41.
285. *Atharvaveda-Saṁhitā,* II.3.6.
286. Ibid., II.3.4; VI.100.2.
287. Ibid., VI.44.3; VI.109, 1, 2.
288. Ibid., Paippalāda recension, XV.15.9.
289. Ibid., I.2.
290. Ibid., I. 17.

discharge.[291] The blood was believed to issue from two types of vessels, the *hirās*[292] which are perhaps distinguished as being smaller than the larger, *dhamanīs*.[293] Both, however, were recognized as existing in large numbers in the body.[294]

The cure for this condition involved the recitation of incantations imploring the blood to stop its flow and the use of sand to surround the vessels and to inhibit the blood-loss.[295]

Skin Disorders: Two types of skin disorders are mentioned in the *Atharvaveda-Saṁhitā*.[296] These are *kilāsa* and *pālita*. The latter term means "pale," and denotes in the *Suśruta-Saṁhitā* white hair caused by age and by pain.[297] In the *Atharvaveda*, however, the word indicates a white-coloured spot on the skin, closely related to *kilāsa*, and is perhaps merely a characterization of it.[298] *Kilāsa*, on the other hand, is more problematic. Sāyaṇa considers it to be a skin-disease characterized by cutaneous whiteness; and most Western interpreters view it a type of "leprosy."[299]

There are three types of *kilāsa* mentioned in classical Indian medicine. It is variety of *kuṣṭha* or skin-disease that includes leprosy.[300] The symptoms of the Atharvavedic *kilāsa* are

---

291. Ibid., Paippalāda recension, XIX.4.15, and *Nirukta*, 3.4.
292. *Atharvaveda-Saṁhitā*, VII.35(36).2.
293. Ibid., verse 1, 2.
294. Ibid., verse, 3.
295. Ibid., Paippalāda recension, I. 94.4.
296. Ibid., I.23.24.
297. *Nidānasthāna*, 13.32-33.
298. *Atharvaveda-Saṁhitā*, I.23.2.
299. A.A. Macdonell, and A.B. Keith, *Vedic Index*, vol. I, p. 158.
300. *Caraka-Saṁhitā*, *Cikitsāsthāna*, 7.173; *Suśruta-Saṁhitā*, *Nidānasthāna*, 5.14.

cutaneous white marks or spots[301] which are said to arise from within the body and to be caused by a curse.[302] Such a description refers to the general skin disorder known as leukoderm, a conditon of defective pigmentation of the skin, especially a congenital absence of pigment in patches or bands.[303] Unlike leprosy, therefore, leukoderma is less severe and does not produce skin-lesions.

The healer uses as spell or spells to cure the skin disorders.[304] He takes the help of a dark, even-coloured herb which appears to possess a dyeing or tincturing quality.[305] A mythological episode has been elaborated for strengthening the effectiveness of the herb. A female *asura* first produced the medicine for *kilāsa* and brought about its destruction. She was conquered in battle and gave the trees an eagle's gall-coloured appearance. This a *asurī* destroyed the *kilāsa* and restored an even colour to the skin.[306] The healer goes on to recount the herb's lineage, both the mother and the father have the same name as the herbs, i.e. "even-coloured."[307] Thereupon, the herb is requested to restore the skin to its natural evenness of colour by staining it dark or gall-coloured.[308] From the descriptions of the healing ritual, it also appears that the plant is uprooted from the ground. Although the charm does not indicate how the herb was applied, one would assume that it was made into a decoction and rubbed on to the skin.[309]

---

301. *Atharvaveda-Saṁhitā,* I.23.2, 3, 4.
302. Ibid., I.23.4.
303. J. Filliozat, op. cit., p. 104.
304. *Atharvaveda-Saṁhitā,* I.23 and 24.
305. Ibid., I.23.1.4; I.24.4.
306. Ibid., I.24.1.2.
307. Ibid., I.24.3.
308. Ibid., I.24.3-4.
309. K.G. Zysk, op. cit., p. 82.

Apacits (*Rash with Pistules*): The *Atharvaveda-Saṁhitā*[310] contains charms against the skin affliction known as *apacit* (feminine). This is a rather obscure malady because of its confounding characteristics. Sāyaṇa has defined the word as *gaṇḍamālā*, or "scrofulous swellings" which are often located about the neck. This view is also supported by Karambelkar.[311] According to Bloomfield, *apacit* probably represents the disease *apacī* mentioned in the *Suśruta-Saṁhitā*.[312] Filliozat has shown it to be more particularly a case of adenopathy.[313]

The *apacit*s are characterized as raised bumps or pustules[314] called *gurvikā*[315] and *agrū* (a female demon).[316] There exist different coloured *apacit*s like white, black and red.[317] According to Filliozat, the black colour may be a gangrenous tinge which the abscess assumes just before rupturing and the red colour could be characteristic of the swelling before it reaches the abscessed stage.[318] There is also a barren *apacit*[319] who is called the black one's daughter. This may describe the state of the swelling before it suppurates or after it has done so, when the pus cannot be seen. The *apacit*s are associated with oozing boils or sores[320] and seem to be located amongst the hairs of

---

310. *Atharvaveda-Saṁhitā*, VI.25.83; VII.74 (78) 1, 2; VII.76(80) 1, 2.
311. V.W. Karambelkar, *The Atharvaveda and the Āyurveda*, Nagpur, 1961, 170f.
312. *Suśruta-Saṁhitā*, *Nidānasthāna*, II.8-9.
313. J. Filliozat, op. cit., pp. 91-92.
314. *Atharvaveda-Saṁhitā*, VI.25.1-3.
315. Ibid., Paippalāda recension, I.59.3.
316. Ibid.
317. Ibid., VI.83.2, 3.
318. J. Filliozat, op. cit., pp. 91-92.
319. *Atharvaveda-Saṁhitā*, VI.83.3.
320. Ibid., VI.83.3.

the head.[321] They also appear on the nape of neck, about the neck, on the shoulders, the abdomen, along the sides and on the *vijāman* (perhaps meaning twin) joints beginning with the armpits and moving down the body, including perhaps the pudenda.[322] They seem to have occurred in large numbers, but were considered to have increased in number as they spread down the body,[323] suggesting perhaps a type of rash with pustules.[324]

The *apacit*s are capable of flying[325] and making noise.[326] So the early interpreters have suggested that the *apacit*s represent some type of flying and buzzing insect.[327] Although the arguments of Bloomfield and Filliozat are quite convincing, the fact remains that these two traits do not correspond with the description of the glandular swellings commonly known as adenopathies. This apparent contradiction is gleaned from the procedure of healing noted below.

The healer is of the opinion that the swellings or pustules, which cover the body in great numbers from the nape of the neck down to the last twin joint, may have resembled the rash caused by the bites of noxious, parasitic insects which suck the blood of their host and whose wings make a sort of buzzing or humming noise.[328] Such insects are identified as *tarda* (grain-infesting insect) and the mosquito (*maśaka*).[329] It is clear that the ancient Indian looked on these noxious insects

321. Ibid., VI.83.1.
322. Ibid., VI.25.1-3; VII.74(78). 2.
323. Ibid., VI.25.1-3.
324. K.G. Zysk, op. cit., p. 83.
325. *Atharvaveda-Saṁhitā,* VI.83.1, 3.
326. Ibid., VI.25.1-3.
327. A.A. Macdonell and A.B. Keith op. cit., vol. 1, p. 24.
328. *Atharvaveda-Saṁhitā,* Paippalāda recension, I.59.2.4.
329. Ibid.

as the cause of this disease. By making the pests fly away, vanish or more colloquially, "buzz-off,"[330] the healer would have effectively initiated a cure.

Hair-loss: The *Atharvaveda-Saṁhitā* includes charms for strengthening of hair and for the promotion of its growth.[331] Hair is lost either naturally or accidentally. The cure for such a condition involved the use of plants,[332] one of which appears to have been *nitatnī*. This plant may have been concocted and ritually sprinkled over the head of the patient suffering form the loss of hair.[333] Analysing the mythology surrounding the herb *nitatnī*, Zysk points out that the Atharvavedic charms may have originally been employed in rites to restore the hair of women.[334]

Thus, the above discussions of the internal and external diseases reveal that the Vedic Indians were capable of identifying the diseases and finding their remedies. The medicines used by the healers were either of a watery nature or of a vegetal origin. Hence the healing tradition of the Vedic period was based on waters, *Jālāṣa* and the medicinal herbs. In addition to these, some other medicines were also used to cure the ailments. Such treatment included ointment (*añjana*),[335] the mineral lead (*sīsā*)[336] and wind.[337] Elsewhere, we learn that the products derived from a cow were also considered to be medicinal.[338] The Vedic Indians considered all medicines to be

330. Ibid., VI.83.1.
331. Ibid., VI.21.136, 137.
332. Ibid., VI.21.
333. Ibid., VI.136.3.
334. K.G. Zysk, op. cit., p. 87.
335. Ibid., p. 90.
336. Ibid.
337. *Ṛgveda*, I.89.4; X.186.1.
338. Ibid., X.100.10; X.175.2.

derived from three sources, i.e. heaven, earth and the waters.[339]

A complete charm is traced in the *Atharvaveda* which focuses on the healing properties of water.[340] This charm (*AVS,* VI.24.1, 2) was recited primarily by the patient and its aim was to eradicate the internal diseases and symptoms including *hṛddyota* (chest-pain or perhaps angina pectoris) and all the demons which afflict him in the eyes, in the heels and in the front of the foot.[341]

Another important medicine is *jālāṣa* which refers to Rudra's remedy.[342] The word *jālāṣa* as an adjective is also traced in the *Ṛgveda.*[343] Such type of medicine has the qualities of cooling.[344] Following a *Kauśika-Sūtra,* Bloomfield has suggested that *jālāṣa* refers to urine.[345] But, Geldner has opined that it is rainwater conceived as cosmic urine.[346] The charm of the *Atharvaveda-Saṁhitā* (VI.57.1) is devoted principally to this medicine, used to cure the sores caused by Rudra's arrows. This notion is further supported by the charm of the *Atharvaveda-Saṁhitā* (VI.44.3) where Rudra's urine is mentioned for healing of bleeding flash-wounds. Ostensibly, Rudra's urine refers to *jālāṣa.*[347]

Thus, Rudra's disease was cured by Rudra's medicine (*jālāṣa*) which was sprinkled on and about the affected area.[348]

339. Ibid., I.34.6
340. *Atharvaveda-Saṁhitā,* VI.24.
341. Ibid., VI.24.1,2.
342. *Ṛgveda,* I.43.4; *Atharvaveda-Saṁhitā,* II.27.6.
343. *Ṛgveda,* II.23.12; VII.35.6.
344. *Nighaṇṭu,* 1.12.10.
345. *Kauśika-Sūtra,* 31.11-15.
346. A.A. Macdonell and A.B. Keith, *Vedic Index,* vol. I, pp. 279-81.
347. K.G. Zysk, op. cit., p. 93.
348. *Atharvaveda-Saṁhitā,* VI.57.2.

This prescribed treatment makes us believe that Rudra's disease involved sores, wounds, or more generally swellings spread about the limbs and exposed parts of the body and that Rudra's medicine, *jālāṣa,* was a real remedy. The cooling treatment by rain water connects *jālāṣa* with Rudra's urine, though the link is purely metaphorical.

The ritual tradition, however, makes a concrete connection between Rudra's medicine, *jālāṣa* and Rudra's urine (*mūtra*) and has, therefore, incorporated the hymn secondarily into a cure for a boil which has yet to suppurate (*akṣata*).[349] It is difficult to conceive that the fresh urine prescribed in the rite could be cooling. Urine, mostly from animals, is a common Āyurvedic remedy for, among other things, jaundice, leprosy and various skin diseases[350] and appears rather to be more a part of the *materia medica* of the later tradition, suggesting that the ritual of the *sūtra* is probably more recent than that implied in the hymn itself.[351]

The healing tradition of the Vedic period also reveals that the medicinal plants and herbs (*virudh, oṣadhi*)[352] were always a part of the healer's *materia medica.* This keen interest in the beneficial properties of the native flora led to the development of a rather large pharmacopoeia. The manner in which the plants were described points to the early stages of Indian scientific thought. The medicinal values of various plants and herbs were analysed by the healers. Such analysis also distinguished the healing virtues of these simples from each other and from trees (*vanaspati*). The healer often included ecological and taxonomical distinctions. The glorification and

349. Ibid., VI.57.

350. U.C. Dutt et al., *The Materia Medica of the Hindus,* rev. edn., Calcutta, 1922, pp. 285-87.

351. K.G. Zysk, op. cit., p. 94.

352. Ibid., p. 96.

praise of simples are clearly explained in the Vedic hymns.[353]

The processing of the simples for the extraction of medicine is done through three stages, i.e. acquisition, preparation and employment. The healers were collecting the simples from distant places or by trade. They also engaged in the uprooting and collection of auspicious plants from their local flora.[354] An integral part of the acquisition of plants from various places was the ancient India's knowledge of them according to a primitive system of classification based on gross morphology and habitat, which is fully appreciated in the Atharvavedic and Ṛgvedic hymns.[355]

The collected plants were then combined (often pulverized) and made (decocted or concocted) into medicines[356] or fashioned into amulets[357] as "companions of the charm"[358] or in order to "help the charm"[359] In fact, the healer (*bhiṣaja*) is characterized as a shaker (*vipra*) who knows both the preparation of the medicines from the plants and the correct recitation of the healing words.[360]

Often a solution was prepared from the extracts of the plants and herbs. Usually, a patient drank the solution in the prescribed amount. The dominant form in which the natural plants were used, however, was as an amulet or talisman. These simples were occasionally employed as important ingredients in poultices or compresses. Evidences also show

353. *Ṛgveda,* 10.97; *Atharvaveda-Saṁhitā,* 8.7.

354. *Ṛgveda,* 10.97.20.

355. *Atharvaveda-Saṁhitā,* VIII.7.4.9, 13, 20, 23, 27; *Ṛgveda,* X.97.2, 3, 5, 7, 9, 15, 18, 19, 21.

356. *Atharvaveda-Saṁhitā,* VIII.7.5, 18, 22. *Ṛgveda,* X.97.21.

357. *Atharvaveda-Saṁhitā,* VIII.7.14.

358. Ibid., VIII.7.7.

359. *Ṛgveda,* X.97.14.

360. Ibid., X.97.6, 22.

that the plants were held in the hand of the healer, perhaps as a type of amulet, and ritually waved over the patient in order to drive away the affiliction which in turn was carried away by birds, or expelled with the passing of wind from the anus.[361]

It is significant to note that the *oṣadhi* or herb was personified, divinized and looked upon as a general luck-bringer.[362] Among the herbs encountered, Arundhatī was considered the most auspicious. The various forms of this herb were very much beneficial in the treatment of broken limbs and flesh wounds. Therefore, some mythological treatment was attached to this herb.[363] Due to the life-saving abilities of the simples, the ancient Indians had a high esteem for their flora.

Besides the above, the Vedic people had knowledge in anatomy, physiology and embryology. Earlier we have already discussed about their knowledge in biology. The hymns of the *Atharvaveda*[364] describe the anatomical features of the medical science of the Vedic period. According to Hoernle, there is a close corroboration of the system of bones described in the *Atharvaveda* with that found in the *Caraka-Saṁhitā* of the Āyurveda.[365] Many organs and bones, in the *Atharvaveda,* were already given distinct names. The poets of the *Atharvaveda* also had knowledge in the anatomy of the cow.[366] In the *Vājasaneyī-Saṁhitā* and *Maitrāyaṇī-Saṁhitā,* the bones of the horse have been enlisted.[367]

---

361. Ibid., X.97.11-13.
362. Ibid., X. 97, 4, 5, 6, 8, 17.
363. K.G. Zysk, op. cit., pp. 97-98.
364. *Atharvaveda,* II.33 and X.2.
365. A.F.R. Hoernle, *Studies in the Medicine of Ancient India: Osteology,* London: Oxford, 1907.
366. *Atharvaveda,* X.9.
367. *Vājasaneyī-Saṁhitā,* XXV, 1-9; *Maitrāyaṇī-Saṁhitā,* III.15.

Evidently, the Vedic seers had a first hand knowledge of the anatomy of human and animal bodies. As per the views of Weber,[368] the anatomical observations of the Vedic people were the result of the dissection of the victim at the sacrifice and the dedication of its different parts to different deities.

The *Atharvaveda* also deals with the physiology to some extent.[369] There was an understanding of a general flow of liquid in the body and this fluid, in different parts, is differently coloured as red, rosy, copper-dark, etc.[370] Embryology is another striking subject depicted in the *Atharvaveda.* This text presents a long list of charms covering the whole field from conception to birth and nourishment of the child. The *Strīkarmāṇī* of the *Atharvaveda* have charms and spells for all stages of embryonic development.[371]

Though a concise view of the Vedic medicine has been presented here in this chapter, still there remain several points demanding further investigation. The significant part of this healing tradition is the Vedic toxicology. Several hymns of the *Atharvaveda* and a few of the *Ṛgveda* concern themselves with poisoning usually caused by animals, and with the remedial measures to cure it. Evidently, India's long and renowned tradition of toxicology has been derived from the basic knowledge of poisons and poisonous animals latent in the Vedas.

---

368. A. Weber, *The History of Indian Literature,* London, 1878, p. 30.
369. *Atharvaveda,* X.2.11.
370. S.N. Dasgupta, *Āyurveda-Vijñāna, Prabāsī,* 1934, vol. XXXIV, part I, no. 3, pp. 349-57.
371. V.W. Karambelkar, op. cit., pp. 102-13.

7

Agriculture

Introduction

A considerable portion of the *Ṛgveda* belongs to a pre-agrarian stage of civilization. Hence it has many hymns on the increase, health and safety of cattle and horses, but a few hymns on argiculture. On the other hand, the hymnś of the *Atharvaveda* deal with the various aspects of agriculture. In the *Atharvaveda* we frequently come across plants with many new names together with their use in magic. The word *kṛṣi* mentioned in the *Ṛgveda* denotes "ploughing." The cultivation of the soil was no doubt known to the Indians before they separated from the Iranians, as is indicated by the identity of the expressions *yavaṁ kṛṣ* and *śasya* in the *Ṛgveda* with *yao kareṣa* and *hahya* in the *Avesta,* referring to the ploughing of the fields and harvesting of the crops to acquire grains.[1] But it is not without significance that the expressions for ploughing occur mainly in the first[2] and tenth[3] books of the *Ṛgveda* and only rarely in the so-called "family" books (II-VIII).[4] In the *Atharvaveda, Pṛthī Vainya* is credited with the origination of

1. A.A. Macdonell and A.B. Keith, *Vedic Index of Names and Subjects,* vol. I, Delhi: Motilal Banarsidass, rpt., 1995, p. 181 and fn. 1.
2. Forms of the root *kṛṣ,* "to plough," occur in *Ṛgveda,* I.23.15; 176, 2.
3. *Ṛgveda,* X.34.13; X.117.7. In X.146.6; *akṛṣivala,* "not agricultural," occurs, cf. X.101.4.
4. *Kṛṣ* is also found in *Ṛgveda,* VIII.20.19; VIII.22.6; in the family books only in IV.57.4; and as *vi-kṛṣ* in IV.57.8.

ploughing,[5] and even in the *Ṛgveda* the Aśvins are spoken of as concerned with the sowing of grain by means of the plough.[6] In the later Saṁhitās and the Brāhmaṇas ploughing is repeatedly referred to.[7]

Even in the *Ṛgveda*,[8] there is clear proof of the importance attached to agriculture. In the *Pañcaviṁśa Brāhmaṇa*,[9] the Vrātyas, Hindus without the pale of Brāhmanism, are described as not cultivating the soil.

Further the word *kṛṣṭi* mentioned in the *Ṛgveda*[10] denotes "people" in general. The same word also appears in the *Atharvaveda*.[11] The common and regular use of this word to mean "people" apparently reveals that the Āryans, when they invaded India, were already agriculturists, though all of them did not devote themselves to this occupation.

The *Atharvaveda* actually represents the life of the ancient Indian agriculturist community. Excavations in the past by Indian archaeologists in collaborations with their Western counterparts in the central and southern regions of India have yielded a hoard of remains pertaining to some ancient agriculturists and cattle-breeding communities.[12] The details

5. *Atharvaveda*, VIII.10.24.
6. *Ṛgveda*, I.117.21.
7. *Atharvaveda*, II.4.5; VIII.2.19; VIII.10.24; X.6.12; XII.2.27; etc. *Taittirīya-Saṁhitā*, VII.1.11.1; *Maitrāyaṇī-Saṁhitā*, I.2.2; III.6.8; *Vājasaneyī-Saṁhitā*, IV.10; IX.22; XIV.19-21; *Śatapatha Brāhmaṇa*, VII.2.2.7; VIII.6.2.2; *Taittirīya Brāhmaṇa*, III.1.2.5; In the *Atharvaveda*, VI.116.1, *Kārṣīvaṇa* denotes a "plougher."
8. *Ṛgveda*, 34.13; 117.7; cf. Hopkins, E.W., *India, Old and New*, p. 208.
9. *Pañcaviṁśa Brāhmaṇa*, XVII.1.
10. *Ṛgveda*, I.52.11; 100.10; 160.5; 189.3; III.49.1; IV.21.2; etc.
11. *Atharvaveda*, XII.1.3.4.
12. Ināmgāon, Dist. Pune, Central India Excavation; Excavation near Budhihala, Dist. Gulbarga, North Karnataka, south India, 1989-90.

of the remains bear resemblances to what is found narrated in the *Atharvaveda*.[13] Moreover, scientific analysis especially of the clay and ashes from the sites have dated these remains to *c.* BCE 2500-600 which is approximately the period of the *Atharvaveda* of the neolithic age. Such archaeological findings lead us to sketch a picture of the life of the ancient farmer-community in India. The literary evidences and the excavational observations are now set in a coherent and concurrent manner. The agricultural activities of the Vedic people are now discussed here in detail pertaining to the informations available from the Vedic literature.

Farmers

The *Atharvaveda* depicts the agricultural activities of the Vedic people and speaks high of them. The farmers working in the field look glorious. They pray to the food-god for better crops and happiness. With the blessings of the deity, they are confident of their success in farming. They work in the field freely without fear and eliminate the dispute relating to their farm work without any difficulty. The King Soma is praised for recognizing everyone who does hard work in the field. The agriculturist irradiates the path to heaven with the help of Soma. Actually gold grows in the farm in the form of crops. The farm is like a divine cow fulfilling the desires of the farmer. The farmer is identified as an authority in the knowledge and acquirement of food. The farmers of the Vedic period had sufficient knowledge in food-growing. They knew the code of farming which begins with the digging of the soil. They offered the food grains, first collected from their field, to the sacred fire with a belief that the food grains would be as sweet as nectar.[14]

---

13. B.S. Kharade, *Society in the Atharvaveda*, New Delhi: D.K. Printworld (P) Ltd., 1997. p. 1. *Atharvaveda*, X.5.34.

14. *Atharvaveda*, VI.116.1.

The farmers declared themselves as the great sons of the Mother Earth.[15] The *Atharvaveda* says that all the people must cultivate lands. Everyone must work hard and grow nutritious food. Indra, the emperor of gods, is also eager to perform his duties in the field. The common mass of the Vedic period desire to choose their King from amongst the agriculturists. The great King Pṛthī was the first to plough the land. Work is worship. The skill of the farmer and maintenance of farming are highly praised in the hymns.[16]

Land under Cultivation

The *Atharvaveda* depicts the qualities of the soil to be cultivated. According to the descriptions, the soil holds the plants possessing energies of various kinds. There are rivers, oceans and large landscapes on the surface of the earth. The soil impels all of us towards progress. Our forefathers resided on the land under cultivation. The soil feeds us all. Highly irrigated lands grow enough crops and enrich the farmers as well as the nation in which they live.

The *Atharvaveda* mentions the twin gods, Aśvinau who survey the soil. The hilly regions, the forests and farms of the states of the Atharvavedic period are depicted in the earth-hymn of the *Atharvaveda*.[17] This hymn narrates:

> O Earth, the hills and mountains of yours may be decorated with ice and your forests may be auspicious as ever. The lands of yours, protected by Indra and coloured pink, black, red and variously formed may be stable. Your greatness may be unconquered and be offered the sacred-food and be unaffected for ever.[18]

---

15. Ibid., XII.1.12.
16. Ibid., XI.1; XII.1; VI.116; XX.65; 111.12; VIII.10.
17. Ibid., XII.1.11.
18. Kharade, B.S. op. cit., p. 15.

One verse describes the attractive smell of the soil. It is stated that gold on the surface of the earth lies mixed with stones, rocks and the dust. The farm grows crops in all seasons. The towns develop on the surface of the earth. The soil is rich enough to produce wheat and rice. The farmer wishes to reside on such a plot which is free from pins and sticks. He wants to live by the side of his lands watered by canals.[19] Thus, it appears that the Indian farmers are always interested to reside close to their farmhouses. In order to pay full attention to agricultural activities, they need such type of living. Actually, if a farmer resides permanently in his farmhouse, then better farm-work, is possible. According to Atre, it is called farm work only when the farmer stays in the farmhouse, otherwise there exist stones and dusts.[20]

Irrigation

The mention of seas, oceans, rivers and lakes in the Veda provides the various sources of water needed for agriculture and living organisms. The word *samudra* meaning occean is a frequent occurrence in the *R̥gveda* and later. It indicates that the Vedic Indians knew the sea. In many places, *samudra* is metaphorically used, as of the two oceans,[21] the lower and the upper oceans,[22] etc. In some hymns of the *R̥gveda, samudra* denotes the River Indus when it receives all its Punjab tributaries.[23] Among the rivers, we trace the names of Gaṅgā, Gomatī, Paruṣnī, Yamunā, Rasā, Revā, Vitastā, Vipāsa, Sutudrī, Śvetyā, Sarayū, Sarasvatī, Sindhu, Suṣomā, Susartu, etc.[24] Vedic

19. *Atharvaveda,* XII.1.
20. T.N. Atre, *Gāvagāḍā,* Tr̥tīya-vr̥tti, 1959, p. 196.
21. *R̥gveda,* X.136.5; cf. *Atharvaveda,* XI.5.6.
22. *R̥gveda,* VII.6.7; X.98.5.
23. Ibid., I.71.7; III.36.7; III.46.4; V.85.6; VI.36.3; VII.95.2.
24. A.A. Macdonell and A.B. Keith, *Vedic Index of Names and Subjects,* vol. II, Delhi: Motilal Banarsidass, rpt., 1995, p. 588.

people used water of these sources for irrigating their lands under cultivation. According to the descriptions of the *Atharvaveda,* the water from deserted areas, the water, obtained from the rivers, the wells, the tanks and the bores become useful for the common mass. The seasonal rainwater may be prosperous for the living beings.[25]

The *Atharvaveda* mentions that motor-machines of clay-plots were assembled on the well-bores near farms to supply water to the soil under cultivation. Indian agriculture was largely dependent on the supply of rainwater but water was also dammed for use at the time of scarcity. In a verse,[26] it is said that the people collect and store water from the sky, and use it at their need. The Vṛṣṭi-Sūkta of the *Atharvaveda* narrates beautifully the sudden rainfall in the summer, when the farmer becomes prompt in action in his farm. *Vṛṣṭi* is the regular word for "rain" in the *Ṛgveda*[27] and later. The rain starts suddenly with the thunderbolt and the farmers rush towards shelter. The plants grow healthy due to the medicinal properties of the rainwater. The seer says that the fire-energy named Jātavedas in the rainwater is responsible for the curative nature of the plants.[28] Dr. Dange has compared this fire-energy with the fire-deity. He has argued that the lightning-fire, responsible for heating the clouds to cause rain, has been praised here in this incantation by the fire-hermits. He has interpreted the metaphor *adhvaryavo-gharmiṇah* as above. But scientifically, lightning in caused due to sudden collision between two clouds and subsequent fall in the density of clouds.[29]

The water-cycle occurring in nature has been well

---

25. *Atharvaveda,* I.6.4.
26. Ibid., VII.89.1.
27. *Ṛgveda,* I.116.12; II. 5.6; etc. *Atharvaveda,* III.31.11; VI.22.3; etc.
28. *Atharvaveda,* I.6; I.4; VI.69; IV.15.
29. Kharade, B.S., op. cit., p. 17.

described by the great seer Śāntati. The winds drive the water-streams to fill the earth with water. The torrents of rain strengthen the crops and make them healthy. Atharvan requests the deities of "maintenance" to open the bags of water and enrich the earth with food grains. This rain that comes after a long period of summer heat is stated to be very useful for cultivating the lands.[30]

Preparation of Ploughshares and their Use

The words *phāla*[31] and *stega*[32] meaning ploughshare are traced in the Vedic literature. Today's popular word *lāṅgala* used by the farmers is also mentioned in the *R̥gveda*[33] and later.[34] It is described in a series of passages[35] as "lance-pointed" (*pavīravat* or *pavīravam*), a "well-lying" (*suśīmam*),[36] and "having a well-smoothed handle." The words *sīra*[37] and *sīla*[38] also denote plough. The *R̥gveda* as well as the later Vedic texts mention the word *sīra*. It was large and heavy, as is evident by the fact

30. Ibid.
31. *R̥gveda*, IV.57.8; X.117.7.
32. *Kāṭhaka-Saṁhitā*, XIX.1; cf. *suphāla*, *Atharvaveda*, III.17.5 and *Maitrāyaṇī-Saṁhitā*, II.7.12.
33. *R̥gveda*, IV.57.4.
34. *Atharvaveda*, II.8.4; *Taittirīya-Saṁhitā*, VI.6.7.4; *Nirukta*, VI.26.
35. *Atharvaveda*, III.17.3; *Taittirīya-Saṁhitā*, IV.2.5.6; *Kāṭhaka-Saṁhitā*, XVI.11; *Maitrāyaṇī-Saṁhitā*, II.7.12; *Vājasaneyī-Saṁhitā*, XII.71; *Vāsiṣṭha Dharmasūtra*, II.34.35.
36. The texts have *suśevam;* Roth conjectures *suśīmam*. See Whitney, Translation of the *Atharvaveda*, p. 116. Cf. Zimmer, *Altindisches Leben*, p. 236.
37. *R̥gveda*, IV.57.8; X.101.3,4; *Atharvaveda*, VI.30.1; VI.91.1; VIII.9.16; *Taittirīya Brāhmaṇa*, I.7.1.2; II.5.8.12; *Vājasaneyī-Saṁhitā*, XVIII.7; *Maitrāyaṇī-Saṁhitā*, II.11.4.
38. *Kāṭhaka-Saṁhitā*, XXVIII.8.

that six oxen,[39] or eight,[40] or twelve,[41] or even twenty-four,[42] were used to drag it. The animals which drew the plough were oxen, which were, no doubt, yoked and harnessed with traces. The ox was guided by the *aṣṭrā*, or "good," of the ploughman. Little is known of the parts of the plough. The words *lāṅgala* and *phāla* are still popular among our farmers, suggesting the components of the plough. The word *tsaru* denotes the handle of plough in the later Vedic literature.[43]

In some regions, the ploughshares were manufactured out of the hard wood of *khadira* and a handful of butter was repeatedly applied to them so as to make them strong and polished. According to the descriptions of the *Atharvaveda*, "the sharp ploughshare may furrow the soil easily. The cultivation may go smooth by driving the ploughshare with the help of bulls (or horses). Satisfied with the oblations the ploughing may be continually fruitful up to the crop-cutting."[44] After ploughing, rows were formed in the soil and crops were grown in parallel rows. This was to ensure their easy access to water, sunlight and air. The soil thus cultivated and made ready to sow the seeds was designated as *sītā*. Oblations of clarified ghee, nectar and milk were offered to the sacred fire to enrich the soil for better fertilization. Pandit Satavalekar interprets these oblations as the "fertilizers." The big sacrifices might have been performed at the beginning of the farming

39. *Atharvaveda*, VI.91.1; VIII.9.16; *Taittirīya-Saṁhitā*, V.2.5.2; *Kāṭhaka-Saṁhitā*, XV.2; XX.3; *Satapatha Brāhmaṇa*, VII.2.26; XII.8.2.6.

40. *Atharvaveda*, VI.91.1.

41. *Taittirīya-Saṁhitā*, I.8.7.1; V.2.5.2; *Kāṭhaka-Saṁhitā*, XV.2; *Maitrāyaṇī-Saṁhitā*, II.6.2.

42. *Kāṭhaka-Saṁhitā*, XV.2; cf. Weber, *Indische Studien*, 13, 224; fn.1.

43. *Atharvaveda*, III.17.3; *Taittirīya-Saṁhitā*, IV.2.5.6; *Maitrāyaṇī-Saṁhitā*, II.7.12; *Kāṭhaka-Saṁhitā*, XVI.12; *Vājasaneyī-Saṁhitā*, XII.71; *Vaśiṣṭha Dharmasūtra*, II.34.

44. *Atharvaveda*, III.17.5.

and the remnants in the altar such as the sacred ashes might have been utilised as "fertilizers."[45]

The great sage Viśvāmitra narrates that ploughing the lands and forming rows on the soil is the fundamental process in cultivating the land. The farmer rides on the plough. The bulls in pairs are attached to the wooden-yokes with a single rope and then fastened to the plough at the end. The plough is hard like *vajra* (thunderbolt). The handles of the plough are expected to be stiff as they are made out of *soma*-wood. The *kṛṣi*-deity is invoked to help them and to drive the plough easily.

Vedic people were using the bulls and the bullock-carts in the farm-works. The yoked bull were performing hard work in the field as well as in the farm. The Bhṛgus and the Aṅgiras have mentioned about the limitless hard work performed by the bulls in the farm. The *Atharvaveda* depicts that the bullocks work hard right from their early stage of life to the end. The horses were also employed in the work of cultivation, but the bulls were mainly used for the daily laborious work. The digging instruments were in use during the Vedic period. It is clear from the *Atharvaveda* that both manpower and animal power were used for farmwork.[46]

Use of Manure

The Vedic Indians knew the use of manure in their field for better yielding and growth of the crops. Two words *śakan* and *karīṣa* traced in the Vedic texts denote the kind of manure used by the ancient farmers.[47] The words *śakṛt*[48] and *śakan*[49] stand for

45. Kharade, B.S., op. cit., pp. 17-18.
46. *Atharvaveda,* III.17; X.6; IV.11; VI.92; XX.37; XX.65; IV.7.
47. A.A. Macdonell and A.B. Keith, *Vedic Index of Names and Subjects,* vol. 1, Delhi: Motilal Banarsidass, rpt., 1995, p. 182.
48. *Ṛgveda,* I.161.10; *Atharvaveda,* XII.4.9; *Taittirīya-Saṁhitā,* VII.1.19.3; etc.
49. In the oblique cases, *śakan* is the base, *Atharvaveda,* XII.4.4;

"dung" in the *Ṛgveda* and later. It is evident that the value of manure was appreciated by the people of Vedic times. The word *karīṣa* means dry cow dung.[50] The *Atharvaveda* describes the value of the natural manure of animals in the fields.[51]

Types of Grain

The Vedic people cultivated various types of crops in their *kṣetra*[52] (field). The *Ṛgveda* leaves us in doubt as to the kinds of grains grown, for *yava* is a word of doubtful signification, and *dhāna* is also vague. In the later Saṁhitās, things are different. Rice (*vrīhī*) appears, *yava* means barley, with a species styled *upavāka*. Beans (*mudga, māṣa*), sesamum (*tila*), and other grains (*aṇu, khalva, godhūma, nīvāra, priyaṅgu, masūra, śyāmaka*) are mentioned, while cucumbers (*urvārū, urvārūka*) were known.[53] It is uncertain whether fruit trees (*vṛkṣa*) were cultivated, or merely grew wild; but frequent mention is made of the jujube (*karkaṇdu, kuvala, badara*).[54] The word *saśya* mentioned in the Vedic literature generally means the corn.[55] It corresponds to the Avestan *hahya*.[56] The names of other grains traced in the Vedic texts are *kulmāṣa* (beans), *garmut* (wild bean), *tandula* (rice grains), *tirya* (sesamum), *śāli* (rice), *plāśuka* (fast growing rice), *upavāka* (*Wrightia antidysenterica*), *khalakula* (*Dolichos uniflorus*), *khalva* (*Phaseolus radiatus*), *gavīdhukā*

→ *Taittirīya-Saṁhitā*, V.7.23.1; *Vājasaneyī-Saṁhitā*, XXXVII.9. cf. Zimmer, *Altindisches Leben*, p. 236.

50. *Śatapatha Brāhmaṇa*, II.1.1.7.
51. *Atharvaveda*, III.14.3-4; XIX.313.
52. *Ṛgveda*, X.33.6.
53. A.A. Macdonell and A.B. Keith, op. cit., vol. I, p. 182.
54. Ibid.
55. *Atharvaveda*, VII.11.1; VIII.10.24; *Taittirīya-Saṁhitā*, III.4.3.3; V.1.7.3; VII.5.20.1; *Maitrāyanī-Saṁhitā*, IV.2.2.
56. A.A. Macdonell and A.B. Keith, op. cit., vol. II, p. 441.

(*Coix barbata*), *śyāmaka* (*Panicum frumentaceum*) and *saktu* (groats), etc.[57]

The Harvest

The Vedic people earned their livelihood mainly from agriculture. The *Atharvaveda* describes the nourishment of the common mass by taking food grains produced from the lands. Atharvan has immensely praised rice as the greatest food-crop for people in general. The seer Jaṭikāyana in his beautiful poetic style has described the healthy rice-crops and he, as evident from the *Atharvaveda-Saṁhitā,* is the first to identify the farmer as one educated in food science. In an invocation, Viśvāmitra wishes that the crops of barley grow in full strength and on an abundant scale. According to the *Atharvaveda,* barely was treated as the food-god. The word *upasadaḥ* is perhaps employed in case of the secondary crops. The remains of burnt wheat and barely have been discovered in the exacavation at Moheṅjodāro and also from those at Ināmgāon near Pune.[58]

The operations of agriculture are neatly summed up in the *Śatapatha Brāhmaṇa*[59] as "ploughing, sowing, reaping, and threshing" (*kṛṣantaḥ, vapantaḥ, lunantaḥ, mṛṇantaḥ*). The ripe grain was cut with a sickle (*dātra, sṛṇi*), bound into bundles[60] (*parṣa*), and beaten out, on the floor of the granary (*khalā*).[61] The grain was then separated from the straw and refuse either by a sieve (*titau*) or a winnowing fan (*śūrpa*).[62] The winnower

57. Ibid., p. 579.
58. B.S. Kharade, op. cit., p. 18.
59. *Śatapatha Brāhmaṇa,* I.6.1.3.
60. Ibid., 78.10; X.101.3; 131.2.
61. *Ṛgveda,* X.48.7.
62. Ibid., X.71.2 and *Atharvaveda,* XII.3.19.

was called *dhānyākṛt*,[63] and the grain was measured in a vessel called *urdara*.[64]

The farm activities during the harvest season have been described in the Svargaudana-Sūkta.[65] All the members of the family of a farmer used to gather there in the farmhouse at the time of harvesting. According to the Sūkta, the rice grains were made free of their stem ends by hammering and churning the stem branches in wooden mortar or stone mortar with a pestle and cleansing them in the mortar with the pestle to separate grains from the husk. Then the mixture was winnowed by using the winnowing basket so as to make them clean. The hymn of the *Atharvaveda* illustrates all these activities as follows.

The rice grains, those filled-up in the mortar or those churned by the pestle or in the leather bag or winnowing basket or winnowed by the Mātariśvā wind, the Hotṛ-priest may offer to the sacred fire as the best oblations.[66]

The husk from the rice grains were separated with the help of wind. So, prayers were offered to the wind-god Maruta. The women-peasants rinsed their palms with water so as to catch the pestle properly when cleansing the rice in the mortar. Hammering with a wooden-staff as is done to separate the dirt from the clothes, the labourers separated the husk from the rice grains. The cleansed rice was then stored in a big soil-pot or in a vessel made of bamboo or iron. A verse of the *Atharvaveda* also refers to the well-constructed ditches.[67]

---

63. *Ṛgveda*, X.94.13.
64. Ibid., II.14.11.
65. Kharade, B.S., op. cit., p. 18.
66. *Atharvaveda*, X.9.26.
67. B.S. Kharade, op. cit., p. 19.

The seasons for agriculture are briefly summed up in a passage of the *Taittirīya-Saṁhitā*.[68] According to its description, barley is sown in winter and ripens in summer. Rice is sown in the beginning of the rains and ripens in autumn. Beans and sesamum are planted at the time of the summer rains and ripen in the winter season. There were two harvests (*saśya*) a year as recorded in the *Taittirīya-Saṁhitā*;[69] the winter crop was ripe by the month of Caitra (March-April) according to the *Kauṣitakī Brāhamaṇa*.[70]

Every year on the sixth new-moon day, in the month of harvest, the rice-cutting feast was arranged. The participants having drunk the *soma*-juice had a heavy meal of rice and ghee along with *biryāṇī* and enjoyed dance with drums, flutes and the trumpet. Atharvan narrates this in a very sophisticated style in the Virāṭa-Anna-Sūkta of the *Atharvaveda*.[71] Even now, each farmer arranges a feast after completion of harvesting.

The Vedic texts also mention the troubles and losses faced by the farmers during farming and harvesting. According to them, moles destroyed the seed; birds and various kinds of reptiles (*upakvasa, jabluja, tarda, dataṅga*) injured the young shoots; excessive rain or drought might damage the crops. The *Atharvaveda* contains spells to prevent these evils.[72] Abhayakāma Atharvan in one of the verses indicates the method of protecting the crops and food grains. Aśvinau, the twin gods, are invovked to guard the agricultural products from the rats. The seer advises the guard to hit the rats on their heads or to put off their teeth. The farmer's anguish

68. *Taittirīya-Saṁhitā*, VII.2.10.2.
69. Ibid., V.1.7.3.
70. *Kauṣītaki Brāhmaṇa*, XIX.3.
71. B.S. Kharade, op. cit., p. 19.
72. *Atharvaveda*, VI.50.142.

over the losses incurred by the grasshoppers has been narrated in the hymn of the *Atharvaveda.*[73]

The farm and the crops were also protected from the vermins by planting the sunflower plant around the field. The plants *sadam-puṣpa* or *sadāphulī* might have been grown as an antidote secondary crop.[74] Nowadays, we also observe large fences of some types of plants designed around the corn fields of some farmers. It is obvious from the above discussions that the sequence of the agricultural activities mentioned in the Vedic literature is still followed today by the Indian farmers.

As the Vedic people were agriculturists and they were depending upon the bulls and bullocks for their farm work, they needed to improve the cattle-wealth. Besides the plant culture, the animal culture was another profession of these ancient Indians. During the time of the *Atharvaveda,* cattle-breeding was an established occupation of the people in the society. The cows and other domestic animals were counted as wealth. The farmers of the Vedic period were fully acquainted with the knowledge of cow-breeding. They felt the need of increasing the cattle wealth for enriching their farm work. According to the descriptions of the *Atharvaveda,* Indra with his wife Śaci visited the cattle-field of Kuvitsa to encourage him in his occupation.[75]

Livestock of the Farmers

The livestock of the Vedic people included not only the cows, oxen, bulls or bullocks but also horses, goats and sheep. The cow was accorded the most respectful place among the domestic animals. The word *go* traced in the Vedic texts denotes the cow or the ox in some cases the products of the

73. Ibid., VI.50.2.
74. *Atharvaveda,* VIII.7.10.
75. Ibid., XX.27.2; III.8.10; etc.

cow.[76] Other Vedic words like *uṣrā, usrīyā, dughā, dhenā, dhenu, rohiṇī, vāsitā, vaśā* and *starī* stand for various types of cows.[77]

Large herds of cattle were well known, as is shown by the *dānastutis*, or "praises of gifts," in the *Ṛgveda*,[78] even when allowances are made for the exaggeration of priestly gratitude. The importance attached to the possession of cattle is shown[79] by the numerous passages in which the gods are asked to prosper them, and by the repeated prayers[80] for wealth in Kine. Hence, too, forays for cattle (*gaviṣṭi*), were well known; the Bharata host is called the "horde desiring cows" (*gavyan grāmaḥ*) in the *Ṛgveda*;[81] and a verbal root *gup*,[82] "to protect," was evolved as early as the *Ṛgveda* from the denominative *go-pāya*, "to guard cows."

The *Atharvaveda* regards the cow as the mother of everyone.[83] As stated in the Atharvavẹdic hymns, *savitṛ* requests the cows and bulls to stay in his cattle-farm permanently. Brahmā welcomes the bulls and cows running towards the cattlefarm. These two animals were considered more important than the horses. It was regarded as pious to listen to the bellowing of the cows and their calves. Atharvan speaks in praise of Kāmadhenu, the divine cow, describing her beauty. The cow, is called *viśvarūpā* and *kāmadudhā*. Among

---

76. A.A. Macdonell and A.B. Keith, *Vedic Index of Names and Subjects*, vol. I, pp. 231-34.
77. Ibid., vol. II, pp. 574-75.
78. *Ṛgveda*, VIII.5.37; cf. *Pañcaviṁśa Brāhmaṇa*, XVII.14.2; *Aitareya Brāhmaṇa*, VIII.21.23; *Śatapatha Brāhmaṇa*, XIII.5.4.8, et seq.
79. *Ṛgveda*, I.43.2; I.162.22; V.4.11; IX.9.9, etc.; *Atharvaveda*, I.31.4; II.26.4; V.29.2; VI.68.3; VIII.7.11; X.1.17; etc.
80. *Ṛgveda*, I.83.1; IV.32.17; V.4.11; VIII.89.2; etc.
81. Ibid., III.33.11.
82. Ibid., VIII.103.9, and *Atharvaveda*, X.9.7-8; XIX.27.9.
83. *Atharvaveda*, X.10.8.

the different types of cows, we trace *śataudanā* and *vaśā* in the *Atharvaveda*. The first one was a kind of breed of cows capable of yielding milk sufficient for hundreds of people, and the second one was qualified to be the best in all respects among the breeds of the cows available at that time.[84]

Like today, there were also different colours of the cows during the Vedic period. The *Ṛgveda* mentions *rohita* (red), *śukra* (light), *pṛṣṇi* (dappled) and *kṛṣṇa* (black) coloured cattle.[85] Various other colours are mentioned in the lists of animals at the sacrifices depicted in the *Yajurveda*, but Macdonell and Keith take those as exceptional.[86] The *Atharvaveda* includes the names of the cows as *śubhrā, kapilā* and *śyāmā* according to their colours.[87]

The term *go* is often applied to express the products of the cow. It frequently means the milk.[88] The milk (*kṣīra*) was either drunk fresh or made into butter, ghee and curd (*dadhi*). The cows were milked thrice a day, early in the morning (*prātar-doha*), in the forenoon (*saṁgava*), and in the evening (*sāyaṁ-doha*).[89] According to *Taittirīya Brāhmaṇa*,[90] the cows were driven out thrice a day to graze. The exact sense of this notice is obscure. Strictly speaking, the cows were driven out from the cattle-shed in the morning, spent the heat of the day in the *saṁgavinī*, wore then driven out during the evening to graze, and finally came or were driven home, as is often mentioned in the *Ṛgveda*.[91]

---

84. B.S. Kharade, op. cit., p. 23.
85. *Ṛgveda*, I.62.9.
86. A.A. Macdonell and A.B. Keith, op. cit., vol. I, p. 233.
87. B.S. Kharade, op. cit., p. 23.
88. *Ṛgveda*, I.33.10; I.151.8; I.181.8; II.30.7; IV.27.5; IX.46.4; IX.71.5.
89. *Taittirīya-Saṁhitā*, VII.5.3.1.
90. *Taittirīya Brāhmaṇa*, I.4.9.2.
91. *Ṛgveda*, I.66.5.

The first milking was productive, the last two scanty.[92] According to the *Aitareya Brāhmaṇa,*[93] among the Bharatas, the herds in the evening are in the *goṣṭha,* at midday in the *saṁgavinī.* This passage as expanded by Sāyaṇa reveals that the herds go home to the *śālā,* or house for animals, at night so far as they consist of animals giving milk; while the others stay out in the *goṣṭha,* or a pen pasturage; but both were together in the cattle-shed during the heat of the day. The time before the *saṁgava,* when the cows were grazing freely on the pasture land, was called *svasara.*[94] After feeding their calves, the cows were allowed to be separated from them. However, they were allowed to join them at the *saṁgava*[95] and sometimes in the evening.[96]

While grazing in the field, the cattle were under the care of a herdsman (*gopā, gopāla*) armed with a goad,[97] but they were liable to all sorts of dangers, such as being lost, falling into pits, breaking limbs,[98] and being stolen. The marking of the ears of cattle was repeatedly adopted, no doubt, to indicate ownership.[99]

Oxen were regularly used for ploughing or for drawing wagons (*anaḍvāh*), in which case they were, it seems, usually castrated.[100] Cows were not properly used for drawing carts, though they at times did so.[101] The seer Kāṅkāyana says that

92. A.A. Macdonell and A.B. Keith, op. cit., vol. I, p. 232.
93. *Aitareya Brāhmaṇa,* III.18.14.
94. *Ṛgveda,* II.2.2; 34.8; V.62.2; VIII.88.1; IX.94.2.
95. Ibid., II.2.2; VIII.88.1.
96. Ibid., II.2.2; and *Gobhila Gṛhyasūtra,* III.8.7.
97. *Ṛgveda,* X.60.3.
98. Ibid., I.120.8; VI.54.5.7.
99. Ibid., VI.28.3; *Maitrāyaṇī-Saṁhitā,* IV.2.9.
100. *Atharvaveda,* III.9.2; IV.138.2.
101. *Śatapatha Brāhmaṇa,* V.2.4.13.

the cow has her own calf in mind everywhere and at any time. The cow is like a treasure of money, gold, food grains, children and calves. Atharvan, referring to torrents of rain as milk-showers, compares all the Vedic deities with the calves. The cows are seen as having reached the highest peak of holiness.

The *Atharvaveda* eulogizes the participation of bulls and bullocks in the activities of the farm-work. The bullocks are honoured the most for their strength and usefulness. The mighty bulls were employed for cultivation and related works. The farmer seems very fond of his young auburn bullcalf.[102]

In addition to the cows, bulls and bullocks, the livestock of the ancient Indians included the goats, sheep, horses, elephants and the buffaloes. The word *aja* denotes goat, *aśva* stands for horse, *gaja* means the elephant, *mahiṣa* or *mahiṣi* stands for buffalo and *eḍaka* denotes ram.[103] There are also some other terms used in the Vedic literature for these animals.[104] Among the domestic animals, we trace cows, goats, sheep, horses, elephants, buffaloes, asses, and cats, etc. in the *Ṛgveda* and later.[105]

Management of Cattle Farms

Śālā in the *Atharvaveda*[106] and later[107] denotes a "house" in the wide sense of the word, including such meanings as "stall" for cattle, "shed" for corn, etc.[108] There were big cowsheds near the farmhouses.

102. *Atharvaveda,* IX.4.22.
103. A.A. Macdonell and A.B. Keith, op. cit., vol. II, pp. 571-73.
104. Ibid.
105. B.L. Ray, *Studies in Sanskrit, Indology and Culture,* Classical New Delhi: Publishing Company, 1998, pp. 17-18.
106. *Atharvaveda,* V.31.5; VI.106.3; VIII.6.10; IX.3.1; XIV.1.63.
107. *Taittirīya Brāhamaṇa,* I.2.3.1; *Satapatha Brāhmaṇa,* III.1.1.6.
108. *Atharvaveda,* III.12.1.

The Process of securing the cattle with a cord was in practice. At some places, the cowsheds were situated by the side of houses in the villages. The cattle entering their shelter, kicking and capering about are beautifully depicted in the *Atharvaveda*. Emphasis has been given on the structure of the cowsheds. These shelters for the cows should be built with proper care so as to maintain the sweet-milking cows in peace. It is mentioned that the cattle going towards this cowshed may be fearless. There should be provisions for properly draining the cow dung. The cows may live here giving nectar-like sweet milk and being free from all diseases.[109] The word *kariṣiniḥ* formed from the root *kariṣin* means cow dung. This also leads to the meaning related to drainage-system as well as the ways to ensure better fertilization. The cattle owner hopes that at all the animals would reside in the cowsheds together and live long. The amulet made from *glomerous* fig tree, the *udumbaramaṇi,* was employed for cattle farms of beautiful, strong cattle full of milk. The huge "wards" held the largest of all the cattle. These wards belonged to the people collectively, right from the head of the village to the common man. In a hymn,[110] the gods are invoked for protecting the high roofs of the cattle sheds. The great seer Kaśyapa has narated about the management of the dairy farms.[111] According to his descriptions, hundreds of dairy managers (or the vessels to milk in), milkmen, cattle riders follow the *vasā*-cow. The deities acknowledge only the *vasā* as they exist due to her presence. V.S. Apte states that the root *kaṁsa* in the word *kaṁsaḥ* means to command and therefore the word can be translated as the commanding authority in the dairy farm or a dairy manager. The employees of the dairy farm were the milkmen, the grazers, the guards and sweepers of the shed.

---

109. Ibid., III.14.3.

110. Ibid., XIX.58.4.

111. Ibid., X.10.5.

As stated, by the seer Uparibabhravā, the potent grass and the tanks full of pure sweet water were provided to the cowsheds.[112]

During Vedic age, there were meadows reserved for the grazing of the domestic animals. It was ensured that the cows and other domestic animals did not enter into the grazing fields of the enemies. The cattle breeders or the farmers were in a position to possess the hills, forests and water tanks needed for feeding their cattle.[113]

Precautions in Cattle Breeding

The *Atharvaveda* also gives stress on better cattle breeding. The farmer must take care of improving the potency of his cattle by providing them healthy environment to breed and grow. Precautions should be taken to protect them from diseases as well as from wild animals.

The bulls, bullocks, horses and oxes need to be healthy and energetic in order to carry on the work relating to cultivation. If these animals will be active in performing the farm works, then the cultivation will be speedier and the production will be more. Likewise, the bulk and freshness of the goats are to be maintained as they are very much in demand for their meat. The Klībasūkta of the *Atharvaveda-Saṁhitā* mentions a rite for clapping the testicles of the animals. According to Pandit S.D. Satavalekar, the hymns of the *Atharvaveda-Saṁhitā* explain the process of cutting down the sperma-genital carriers or pressing down the testicles or injuring the sensation regarding intercourse of the male animals of the above-mentioned breeds. In the hymn the seer has prescribed a medicinal plant for the purpose, but such a

112. B.S. Kharade, op. cit., p. 27.

113. Ibid.

plant has not been indentified yet.[114] However, Pandit Satavalekar has stated the purpose behind this operation.

The *Atharvaveda* narrates that the priest Brahmā takes care of the domestic animals regarding their health and hygiene. When the cow produces one calf after another in regular intervals of a year, then it is supposed that the proper reproductive system is working normally. If a cow gives birth to twins or trio without the menstrual flux, it becomes headache to the farmer and the situation becomes the source of pain for the entire community of the cattleshed.[115]

In order to cure some diseases of the cattle, some medicinal plants were employed. Among them, the plants *arundhatī* and *jivalā* were significant. The plant *arundhatī* was invoked for its very powerful medicinal qualities useful in reducing the swelling of the stomach and dealing with problems relating to milk-yielding capacity.[116] Atharvan recommends *jivalā,* a medicinal plant, for healing the injuries of animals caused by agricultural tools as well as weapons. The seer, further, suggests some important measures to guard the domestic animals from wild beasts of prey such as the wolves and tigers and protect the cattle from thieves and even insects.[117] It is suggested that the paths of the robbers and those of wild animals be destroyed so as to prevent the stealing of the cattle from the cattle farms. As the robbery took place generally at night, Gopatha, a cattle-breeding seer, warns the people in this occupation to be alert at night. The guards and the watchmen may in shifts, one by one, keep watch around the cowsheds, farmhouses and the cattle fields.[118]

---

114. Ibid., p. 28.
115. *Atharvaveda,* III.28.1.
116. Ibid., VI.59.1.
117. Ibid., IV.3.1.
118. Ibid., XIX.48.5.

Precautionary measures were also taken to save the cattle from the attack of leopards, wolves and deceiving agile hunters. Very often such incidents occurred in the night. So, the guards were trained to make sounds like the animals as well as to disguise themselves as scarecrows to frighten and seare away the wild animals. In order to protect the cattle from the robbers, the cattle were stamped on the ears or any other part of the body. This was also done to keep an account of the animals in the cattle-farm. The seer Viśvāmitra invokes Aśvinau to safeguard the cattle.[119]

Thus, it is observed from the Vedic records that animal culture was established both qualitatively and quantitatively during the ancient time. It flourished like the plant culture. The techniques in cattle breeding were fairly developed. Nowadays, people are trained to adapt dairy farming as a profitable profession. But, the Vedic people were very much aware of this fact and followed this occupation besides the agriculture. It is indeed striking that some guidelines regarding this business provided by our ancestors are of value and in practice even today. Rightly the British scholars have expressed their views in this respect. According to them, the Indian farmers had established their farmhouses to the maximum extent possible. By the way of inheriting the technique from their fathers and forefathers, they have known to make the cattle potent by providing them all medicinal facilities available in nature.[120]

Evidently, both the *Ṛgveda* and the *Atharvaveda* refer to *kṛṣi* (agriculture) and to the cattle wealth. As already stated, the terms *go, gopā* and *gopāla,* are traced in the Vedic literature to denote the cow and the milkman. The Vedic Indian grew crops, produced food grains and was habituated to milk and milk products.

---

119. Ibid., VI.141.2.

120. B.S. Kharade, op. cit., p. 32 and fn. 31.

8

Geology

Introduction

THE Vedic literature is a theistic school investing divinity in all its geological and universal agents. It is the storehouse of knowledge of the natural world. The Vedic sages initiated the formulation of the rudiments of a Vedic theory of the earth that culminated in the Upaniṣadic period which invȯlved deep studies and contemplation. Most of the Ṛgvedic and some of the other Vedic literature were all concerned with the earth. The Ṛgvedic compositions were simply geo-poetry to a major extent with very less human code of conduct or corrective spirits, like the Gambler's Sūkta. Drawing upon the Vedic authority, the Upaniṣadic school which may be seen as the rationalistic dimension of nature — the geo-philosophy, as it may be called — was developed. Amongst the six *aṅga*s or adjuncts of the Vedas, importance was given to mathematics and geo-astronomy in preference to all other disciplines. Ample information on the earth and geo-electrical/magnetic, hydrospherical, geothermal and atmospheric shields, the luminaries and planets of the solar system and the starry zodiac of the celestial sphere, etc. are available in the Vedas. In addition, information culled from one of the most important Upaniṣads, i.e. the *Taittirīya Upaniṣad,* has paved the way for tracing the evolution of the earth from space which is confirmed by modern views.

Data about the origin of the earth and the planets, age of the earth, shape of the earth, dimensions of the earth and movements of the earth are also presented by the Vedic hymns. Seismology based on the Vedic theory of the earth can also be predicted.

The most important factor is the tracing of the origin of the Āryans to the Brahmāvartta and the Brahmarṣideśa which are very close to the Spiti Valley of the Himalayas. There is a geological section which brings the history of the earth from the Cambrian period to that of the Cretaccous, measuring a time gap of some 500 million years, which is included in the standard book on geology of those periods. There is some difference between the geology of the Spiti valley indicated to us and the standard geological record of the European stratigraphy. The geology of the Spiti valley, most probably, leads us to believe that the Āryan sages dwelt in that place for millennia. The Indian philosophical approach for all local problems gave them some fanciful Purāṇic interpretations. For example, ammonite shells were found in the Spiti shales up the river Nārāyaṇī in Nepal which, having drained, supplied those shells to the lower stretches of the river joining the Gaṇḍakī. Instead of their correct identification as fossils, they have been worshipped as *śāligrāmas*[1] since ages. According to Krishnan, they (the Spiti Shales) contain numerous fossils, particularly ammonites, which are often found enclosed in nodules. These ammonites called *śāligrāma*s are brought down by the Gaṇḍaka and other rivers in Nepal and are considered sacred by the Hindus. Some of the fossils have a coating of pyrites which gives them a golden colour. These golden-coloured ammonites have been addressed as *svarṇa śāligrāma*s. This confirms that the Hindu thought is essentially spiritual.

Despite spirituality, the Hindu philosophy is most scientific as observed by the great scientist Einstein. According to him, "Science without religion is lame and religion without science

1. M.S. Krishnan, *Geology of India and Burma*, Higginbothams, Madras, 1956.

is blind." The facts and figures expressed in the Vedic hymns reveal that the thoughts of the Vedic seers are all blended with geological truth. The Vedas contain the forests, mountains, rivers, lakes, flora and fauna, and above all the natural environment in which the primitive people were living. The earth-science projected in the Vedic literature adheres to *Bhū Maṇḍala, Graha Maṇḍala* and *Nakṣatra Maṇḍala* and from which we can formulate the geological aspects of the planet "Earth." The data available from the Vedas and the Vedāṅgas were complete in all respects right from the definition of the "Universe" — the term meaning everything living and non-living in the words of Fred Hoyle.[2]

Vedic view of the earth, its origin, shape, dimensions, constitution, movements, quakes/tremours, and its position *vis-à-vis* the solar system, stars and ethereal space prove the geological acumen of the Vedic seers. The heliocentric theory of the Universe is also gleaned from the hymns of the Vedas. With the help of the Veda-based methods, earthquakes can also be predicted much before the real occurrence.[3] It is worth mentioning here that the Vedic literature is a theistic school investing divinity in all its geological and universal agents. Vedic versions of geology are based on the elements of the earth, geo-electrical/magnetic fields, hydrosphere, geothermal and atmospheric shields, the luminaries and planets of the solar system, and the starry zodiac of the celestial sphere.

Geophysical Phenomena

The Vedic divinities Indra, Agni, Maruts, Vāyu, Varuṇa, Dyāvāpṛthvī and Āpaḥ, etc. exhibit geophysical phenomena, which go a long way in describing the origin and evolution of the Universe as well as that of the earth. The counterpart of

---

2. Fred Hoyle, *Frontiers of Astronomy,* London, 1957.
3. S.R.N. Murthy, *Vedic View of the Earth,* New Delhi: D.K. Printworld (P) Ltd., 1997, pp. 31-112.

heaven and earth is Indra.[4] In a reference to Indra, the *Ṛgveda* describes the shaking of the mountains or earthquakes.[5] Such a description is found in many *ṛks*.[6] Almost all the *maṇḍala*s of the *Ṛgveda* mention this aspect of the god Indra and by whom this universe is made to tremble.[7] The most important of all these hymns is the one that says :

> He who fixed fast and firm the earth that strengthened and set at rest the agitated mountains, who measured out the air's wide middle region and gave the heaven support. He man is Indra. — *ṚV*,II.12.2

It is, thus, clear that Indra is not a god but a force which separates the earth from the sky or space and holds them as well as the moon in order, fixing them in their orbit of rotation to prevent a wobbling condition.

The first attribute of Indra is destroying the clouds and causing rains. The second attribute of Indra is causing the earthquake and fixing the earth firmly on its path of movement. From the scientific point of view, these two attributes unveil the characteristics of Indra as noticed by the Vedic seers.

This geophysical phenomenon symbolized as Indra is responsible in structuring the earth. Soon after the consolidation of the earth from its molten conditions orginating out of hot clouds from the sun, the earth underwent what is called Primary Geophysical Differentiation. As a result of this process, the earth got differentiated into an outer shell, an inner mantle and an interior core. The outer shell is essentially made of silicates of alumina and magnesia and hence called SIAL and SIMA; the core is essentially made of iron and nickel

4. *Ṛgveda*, X.111.4-5.
5. Ibid., I.63.1.
6. Ibid., I.80.14.
7. Ibid., II.12.4.

and addressed as NIFE; and the mantle has a composition comparable to that of the chromosphere of the sun. The most interesting feature of this differentiation is the generation of a geomagnetic field due to the earth's core, which generates a shell outside the earth from which all harmful rays of the external world are fittered through paving the way for the origin of the sedimentary cycle and life on earth. It is impossible to fully evaluate the contribution of this process, for its later evolution has been unique in the whole visible universe. The formation of clouds and causing of rains and the cycle of weathering, denudation, transportation of sediments and their deposition in the oceans began in due course.[8]

The word *vidyut* traced in the Vedic literature also represents a geophysical phenomenon. This is the outcome of the long-term interaction between the Vedic sages and the natural phenomena. As Indra causes rains for the growth of crops on the surface of the earth, the ancient seers attribute this phenomenon to Indra.

The iconographic description of Indra explains the above action of the deity more clearly. Indra's vehicle is the elephant which can be compared to the dark clouds; his tawny colour itself is the colour of the rains; his weapon, the thunderbolt is the one causing the rains or generated during the fall of rains; his one hand depicting benediction refers to the all-round prosperity brought about by the rains for humanity.

The second attribute of Indra has to do with firmly fixing the shaking earth and mountains. This is linked with the geological phenomenon as explained by Bhat.[9] Accordingly, in ancient times, the earth, being shaken severely by the

---

8. P.V. Shankara Narayan, *Geomagnetism and Life Processes,* Science Foundation, Madras, 1989.
9. R.M. Bhat, *Varāhamihira's Bṛhat Saṁhitā,* Motilal Banarsidass, 2 vols., 1986.

winged mountains, prayed to the Supreme Creator (Brahmā) to save her from the suffering. Then, the creator spoke to Indra to protect mother earth from the flying mountains. Hearing this, Indra consoled her and told her not to be afraid. He again made her aware of the fact that wind, fire, himself and Varuṇa will shake her in the four parts of the day and night put together respectively in order to reveal the good and bad effects of actions to the world. This story has also relevance in the contemporary context. Though the earth has attained some kind of stability sin some of its landmasses of ancient crystalline substance, it is still unstable along the plate margins and numerous earthquakes originate at these points even to this day.

The Ṛgvedic sages had studied the causes of the earthquakes and were able to speculate their occurrence. Their notions on seismology produce a theory for prediction of earthquakes. According to Varāhamihira,[10] some sages hold that an earthquake is brought about by the huge animals living in the waters of the ocean, while other (like Garga) opine that it is the result of the rest that is resorted to by the elephants of the quarters that are tired by the weight of the earth. Yet other sages like Vasiṣṭha declare that it is caused by the atmospheric wind colliding with another and falling to the earth with a blooming sound. There are still others like Vṛddhagarga who maintain that it is occasioned by some unseen power.

The seer Parāśara observed that the earthquakes are caused by eclipses of luminaries, unnatural phenomena occurring in the planets and special movements of the heavenly bodies.

Varāhamihira noticed that the predictive seismology is based on Wind Circle, Fire Circle and Varuṇa Circle. It is observed that the fruition of an earthquake of Wind Circle

---

10. R.M. Bhat, op. cit.

takes two months, the Fire Circle takes three fortnights, Indra's Circle takes seven days and Varuṇa's Circle takes immediate effect. Ostensibly, any unnatural phenomenon causing the earthquake can be predicted on the basis of the above circles.[11]

The foundation of the modern theory of earthquakes on scientific terms came into existence in 1897 when Oldham made a thorough study of the Assam earthquakes in the Geological Survey of India. From then onwards, the science of seismology has advanced very much; yet there is hardly any theory of predicting earthquakes. In this context, the theory of the earthquakes put forth by the Vedic sages can help us in predicting the earthquakes.

In order to formulate a theory of predicting earthquakes, all the geological changes should be taken into consideration. Specifically, the geomorphological changes, including the climate and environment, are due to the precession of the equinoxes under the general force of universal gravitation. The disposition of major planets having considerable angular momenta can be accounted for. One may find out the centre of the total angular momenta of the solar system at the deep focus earthquakes in the past and determine the positions of fluctuation in the path of the total angular momenta arrived at by finding out the advanced positions of major planets.[12]

Other geological agencies identified by the Vedic seers are Agni, Varuṇa, Maruts, etc. as noted earlier. Agni represents the geothermal field. Agni is the divine fire. The very first hymn of the *Ṛgveda* is a song to the divine fire. According to Macdonell,[13] the sacrificial fire is personified as Agni. He acquires second position to Indra in the *Ṛgveda.* He is addressed in about 200 hymns of this Veda. The

---

11. Ibid.

12. S.R.N. Murthy, op. cit., p. 54.

13. A.A. Macdonell, *A Vedic Reader for Students,* Oxford Press, 1976.

anthropomorphism of his physical appearance is only rudimentary, and is connected chiefly with the sacrificial aspect of fire. Thus, he is butterbacked, flame haired, and has a tawny beard, sharp jaws and golden teeth. Mention is often made of his tongue, through which the gods eat the oblations. With a burning head, he faces in all directions.

Agni is noted to shine like the sun with a lustre resembling that of the dawn and the lightning of the rain-cloud. He shines even in the night and dispels darkness. His flames are described as roaring like ocean waves and he sounds like thunder. He is smoke-bannered and his smoke rises up to the heaven. He is also described as the progeny of the waters.

Since he is generated out of the friction of two twigs by force, Agni is addressed as the son of strength. Agni is supposed to reside in the embryo of waters. The sun is noted to be a form of Agni. The divine fire is addressed as the child of the heaven. So, Agni has a triple origin — on earth, in waters and in the sky. Agni gives form to all things in nature. The best forms may be *ratnas*, because Agni is described as *ratnadhātama.* Actually, the formation of gemstones in the earth is one example. Heat is the main factor in forming the minerals like the gemstones. Agni is the major geological agent which has played a very important role in the origin and evolution of the earth. Minerals being definite physico-chemical entities, the role of temperature and pressure in the formation of gemstones is highly significant.[14] Many hymns of the *Ṛgveda*[15] depcit the origin and nature of Agni. The geothermal concept can be derived from some of these hymns.

The importance of the geothermal field as a principal

---

14. S.R.N. Murthy, op. cit., p. 61.

15. *Ṛgveda,* I.21.4; I.36.3; I.36.20; I.44.3; I.44.5; I.44.10; I.59.2; I.65.4; I.69.1; I.70.21; I.83.7; I.76.4; I.127.3; I.127.6; I.128.3; I.146.1; II.1.1; II.4.7; III.15.5; IV.3.6; etc.

geological agent in bringing the rock to molten lava condition and solidifying them, in making igneous rocks, and hardening the sediments into rocks as well as causing metamorphic rocks is very well known in modern petrology — the study of rocks. The effect of the geothermal field in causing volcanoes, thermal springs, and convection currents which move the continental landmasses is also known. The influences of the solar wind on the geothermal field is clear. Where geological agents turning the chemical compounds into minerals by the application of certain temperature and pressure are concerned, the geothermal field is the most important geological agent which was conceived by the great sages as "divine fire" in the *Ṛgveda*.

The Vedic deities Maruts and Vāyu represent the god of wind. They are described as the great, mighty, young and unageing, fierce, terrible, playful and child-like. They make thunderous noise and cause mountains to quake. They rend trees and devour forests. They shed rains covering the Sun causing darkness. They are also said to remove heat and dispel darkness preparing a path for the Sun.

The mention of the Maruts and Vāyu in the Ṛgvedic hymns[16] makes it clear that the Ṛgvedic sages worshipped the atmospheric winds as divine Marut or divine Vāyu. The wind as a powerful agent is well known in physical geology. The dynamic activity involved in the process of natural weathering, denudation and transportation is vividly, described in physical geology.[17]

The Vedic sages observed the actions of wind in nature. In the first interaction itself, they have been able to evaluate, the action of wind on the dusty earth, the cleaving of rocks,

---

16. Ibid., I.37.6-12; I.39.3, 5; I.85.5, 10; I.88.2-3; etc.
17. A. Holmes, *Principles of Physical Geology*, English Language Book Society, 1964, pp. 743-81.

the transportation of dust and sand to far-off places and the influence of the wind in rains and floods.[18]

The god Varuṇa also acts as a geological agent. As geology is linked with the law of nature, Varuṇa is the lord of law of nature, i.e. gravitation. He is the upholder of the physical and moral order. He established heaven and earth, and by his order heaven and earth are held apart. He is also a regulator of waters. He caused the rivers to flow; by his occult power they pour swiftly into the ocean without filling it. He is described as the god of rivers. He represents the entire hydrosphere that causes the earthquake.

The *Ṛgveda* mentions Varuṇa as the law-maker who is governing all gods. This law is called as *ṛta* in the *Ṛgveda.*[19] This *ṛta* is the law of the universe or the great cosmic order by which the whole of the manifest universe is working. According to Griffiths, "Varuṇa is King of the air and of the sea, the latter being often regarded as identical with the former."[20] The concept of Varuṇa is essentially that of governing the world and keeping it in order rather than one of causing rains and floods and owning oceans. By his power, Varuṇa controls the gods to keep them in their path. The luminaries, the earth and the heaven are held in their assigned position due to the influence of Varuṇa.

Besides the above geophysical phenomena, the theory of the earth has been well treated in the Vedic literature. Geological elements regarding the planet earth are contained in the Vedic hymns. Let us explain the concept of the earth as viewed by the Vedic seers.

---

18. *Ṛgveda*, V.54.9; V.55.4, 5, 7; V.60.2; V.66.7, 9; X.168.1.
19. Ibid., I.25.8, 9.
20. R.T.H. Griffiths, *The Hymns of the Ṛgveda*, Motilal Banarsidass, 1986.

Vedic Theory of the Earth

The *Ṛgveda* eulogizes the glory of the earth along with the heaven. There is only are *sūkta* on *pṛthvī* in the *Ṛgveda* while there are six or seven addressed to the *dyāvāpṛthvī.* However, there is an exhaustive hymn in the *Atharvaveda* on *bhūmi.* Macdonell[21] observes that heaven and earth are the most frequently named pair of deities in the *Ṛgveda.* They are so closely associated that they are invoked as a pair in six hymns.

While the *pṛthvī, bhūmi* and *janitrī* terms have been used in the Vedas to address the earth, some 28 names of the earth appear in the literature by the time of Amarasiṁha.[22] The Ṛgvedic sages believed that the heaven was wrapped up by the earth and they are held apart by Varuṇa. By the time of the *Taittirīya Upaniṣad,*[23] the earth is stated to be the earlier form, heaven the later form, and the space is noted to be their junction negotiated by air or atmosphere. In the *Ānandavallī* or *Bhṛguvallī,* the evolution of the *pañcabhūta*s has been described in simple terms. The field of *Brahman* appears as *ātmā* in the space; from space evolves Vāyu; from Vāyu evolves Agni; from Agni evolves Āpaḥ; from Āpaḥ evolves Pṛthvī. This theory of evolution of the earth has been largely adopted by almost all the post-Vedic literature. It is a fact that modern science also supports the view that from space originates all celestial bodies. Thus, the origin of the earth has been understood in the Vedic and the Upaniṣadic literature.[24] The *Ṛgveda* also mentions that the earth is unsupported. Though the Vedic notion of motionless earth is not correct, the earth

---

21. A.A. Macdonell, op. cit.

22. S.R.N. Murthy, *An Integrated Theory of the Earth,* Bangalore: Kalpataru Research Academy, 1987.

23. *Taittirīya Upaniṣad,* Śikṣāvallī, 3rd *anuvāka.*

24. *Ṛgveda,* I.159.1; I.160.1; I.185.1-2.

appears motionless relative to the bodies moving on the earth.[25] This has been rectified in the *Aitareya Brāhmaṇa* later.

By the time of the *Atharvaveda,* the sages appear to have advanced in their notion of the earth. They realized that the day and night might happen due to the movement of the earth about its axis. In the Bhūmi Sūkta, the characteristics of the earth have been described. The earth is held in its position by gravitation. The word *ṛta* means the law of gravitation.[26]

There are a few references to the earth in the *Yajurveda.*[27] In *kāṇḍa* 4, *anuvāka* 5, it is said that the sage makes a request that inorganic material like rocks, soil, mountains, hills, sands, vegetation, gold, silver, iron, lead, tin, copper and steel be made available to him for the performance of sacrifices. It is, thus, evident that the Yajurvedic sages knew the elements of the earth. The use of metals were prevalent. The examination of the ground of mountains and hills as well as of the soil, especially for the metallic ores of gold, silver, iron, lead, copper and steel has been stressed. The sages might have located the ores of all these metals and have studied their metallurgical properties, otherwise they would not have been able to mention the metals by name. Bronze and brass alloys have not been mentioned in the *Yajurveda;* probably they are later to the Yajurvedic period. The most important issue is the availability of tin ore, cassiterite (called *kastīra* in Sanskrit). It is suggested by Hegde that the Tosham hill deposit might have accounted for a small quantity of alluvial tin in the area of Āryan origin.[28] But the pan-Indian civilization might have

25. Ibid., I.185.2.

26. Ibid., X.85.1.

27. S.D. Satavatekar, *Taittirīya-Saṁhitā,* Swādhyāya Maṇḍala, Pāradi, Gujarat, 1990, p. 397.

28. K.T.M. Hegde, *An Introduction to Ancient Indian Metallurgy Bangalore,* 1991, p. 86.

accounted for tin from Burma (now Myanmar), Malaya, Sumatra and other places in the east and Afghanistan, Baluchistan in the mid-east. According to Murthy,[29] India within her present territory has very little quantity of tin ore.

The Vedic School believed that the earth is a representative of the universe and named the earth Viśvambharā. When, once the relationship of the earth to the universe was established, the idea that the earth is a separate entity to be studied exclusively was given up. Even in the Dyāvāpṛthvī-hymn, the earth is considered along with the heaven. This concept of the earth in relation to the universe is as old as the *Ṛgveda* which paved the way for a geo-cosmic theory in the Orient. The idea of a disc-like earth floating on water is as old as the Babylonian period. It was modified by Homer into a "spherical universe." Pythagoras also considered the earth as spherical and this view was accepted by Plato and Aristotle. This paved the way for a scientific cosmogony in the West during the middle of the seventeenth and eighteenth centuries CE. The most important "theory of the earth" in that period was given by Descartes in his *Philosophe Principle* (1644) as pointed out by C.A. Ronan.[30] He said that the various bodies of planets were originally glowing masses like the sun, the earth being no exception, and they possessed a nucleus of incandescent self-luminous mass of matter of which the middle zone was composed of an opaque solid substance which had initially been liquid in condition and the outer zone was of solid crust.[31] Finally, the disposition of various planets around the sun was explained by him. He expressed some ideas about volcanoes and the occurrence of earthquakes — as due to the escape of

---

29. S.R.N. Murthy et al., "Tin in Ancient India," *Journal of Geological Society of India*, vol. 38, no. 1, 1991, p. 106.

30. C.A. Ronan, *The Astronomers*, London, 1964, p. 32.

31. S.R.N. Murthy, *An Integrated Theory of the Earth*, Bangalore: Kalpataru Research Academy, 1987.

internal heat of the earth along with volatiles. Ronan informs us that Leibnitz developed the theory.[32] He observed that the mountains were formed by the irregular development of the early crust and the erosion of these parts caused the sedimentary rocks among other things, while no such notion was there in the Orient.

Vedic Heliology

It is very interesting to study the subject of the Vedic heliology. The sun directly influences the earth and various terrestrial activities. The slightest change in temperature, for instance, will affect the people to an enormous extent. Actually, almost all chemical, physical and biological changes that are taking place on the surface of the earth can directly be related to the solar influence. On the basis of the information available from the Vedic period to the recent times on the influence of the sun on the earth, sound principles can be formulated for the future interpretation of the terrestrial changes, a foundation aspect of the "Theory of the Earth."[33] Thus, the Vedic study of heliology can be of utmost importance as the greatest contribution from the oldest school of thought on the earth.

Murthy holds that an integrated study of the ancient Indian and modern contributions in heliology can pave a way for the fruitful interpretation of the earth's surface changes as well as the changes in its interior. It is only the surface changes that are well known; the internal changes caused by the heliological influence on the geomagnetic storms and convection currents, etc. are not yet known. In this connection, the Vedic and post-Vedic concepts may help in the formulation of the "Theory of the Erath."[34]

32. Leibnitz, *Acta Eruditarium*, 1639.
33. S.R.N. Murthy, *Vedic View of the Earth*, New Delhi: D.K. Printworld (P) Ltd. 1997, p. 141.
34. Ibid.

Vedic Selenology

The study of the influence of the moon on the terrestrial changes is the subject of the Vedic selenology. Such studies open up many unknown facts related to earth-science. The lunar influence on the earth observed from the Vedic times to that of Varāhamihira have been presented by him in his *Bṛhat-Saṁhitā.* Though the lunar influence on the earth may be lesser than the influence of the sun on the earth, the luni-solar influence is most important. This is because of the fact that the combined influence is responsible for much of the changing scenery on the earth, i.e. the environmental changes on it. The sociological influences of the moon are also very important. In addition to these, the interaction among the bary-centre (the centre of the earth-moon system), the magnetic centre of the earth and the gravity centre of the earth causes many significant geological changes.

Modern selenological studies have brought forth a wealth of data on the origin and evolution of the moon. The absence of a strong seleno-magnetic field and a low intensity gravity field on the moon have resulted in the absence of any life on it similar to that on the earth. The evolution of rocks on the moon also stopped some time after its origin.[35]

The Effects of Eclipses

The formation of solar and lunar eclipses brings about a lot of changes on the earth. The cult of eclipses forms the main theme of the Vedas. There are spells and charms to avert calamities caused due to eclipses. Until the origin of the text of the old *Sūrya Siddhānta* (since nothing about eclipses is evident from the text of *Vedāṅga Jyotiṣa* of Lagadha), it appears that the Vedic sages were under the erroneous assumtion that the Rāhu gulped down the luminaries during the eclipses. This theory was well-developed by the astronomers of the post-Vedic

35. Ibid, p. 143.

period to ascertain the terrestrial changes followed by different types of eclipses which have been summarised by Varāhamihira in his *Bṛhat-Saṁhitā*.[36]

The Effects of the Stars

Terrestrial changes are also brought about by the stars present in the universe. The Vedic sages made a thorough study of the stellar path forming a background or frame for the *graha*s and recognised some 27 or 28 stars/groups and gave them names based on certain observations. Therefore, the theory of the earth as a representative of the universe is complete only when it is studied in the background of the universal manifestation.

The Ṛgvedic seers were well-acquainted with the stars of the Zodiac. According to the *Ṛgveda,* the stars disappear along with the night. When the sun rises[37] even as the Moon remains nearer to them,[38] i.e. transiting the stars, describing the motion of the lunar and solar bodies on the starry path. The Vedic sages have rightly identified the transit of the sun through the arc of Kṛttikā which is the hottest period and named the presiding deity of this star as divine fire. Different kinds of halos and rainbows and their weather indications are also stated.[39] It is mentioned that the occurrence of rainbow or halos in the arc of the stars increases rains.

The arc of the Swāti star coincides with the solar movement from the last week of October to the first week of November. This was noted by the Vedic sages as a period of severe wind action. Hence, the deity of the star is Vāyu. The *Ṛgveda* mentions the effects of this star, attributing a *ṛk* to god Vāyu

36. R.M. Bhat, *Varāhamihira's Bṛhat-Saṁhitā,* Motilal Banarsidass, 2 vols., 1986.
37. *Ṛgveda,* I.50.2.
38. Ibid., X.85.2.
39. R.M. Bhat, op. cit.

and another to Indra-Vāyu.[40] Association of Indra with Vāyu is significant here since the severe action of the wind is probably a result of the reaction of the geomagnetic field with the solar magnetic influence charged by the Swāti star.

The Indrāgni is the presiding deity of the star Viśākhā.[41] Indra-Agni have been described as brothers born of a father with their mother everywhere. This may mean that the geoelectric (magnetic) field and the geothermal field have a common origin and they are omnipresent (owing to their mother who is everywhere).

Thus, the starlore of the Vedic literature is something like a testimony of the universal knowledge of the Vedic sages who had acquainted themselves with the terrestrial and planetary bodies. The material universe with its multitheistic concept later helped them to make observations on the ultimate reality underlying the universe.

The Geological Agents

The Vedas describe the actions of the geological agents like heat, wind, and water in the form of rivers, oceans, etc. Such descriptions are the first lessons in terms of modern physical geology, but these are not in the lines of Western thinking. There appears to be a peculiar mix, and a total or overall picture of the earth subjected to various natural geological and geophysical agencies is presented. For example, the influence of heat on the earth (the geothermal aspect) is part of the Agni Sūktas; the influence of water on the earth (the hydrosphere-related activity) is part of the Varuṇa Sūkta, Nadī Sūktas, Parjanya Sūktas, Samudra Sūktas, etc.; the action of wind in the atmosphere is part of the Vāyu Sūktas; and the role of water in the hydrological cycle causing rain is the essence of the Indra Sūktas.

---

40. *R̥gveda*, IV.447.1-2.

41. Ibid., VI.59.6-7.

Most of the *Ṛgveda* and parts of the other Vedas deal with the various geological and geophysical activities and are centred around the earth. Ostensibly, all the data collected from these sources can easily lead us to formulate a "Theory of the Earth."

The Age of the Earth

Many scientists have estimated the age of the earth from different points of view. Kelvin holds that the earth is about 40 million years old to account for the dissipation of original heat and in consideration of its present status. Then, Jolly estimated that the age of the earth is not less than 100 million years considering the purity of the original oceans which are becoming increasingly saline due to the salt transported and added to the oceans by the rivers of the earth. As per the stratigraphic record on the details of the fossils, the age of the earth is not less than some 600 million years.[42] Based on radiometric methods, the age of the earth has been estimated to be about 4500 million years.[43]

Arthur Holmes has been recognised as the architect of modern geochronology. His observations on the age of the earth from Vedic texts is something which the Vedic and post-Vedic students of the earth-science must be proud of. It is also a fact that the accuracy that the Vedic Chronology has maintained is not seen in the modern scientific deliberations. Even the most accurate geochronological dating of the earth in the present state of our knowledge would go by a margin of + or – 100 million years or so.[44]

Vedic way of calculating time appears to be totally based on the movements of the heavenly bodies. Time has been

42. B. Kummel, *History of the Earth*, New Delhi: Eurasia Publishing House, 1961.
43. S.R.N. Murthy, op. cit., p. 236.
44. R.M. Bhat, op. cit., p. 1106.

calculated taking into account the motion of the earth relative to the motion of the celestial bodies.

The Vedic sages also recognised five types of years, viz. the solar, the Lunar, the Sāvana (360 days), Nakṣatra and Bārhaspatya, the last based on the movements of the planet Jupiter. The last one is in vogue probably from the time of Varāhamihira. This forms a cycle of 60 years commencing from Prabhave and ending with Akṣaya.

Shape of the Earth

The Babylonians and the Greeks believed in a disc-like Earth.[45] Aristotle was the first to suggest that the Earth is round for during an eclipse of the moon, the shadow of the Earth is curved. His five elements appear to be direct derivatives of the *Taittirīya Upaniṣad*. These five elements are fire, air, water, the ground and the space (*antarikṣa*). Eratosthenes in the third century BCE determined the circumference of the earth, which is very close to the modern value. Ptolemy places himself fairly and squarely on the side of Aristotle and accepts a spherical earth immovable in the centre of a spherical universe.

The change in the concept of the disc-like earth to spherical earth took place in Europe about fifth/sixth century BCE during the period of Pythagoras. Even then, they did not know how the spherical earth could exist in space unsupported until Newton explained it by his "Theory of Gravitation" in CE 1686. The concept of the global earth has been supported even today with the advancements in astronomy, geology and allied sciences.

Dimensions of the Earth

Ancient scholars before Aristotle had taken interest in calculating the circumference of the earth. But, it is Hipparchus

---

45. C.A. Ronan, *The Astronomers*, London, 1964, p. 232.

who has been credited for a calculation close to modern values in 240 BCE.[46] According to the demonstration of Newton, the earth is not a perfect sphere but an oblate spheroid. The circumference of the earth as per the *Pañcasiddhāntikā* of Varāhamihira is equal to 3200 *yojana*s, 9 – 1/9 *yojana*s correspand to one degree and 800 *yojana*s to 90 degree. We have

1 *yojana* = 4 *krosa*s

1 *krosa* = 2000 *daṇḍa*s or fathoms

1 *daṇḍa* = 2 yards

Hence, 1 *yojana* = 2×2000×4 Yards

$$= \frac{16000}{1760} \text{ miles}$$

$$= (100/11) \text{ miles}$$

Again, 1 mile = 1760×3 = 5280 ft

1 ft = 12 inch

1 inch = 2.54 cm

So, 1 *yojna* =

$$\frac{100\times5280\times12\times2.54 \text{ cm}}{11}$$

$$= \frac{100\times5280\times12\times2.54\times10^{-2}\text{m}}{11}$$

$$= \frac{100\times5280\times12\times2.54\times10^{-2}\times10^{-3} \text{ km}}{11}$$

$$= \frac{5280\times12\times2.54\times10^{-3} \text{ km}}{11}$$

$$= 14630.4\times10^{-3} \text{ km}$$

---

46. Ibid.

Then, the circumference of the earth comes to $3200 \times 14630.4 \times 10^{-3}$ km, i.e. 46817.28 km.

Subbarayappa and Sarma[47] have presented the views of the modern *Sūrya Siddhānta*, Brahmagupta, Deva Keralam, Bhāskara II, Nīlakaṇṭha and others regarding the circumference of the earth. The modern *Sūrya Siddhānta* and Bhāskara II opine that the circumference of the earth in 4967 *yojana*s and the surface area of the earth in 785034 square *yojana*s. The Deva Keralam and Bhāskara I gave 3299 *yojana*s. as the circumference of the earth. According to Nīlakaṇṭha, the diameter of the earth is 1050 *yojana*s.

Modern calculations give a little less than 40,000 km as the circumference of the earth. This would give 111–1/9 km per radian, comparable to 8 and 8/9 *yojana*s. On the same lines, the diameter of the earth would be 13155 km or nearly, 8220 miles. Nīlakaṇṭha arrived at this data by about CE 144 as observed by Subbarayappa and Sarma.

Constitution of the Earth

The chief elements of the earth as viewed from the Vedic cosmogony and cosmology are air, fire, water, the ground and the space (*antarikṣa*). Vedic deity Maruts and Vāyu represent the air or atmosphere, Agni represents fire, Āpaḥ represents water, the Pr̥thvī represents the ground and the sky or space is represented by *antarikṣa*. The space is the medium that accomnodates the manifest universe. It is characterized by the quality of sound according to *Taittirīya Upaniṣad*. It is note the earth originated through Vāyu, Agni and Āpaḥ.

The terms *pr̥thvī, bhūmi* and *janitrī* have been used in the Vedas to address the earth, some 28 names of the earth appear

47. B.V. Subbarayappa, and K.V. Sarma, *Indian Astronomy — A Source Book*, Nehru Centre, Bombay, 1985, p. 338.

in the literature by the time of Amarasiṁha.[48] The Ṛgvedic sages believed that the heaven was wrapped up by the earth and they are held apart by Varuṇa. There is one *sūkta* on *pṛthvī* in the *Ṛgveda* while there are six or seven addressed to the *dyāvāpṛthvī*. However, there is an exhaustive hymn in the *Atharvaveda* on *bhūmi*. According to Macdonell,[49] Heaven and Earth are the most frequently named pair of deities in the *Ṛgveda*. They are so closely associated that they are invoked as a pair in six hymns.

The Vedic concept of the origin of the universe is based on two theories, namely

(i) Water theory, and

(ii) Golden-Egg theory.

According to Water theory, initially there was nothing except water.

The evolution starts from water. Darwin's theory of evolution supports this view. On the other hand, this material world has been originated from the cosmic golden-egg. The earth is described as *hiraṇyagarbha*, i.e. in the core of the earth, there exist *hiraṇya* (gold). The earth is also addressed as *hiraṇyagarbha* meaning that the earth has a gold bosom. The earth is praised as *jagato niveśanī* — one in whom the entire universe is present.

From the episode of Indra-Vṛtra fight, it is evident that Indra represents the force and Vṛtra (the demon) represents the inertia. Indra killed Vṛtra in the fight, i.e. the inertia was broken and the evolution was sprung. Based on this concept, it would be reasonable to presume that the earth has a gold-womb. The modern school describes the earth as made of

---

48. S.R.N. Murthy, *An Integrated Theory of the Earth*, Bangalore: Kalpataru Research Academy, 1987, p. 127.

49. A.A. Macdonell, *A Vedic Reader for Students*, Oxford Press, 1976.

crust, mantle and core shells and the core compensating for the lesser density of the crust by being denser to the tune of 11 or 13 so, but it is only a conjecture. The core is known to be made up of nickel and iron called NIFE. The crust of the earth is the shell which is above the "Moho" level which may vary from 35 to 60 km at the surface. The mantle is known to extend up to 2900 km from the surface where the boundary of the core commences towards the centre. These have been recognised by the propagation of earthquake waves within the earth, and it is noted that as "S" waves do not transverse the core, the core must be at least partly liquid in condition.[50]

According to Bullen,[51] the core of the earth below 5000 km contains solid material and it could transmit the transverse waves. But the core is found not to transmit transverse waves because of its plastic condition. It has been suggested that the "S" waves arriving at the boundary of the core do not enter it but transform into longitudinal waves by refracting and transit the core. Studies on propagation of earthquake waves within the earth provide a lot of information regarding the core and the mantle of it.

Thus, the earth has all the characteristies of previous stages of evolution which include qualities of sound, touch, form, juices and smell, etc. The earth is described as wide, supporting forests, hills and mountains. It contains herbs to protect in. It contains oceans and rivers to provide water for the growth of crops and for the existence of all living beings. The earth is said to be, at places, white, dark, tawny and of variegated colour. The earth is described as raised at some places and lowered at other places. The earth is depicted as the progenitor of the people and animals with 2 or 4 ft. The divine fire is

50. B. Gutenberg (ed.), *Internal Constitution of the Earth,* Dover, 1951, p. 439.

51. C.F. Richter, *Elementary Seismology,* New Delhi: Eurasia Publishing House, 1958, p. 768.

noted to be in the earth and in herbs, waters and rocks. The earth with such divine fire is prayed to give a long life. The earth is made up of rocks and dust. Obviously, the earth holds almost all secrets of nature which pave a way to understand the mystery of this universe. The geological agencies like geothermal, geomagnetic, hydrothermal and wind are present within the earth and the Vedic sages have well-understood their activities in bringing about the variable changes inside the core of the earth.

Movement of the Earth

The geocentric theory of the universe was prevalent in ancient times, though the *Ṛgveda* mentions that the sun moves and also attracts the celestial dust (including celestial bodies) through the fragments.[52] The movement of the sun is supported by the *Chāndogyopaniṣad*. But, the concept of the geocentric theory was so firmly rooted that the scientists later did not veuture to think about the motion of the earth. However, Varāhamihira mentioned that some other's conceived the idea of motion of the earth as if it is placed in a revolving engine. This indicates, that some *siddhānta*s prior to Varāhamihira mentioned the revolution of the earth, but Varāhamihira did not accept it. But he has not mentioned who actually believed in the revolution of the earth prior to his time.[53]

Āryabhaṭṭa observed that the earth revolved about its axis causing day and night.[54] This view of Āryabhaṭṭa was not appreciated by Bhāskar II who wrote *Siddhānta Śiromaṇi* in CE 1077. But, he holds that the earth has got force of attraction. By this force the earth attracts heavier bodies towards it.

52. *Ṛgveda*, I.35.2.

53. G. Thibaut, and S. Dwivedi, *Pañcasiddhāntikā of Varāhamihira*, Varanasi, 1968.

54. *Āryabhaṭīyam*, Golapāda Chapter, v. 10.

During this action, it appears that the body is falling on to the earth. However, the space is extended to all four sides. As such, how does the fall of the earth take place?[55]

The concept of the rotation of the earth was adopted by the author of *Brahmasphoṭasiddhānta* — Brahmagupta in CE 598. Following this, Subbarayapa and Sarma state that the sphere of the star is fixed. It is only the earth that regularly rotates once a day, causing the rising and setting of the stars and the planets.[56] Āryabhaṭṭa has accepted the rotation of the earth. Modern *Sūrya Siddhānta* mentions eight kinds of movements of the planets, but does not refer to the motion of the earth.[57] Actually, today's scientific observation go in favour of revolution of the earth around its own axis as well as around the sun. Like the other planets, the earth revolves around the sun in its own orbit. The axial rotation of the earth causes day and night whereas its revolution around the sun causes the change of the seasons. Ostensibly, the Vedic concept of the stable-earth has been changed, in course of time, to the movable earth supported by prolonged theoretical as well as experimental observations. In this context, the contribution of Kepler, Galileo, Copernicus and Newton are of great importance.

Conclusion

The geological aspects of the Vedic literature are gleaned from the study of the cosmology, cosmogony, agriculture, meteorology, seismology and above all the Vedic theory of the earth. The speculations of the Vedic seers regarding prediction of rains, cultivation of crops, prediction of

---

55. U.N. Singh, Pandit, *The Siddhānta Śiromaṇi, Golādhyāya,* Bombay, 1905, p. 112.
56. B.V. Subbarayappa, and K.V. Sharma, op. cit.
57. K. Chowdhury, *Sūrya Siddhānta,* Kashi Sanskrit Series, No. 144, Banaras, 1946, p. 298.

earthquake, prediction of volcanic activity, etc. form the basis of the geophysical phenomena taking place in nature. The earth-science was a special subject studied by the Vedic people who were the lovers of the nature in which they lived. The Vedic divinities like Indra, Varuṇa, Maruts, Vāyu, Āpaḥ, Parjanya, Pr̥thvī, Dyāvā-Pṛthvī, etc. are the symbolic representations of the many geophysical phenomena that occur in the nature. Further study in this line can open up many untrodden areas of geology buried under the level of Vedic philosophy and materialism.

9

Environmental Science and Ecology

Part I : Environmental Science

Introduction

THE Vedas, Saṁhitās, Āraṇyakas (forest texts), the Upaniṣads, Brāhmaṇas, Kalpasūtras and the Vedāṅgas are full of descriptions of our nature and natural beauty. The four Vedas, namely *Ṛg, Yaju, Sāma* and *Atharva* deal with some cities, towns, countries, states, rivers, mountains, lakes, forests, trees, birds, animals, earth, water, air, fire, climate as well as some place names. Being the primary sources of human civilization and knowledge, the Vedas and the Vedic texts are the anthologies of our rich natural resources. This, in turn, provides environmental studies from the Vedas. Moreover, the geographical account depicted in the Vedas throws sufficient light on our environmental knowledge. No specific observation has been made so far on the Vedic environment. Here, in this chapter, an attempt has been made to discover the environment portrayed in the Vedas and the ecology buried underneath the hymns.

The *Ṛgveda* or "Veda of Verses," is the most ancient and most important text of Vedism. It exists in the form of a collection of 1028 hymns (*sūkta*s), divided into ten "circles" (*maṇḍala*s). The chief subject of the *Ṛgveda* is to eulogize the glory of the gods and goddesses. The deities of the *Ṛgveda* are mainly Agni (the fire), Indra, Varuna, Viṣṇu, Rudra, Savitā,

Marut, Sūrya (the sun), Vāyu (the air), Soma, Dyāvāpṛthvī (the world), Mitra, Pūṣan, Uṣā (morning), Parjanya, Aśvin, Yama, etc. Among these, it is seen that most of the deities relate to our environment, so to say our existing natural resources. As the Vedas are the sacred texts of the Āryan culture, it is quite evident that the Āryans were worshipping the components of natural creations. It is true that the physical environments outlined in the Vedic hymns and *sūtra*s play an important role in shaping habits, customs and manners of people. The pattern of culture is largely determined by geographical conditions and hence by the environment in which we live. An adequate knowledge of the Vedic environment is, therefore, a sign of the Āryan culture.

The Vedas depict the universe which is divided into three parts, each sometimes duplicated and even triplicated. They are the earth, the *antarikṣa* and the sky. Space is conceived in fact as like an ocean, divided into two, three or four seas. For the sun, the common Vedic conception is that it has a bright and a dark face. The *nakṣatra*s or lunar mansions appear perhaps in the most recent parts of the *Ṛgveda*. The astronomical phenomena are hidden behind mythical forms.

Oceans in Ṛgveda

Ṛgveda describes four oceans as is evident from the frequent use of the word *samudra* (literally "gathering of waters") in it and in later texts. It is of importance in so far as it indicates that the Vedic Indians knew the sea. Max Müller[1] and Lassen[2] asserts it. Zimmer[3] admits it in one passage of the *Ṛgveda*[4] and

1. *Sacred Books of the East*, 32, 61 ff. quoting *ṚV* I.71.7; I.190.7; V.78.8; VII.49.2; VII.95.2.
2. A.A. Macdonell and A.B. Keith, *Vedic Index of Names and Subjects*, vol. II, Delhi: MLBD, 1982, p. 432.
3. A.A. Macdonell, *Sanskrit Literature*, pp. 143-44.
4. *Ṛgveda*, VII.95.2.

of course later.[5] He is inclined to restrict the knowledge of the Vedic Indians about the ocean. He points out that in many places *samudra* is metaphorically used, as of the two oceans,[6] the lower and the upper oceans,[7] etc. In other passages he thinks that *samudra* denotes the river Indus when it receives all its Punjab tributaries.[8]

Out of the four oceans, there was one such ocean in which the rivers Sarasvatī and Sindhu met. According to Bhūgarva Śāstrī, this Rājapūtānā ocean existed before 25,000 years. But this ocean is not found today. There are references to the treasures of the ocean,[9] perhaps pearls or the grains of trade[10] and the story of Bhujya seems to allude to marine navigation.

Rivers and Lakes in R̥gveda

The names of rivers alone permit of certain identification. The river par excellence in the *R̥gveda* is the Sindhu (Indus), which is known at last in the upper and middle course. The "five rivers" which later gave to the Punjab its name are mentioned as early as the hymns: Vitastā (Jhelum), Asiknī (Cenāb), Paruṣṇi, later Irāvatī (Rāvī), Vipāśa (Beas) and Śutudri (Sutlej). The River Sarasvatī[11] mentioned in the *R̥gveda* is assumed to be the modern Sursuti, between the Sutlej and the Jamunā. With the Indus and its five tributaries it forms the "seven

---

5. *Atharvaveda,* IV.10.4; VI.105.3; XIX.38.2; *Taittirīya-Saṁhitā,* VII.4.13.1.
6. *R̥gveda,* X.136.5.
7. Ibid., VII.6.7; X.98.5.
8. Ibid., I.71.7; III.36.7; III.46.4; V.85.6; VI.36.3; VII.95.2; VIII.16.2; VIII.44.25; IX.88.6; IX.107.9.
9. Ibid., I.47.6; VII.6.7; IX.97.44.
10. Ibid., I.48.3; I.56.2; IV.55.6.
11. Ibid., III.23.4; X.64.9; X.75.5. Also A.A. Macdonell and A.B. Keith, *Vedic Index of Names and Subjects,* vol. II, Delhi: MLBD 1982, p. 434 and 435.

rivers of the Veda."[12] The Yamunā[13] (Jamunā) itself is very seldom mentioned, and the Gaṅgā[14] (Ganges) only once.

Āpayā is the name of a river mentioned only once in the *Ṛgveda*,[15] when it occurs between the Dṛṣadvatī and the Sarasvatī. According to Roth, Sarasvatī is called the "foremost of rivers" (*nadītamā*)[16] and is referred to as a large river. Max Müller identifies that word Anitabhā of *Ṛgveda* as a river.[17] Ārjikīyā (feminine word) designates the river of the Land. Roth[18] accepts this as river in one passages[19] only. Hillebrandt thinks it may have been the upper Indus, or the Vitastā (the Jhelum), or some other stream. Brunnhofer[20] identifies it with the Arghesan, a tributary of the Arghanab. In the hymn of the *Ṛgveda*[21] which celebrates the rivers, Ludwig[22] finds a reference to an affluent of the Indus called Ūrṇāvatī. This interpretation, however, seems certainly wrong. Roth[23] renders the word merely as "woolly" and Zimmer[24] rejects Ludwig's explanation on the ground that it throws the structure of the hymn into

12. Ibid., VIII.24.27.
13. Ibid., V.52.17; VIII.18.19; X.75.5.
14. Ibid., X.75.5.
15. Ibid., III.23.4.
16. Ibid., II.41.16.
17. Ibid., V.53.9.
18. A.A. Macdonell and A.B. Keith *Vedic Index of Names and Subjects*, vol. I, Delhi: MLBD, 1982, pp. 62-63.
19. *Ṛgveda*, X.75.5.
20. *Iran and Turan*, 52 of Max Müller, *Sacred Books of the East*, 32, 398; 399.
21. *Ṛgveda*, X.75.8.
22. *Translation of the Ṛgveda*, 3200.
23. A.A. Macdonell and A.B. Keith, *Vedic Index of Names and Subjects*, vol. I, Delhi: MLBD, 1982, p. 106.
24. *Ṛgveda*, V.53.9.

confusion. Pischel makes the word an epithet of the Indus, "rich in sheep." Krumu is the name of a stream mentioned twice in the *Ṛgveda* — once in the fifth book and once in the last, in the *Nadī-Stuti,* or "Praise of rivers."[25] There can be little doubt that this river is identical with the modern Kurum, a western tributary of the Indus.[26] Gomatī is mentioned as a river in the *Nadī-Stuti* or "Praise of Rivers," in the tenth *maṇḍala* of the *Ṛgveda.*[27] Later Geldner[28] identifies this river with Gumtī which flows through Kurukṣetra,[29] as the centre of Vedic civilization. Tṛṣṭāmā is mentioned as a stream in the *Ṛgveda.*[30] Paruṣṇī is the name of a river mentioned in the *Nadī-Stuti.*[31] This river is called a "great stream" (*mahānadī*) in the eighth book of the *Ṛgveda.*[32] The name is certainly that of the river later called Rāvī (Irāvatī) as recognized by Yāska.[33] Marud-Vṛdhā is the name of a stream mentioned in the *Ṛgveda*[34] along with the Asiknī and the Vitastā. Mehatnū is the name of a stream in the *Ṛgveda.*[35] It must apparently have been a tributary of the Sindhu (Indus), entering that river before the Krumu (Kurum) and Gomatī (Gomal). It may conceivably have been

---

25. Ibid., X.75.6.
26. Macdonell and Keith, *Vedic Index of Names and Subjects,* vol. 1, Delhi: MLBD, 1982, p. 199.
27. *Ṛgveda,* X.75.6.
28. *Vedic Index of Name and Subjects,* vol. I, Delhi: MLBD, 1982, p. 238.
29. Hopkins, *Journal of the American Oriental Society,* 19, 9 ff.; Macdonell, *Sanskrit Literature,* 174; Keith, *Journal of the Royal Asiatic Society,* 1908, 1141.
30. *Ṛgveda,* X.75.6.
31. Ibid., X.75.5.
32. Ibid., VIII.74.15.
33. *Nirukta,* IX.26.
34. *Ṛgveda,* X.75.5.
35. Ibid., X.75.6.

a tributary of the Krumu. *Ṛgveda* includes a river named Yavyāvatī.[36] It is also noticed in *Pañcaviṁśa Brāhmaṇa.*[37] Rasā is found in three passages of the *Ṛgveda,*[38] clearly as the name of a real stream in the extreme north-west of the Vedic territory. *Reva* is the name of the Narmadā (Nerbuddha) river, otherwise occurring only in post-Vedic literature.[39] Vitastā, the most westerly of the five rivers of the Punjab, is only mentioned in the *Ṛgveda.*[40] Vipāśa is the name of the river mentioned twice in the *Ṛgveda.*[41] It is modern Beas in the Punjab; the Hyphasis, Hypanis or Bipasis of the Greeks. Vibālī is found once in the *Ṛgveda,*[42] apparenty as the name of an unknown stream. According to Sāyaṇa, Śiphā found in the *Ṛgveda* is also a river.[43] Śutudrī of *Ṛgveda*[44] is the name of the most easterly river of Punjab, the modern Sutlej. In the post-Vedic period, the names of this river appears transformed to Śatadru. Śvetyā of *Ṛgveda*[45] appears to be a stream, most probably a tributary of the Indus. We find the river Sarayū thrice in the *Ṛgveda.*[46] This river appears in one passage with Sarasvatī and Sindhu,[47] and in another with Rasā, Anitabhā, and Kubhā.[48] *Ṛgveda* mentions

36. Ibid., VI.27.6.
37. *Pañcaviṁśa Brāhmaṇa,* XXV.7.2.
38. *Ṛgveda,* I.112.12; V.53.9; X.75.6.
39. Cf. *Indian Antiquary,* 30.273, n. 17.
40. *Ṛgveda,* X.75.5.
41. Ibid., IV.30.11.
42. Ibid., IV.30.12.
43. Ibid., I.104.3.
44. Ibid., III.33.1; X.75.5.
45. Ibid., X.75.6.
46. Ibid., IV.30.18.
47. Ibid., X.64.9.
48. Ibid., V.53.9.

Sindhu as a stream.[49] Su-Vāstu is the name of a river in the *Ṛgveda.*[50] It is clearly the soastos of Āryans[51] and the modern Swāt, a tributary of the Kubhā (Kabul river) which is itself an affluent of the Indus. Max Müller and Keith identify Su-ṣomā as a river described in the *Ṛgveda.*[52] Su-Sartu found in the *Nadī-Stuti* of *Ṛgveda* has also been identified with a river.[53]

Thus we come across a number of rivers depicted in the *Ṛgveda.* These rivers are regarded as sacred and never being dried up. Many battles have been fought on the banks of these rivers and different clans, towns, cities and villages are found to have been settled by the sides of the Ṛgvedic rivers and streams. Obviously, the environmental suitability surrounding these rivers and streams promoted the civilization to grow.

Countries, Cities, Towns and Holy Places in Ṛgveda

The seven-continent theory is regarded by the scholars as conventional even in the *Ṛgveda.* Similarly the place-name Gayā[54] is intimately associated with the terms Gayā-Śīras or Gayā and Gayā-Śīrṣa or Gayā. It is well known from the *Ṛgveda* or *Atharvaveda.* The unanimous testimony of the Purāṇic writers and medieval lexicographers suggests that the Gayā region was known to the Ṛgvedic seers as Kīkaṭa. Ūrjayantī is regarded by Ludwig in one passage of the *Ṛgveda*[55] as the name of a fort, the stronghold of Nārmara.

Kurukṣetra (land of the Kurus) is always regarded in the

---

49. Ibid., I.97.8; I.125.5; II.11.9; II.253.5; III.53.9.
50. Ibid., VIII.19.37; *Nirukta,* IV.11.
51. *Indica,* IV.11.
52. *Ṛgveda,* I.75.5. Also *Vedic Index of Names and Subjects,* vol. II, p. 460.
53. *Ṛgveda,* I.75.6.
54. *Ṛgveda,* X.63.17; X.64.17.
55. Ibid., II. 13, 8.

Brāhmaṇa texts[56] as particularly sacred country. Within its boundaries flowed the rivers Dṛṣadvatī and Sarasvatī as well as the Āpayā.[57] Here, too, was situated Śaryaṇāvant,[58] which appears to have been a lake, like that known to the *Śatapatha Brāhmaṇa* by the name of Anyataḥ-plakṣā.[59] According to Pischel, there was also in Kurukṣetra a stream called Pastyā,[60] which he sees in certain passages of the *Ṛgveda*. The boundaries of Kurukṣetra are given in a passage of the *Taittirīya Āraṇyaka*[61] as being Khāṇḍara on the south, the Tūrghna on the north, and the Parīṇah on the west. According to Max Müller and Keith, it corresponds to the modern Sirhind.[62]

The place having *pañca-nada* (five streams) often refers to Punjab as the home of the *Ṛgveda*.[63] Plakṣa Praśravaṇa is the name of a locality, forty-four days' journey from the spot where the Sarasvatī disappears. In the *Ṛgveda sūtras*,[64] the locality is called Plakṣa Praśravaṇa, and is apparently meant to designate the source of the Sarasvatī rather than the place of its reapperance. Bhajeratha has mentioned in one passage of the *Ṛgveda*[65] where Ludwig[66] thinks a place-name is meant.

Forts with a hundred walls (Śatabhujā) are spoken of in

---

56. *Pañcaviṁśa Brāhmaṇa*, XXV.10; *Śatapatha Brāhmaṇa*, IV.1.5.13; XI.5.1.4; XIV.1.1.2; *Aitareya Brāhmaṇa*, VII.30; *Maitrāyaṇī-Saṁhitā*, II.1.4; IV.5.9.
57. Cf. *Ṛgveda*, III.23.2
58. *Vedic Index of Names and Subjects*, vol. I, p. 169.
59. *Śatapatha Brāhmaṇa*, XI.5.1.4.
60. *Vedic Index of Names and Subjects*, vol. I, p. 170.
61. *Ṛgveda*, V.1.1.
62. *Vedic Index of Names and Subjects*, vol. I, p. 170.
63. Ibid., p. 468.
64. Ibid., vol. II, p. 55.
65. *Ṛgveda*, X.60.2.
66. *Vedic Index of Names and Subjects*, vol. II, p. 94.

the *Ṛgveda*.[67] Pischel and Geldner,[68] however, think that there were towns with wooden walls and ditches like the Indian town of Pāṭaliputra known to Megasthenes[69] and the Pāli texts.[70] The word *nagara* is of late occurrence. On the whole it is hardly likely that in early Vedic times city life was much developed. Pura[71] and Mahāpura[72] traced in *Ṛgveda, Yajurveda* Saṁhitās and Brāhmaṇas denote "fort" and a "great fortress."

Mountains and Forests in Ṛgveda

The mountain ranges have also been described in the *Ṛgveda*. Giri is a word that occurs repeatedly in the *Ṛgveda*.[73] Thus reference is made to the trees on the hills, hence called "tree-haired" (*vṛkṣa-keśāḥ*),[74] and to the streams proceeding from the hills to the sea (*samudra*).[75] The term is frequently coupled with the adjectival *parvata*.[76] The *Ṛgveda* mentions the waters from the hills,[77] and the *Atharvaveda*[78] refers to the snowy mountains. Actual names of the mountains, as Mūjavant, Trikakud, Himavant, are very rare. References to Krauñca, Mahāmeru, and Maināga, are confined to the *Taittirīya Āraṇyaka,* while

67. *Ṛgveda,* I.166.8; VII.15.14.
68. Cf. *Vedic Index of Names and Subjects,* vol. I, p. 539.
69. Ibid.
70. Ibid.
71. Ibid., vol. II, p. 14.
72. Ibid., 141.
73. *Ṛgveda,* I.56.3; I.61.14; I.63.1; IV.20.6; VI.24.8, etc.
74. Ibid., V.41.11.
75. Ibid., VII.95.2.
76. Ibid., I.56.4; VIII.64.5; *Atharvaveda,* IV.7.8; VI.12.3; VI.17.3; IX.1.18, etc.
77. *Ṛgveda,* VI.66.11.
78. Ibid., XII.1.11.

Nāvaprabhraṁśana can no longer be considered as a proper name.[79]

Bühler[80] points out that the Pāripātra mountains are a part of the Vindhya range in Mālwā. In the *Ṛgveda*,[81] *soma* is described as Maujavata, "coming from the Mūjavants," or, as Yāska[82] take it, "from Mount Mūjavant." Sāyaṇa[83] agrees with Yāska in taking Mūjavant as the name of a mountain. Hillebrandt[84] is justified in saying that the identification of Mūjavant by Zimmer[85] with one of the lower hills on the south-west of Kaśmīr lacks evidence. It is not reasonable to deny that Mūjavant was a hill from which the people took their name. Yāska[86] suggests that Mūjavant is equivalent to Muñjavant, which actually occurs later, in the Epic[87] *Mahābhārata* as the name of a mountain in the Himalayas. *Taittirīya Āraṇyaka*[88] includes "Maināka" which is taken as the name of a mountain among the Himalayas.

Himavat meaning "snowy" is traced in the *Ṛgveda*.[89] This word refers to the mountains now called Himalayas.[90]

79. *Atharvaveda*, XIX.37.8 with Whitney's note in his Translation; Macdonell, *Journal of the Royal Asiatic Society*, 1909, p. 1107; Cf. Macdonell and Keith, *Vedic Index of Names and Subjects*, vol. I, p. 227.
80. Cf. *Sacred Books of the East*, 14.2, 3; 146, 147.
81. *Ṛgveda*, X.34.1.
82. *Nirukta*, IX.8.
83. Sāyaṇa on *Ṛgveda*, I.161.8.
84. Cf. *Vedic Index of Names and Subjects*, vol. II, p. 170.
85. Ibid.
86. Cf. *Siddhānta Kaumudī on Pāṇini*, IV.4.110 where instead of Maujavata in *Ṛgveda*, X.34.1, Mauñjavata is read.
87. *Mahābhārata*, X.785; XIV.180.
88. Cf. Weber, *Indian Literature*, p. 93.
89. *Ṛgveda*, X.121.4.
90. *Vedic Index of Names and Subjects*, vol. II, p. 503.

According to Sieg,[91] a hymn of the *Ṛgveda* describes a forest fire. These fires generally occur in spring.

The mountain ranges with their dense forests streams, valleys, snow-beds, animals, birds and insects maintain the environmental equilibrium of this creation, which, in turn, provides the living beings an ecological surrounding to live in. The environment protrayed in the Vedas, specially most part in the *Ṛgveda,* throws adequate light on the natural resources around us and tends to prompt human instinct to explore such a vast sphere of nature for shaping the civilizations.

Flora and Fauna in Ṛgveda

The flora and fauna, too, have permeated the national religious life in a very intimate way. Birds and animals are the vehicles of gods and goddesses; the elephant plays a very important role in religious processions, and the lotus is frequently used in artistic designs and religious symbolism. *Ṛgveda* mentions a large number of trees, plants, grains and grass in connection with the performance of sacrifices.

The cow has all along been a very popular animal with the Indo-Āryans. Other animals found mention in the Vedic literature are goats, sheep, horses, elephants, asses, cats, etc. These were used as domestic animals. Wild animals like tigers, wolves, jackals, etc. are included in the Vedas. The serpent was a much dreadful reptile. It was most probably due to the fear of this reptile that the Āryan people were compelled to perform certain sacrifices, such as the *Śravaṇā,* to propitiate snakes. Besides these, birds, aquatic creatures and insects of certain species are included in the Vedic literature. Right from the times of the *Ṛgveda,* the frog attracted the attention of the

91. Ibid., vol. I, p. 355, *Ṛgveda,* X.142.

Āryan poets. *Ṛgveda* includes a plant named *araṭu*[92] from the wood of which the axle of a chariot was sometimes made. *urvāruka* (cucumber) is found in the *Ṛgveda*.[93] This word denotes the fruit. Roughly speaking, the vegetable world is divided in Vedic literature[94] between *oṣadhi* or *vīrudh* "plants" and *vana* or *vṛkṣa* "trees."

Kiyāmbu is the name of one of the water-plants which are to grow, according to a funeral hymn in the *Ṛgveda*,[95] on the place where the body of the dead was burned. *Pāka-dūrvā* is, in a verse of the *Ṛgveda*,[96] included with *kiyāmbu* and *vyālkaśa* among the plants used for growing on the spot where the corps has been consumed to fire.[97] Puṇḍarīka denotes the blossom of the lotus in the *Ṛgveda*.[98] *Puṣkara*[99] is a name in the *Ṛgveda*, which denotes the blue lotus flower. *Prasū* in the *Ṛgveda*[100] denotes the young shoots of grass or herbs used at the sacrifices. *Bhāṅga* is described as an epithet of *soma* in the *Ṛgveda*,[101] presumably in the sense of "intoxicating," which then came to designate hemp. Besides, *Ṛgveda* mentions the plants like *vīrudh*,[102] *vratati*,[103] and *śīpāla*[104] (water plant). The animals

92. *Ṛgveda*, VIII.46.27.
93. Ibid., VII.59.12.
94. Ibid., X.97.
95. Ibid., X.16.13.
96. Ibid.
97. Bloomfield, *American Journal of Philology*, II, 342-50; *Journal of the American Oriental Society*, 15, XXXIX quoted in *Vedic Index of Names and Subjects*, vol. I, p. 513.
98. *Ṛgveda*, X.142.8.
99. Ibid., VI.16.13; VII.33.11.
100. Ibid., I.95.10; III.5.8; VIII.9.3; VIII.35.7; VII.6.20.
101. Ibid., XI.6.15.
102. Ibid., I.67.9; I.141.4; II.1.14; II.35.8.
103. Ibid., VIII.40.6. This is a "Creeping Plant."
104. Ibid., X.68.5.

and birds found mentioned in this Veda are *uṣṭi*[105] (buffalo), *ṛkṣa*[106] (bear), *ṛṣya*[107] (stag), *eta*[108] (deer), *kapi*[109] (monkey), *kaśikā*[110] (weasel), *gardabha*[111] (ass), *gavaya*[112] (species of ox), *chāga*[113] (goat), *tsaru*[114] (crawling animal), *dāna*[115] (a chariot horse), *padi*[116] (bird), *piśa*[117] (deer), *praṣṭi*[118] (side horse), *basta*[119] (goat), *maṇḍūka*[120] (frog), *madhyamavaḥ*[121] (horse), *mayūra*[122] (peacock), *marya*[123] (stallion), *mahiṣa,*[124] (buffalo) and many other names actually appearing in the Vedic environment. *Meṣa* denotes "ram" in

105. Ibid., X.106.2.
106. Ibid., V.56.3.
107. Ibid., VIII.4.10.
108. Ibid., I.165.2; I.169.6, 7; V.54.5; X.77.2.
109. Ibid., X.86.5.
110. Ibid., I.126.5.
111. Ibid., III.53.23.
112. Ibid., IV.21.8.
113. Ibid., I.162.3.
114. Ibid., VII.50.1.
115. Ibid., V.27.5; VII.18.23; VIII.46.24.
116. Ibid., I.125.2.
117. Ibid., I.64.8.
118. Ibid., I.39.6; VIII.27.8.
119. Ibid., I.161.13.
120. Ibid., VII.103.1; X.166.5.
121. Ibid., II.29.4.
122. Ibid., III.45.1.
123. Ibid., VII.56.16; VIII.43.25.
124. Ibid., VIII.58.15; IX.92.6; IX.96.6; X.123.4.

the *Ṛgveda*[125] and later,[126] while *meṣī* means "sheep."[127] Both words are also used to denote the "wool" of the sheep, specially as employed for the *soma* filter. *Rāsabha*[128] in the *Ṛgveda* denotes an "ass." *Rohita*[129] (red horse), *lodha*[130] (red goat), *lopāśa*[131] (jackal), *varāha*[132] (boar), *vāraṇa*[133] (elephant), *vṛścika*[134] (scorpion), *vṛṣabha*[135] (bull), *śaśā*[136] (hare), *śvān*[137] (dog), *śvapada*[138] (beast of prey), *sarīsṛpa*[139] (reptile), *sārameya*[140] (dog), *sālāvṛka*[141] (wild dog), *siṁha*[142] (lion) *sūkara*[143] (wild bear) *sūcīka*[144] (stinging

---

125. Ibid., I.43.6; I.116.16; VIII.2.40; X.27.17, etc.
126. *Atharvaveda,* VI.49.2; *Vājasaneyī-Saṁhitā,* III.59; XIX.90; XXIV.30; *Taittirīya-Saṁhitā,* VII.4.12.1.
127. *Ṛgveda,* I.43.6; *Vājasaneyī-Saṁhitā,* III.59; XXIV.1; *Taittirīya Brāhmaṇa,* I.6.4.4, etc.
128. *Ṛgveda,* I.34.9; I.116.2; I.162.21; III.53.5; VIII.85.7.
129. Ibid., I.94.10; I.134.9; II.10.2; III.6.6, etc.
130. Ibid., III.53.23.
131. Ibid., X.28.4.
132. Ibid., I.61.7; VIII.77.10.
133. Ibid., VIII.33.8; X.40.4.
134. Ibid., I.191.16.
135. Ibid., I.94.10; I.160.3; VI.46.4.
136. Ibid., X.28.2.
137. Ibid., I.161.13; I.182.4; II.39.4, etc.
138. Ibid., X.16.6.
139. Ibid., X.162.3.
140. Ibid., VII.55.2.
141. Ibid., X.73.2; X.95.15.
142. Ibid., I.64.8; I.95.5; III.2.11; III.9.4; III.26.5; IV.16.14, etc.
143. Ibid., VII.55.4.
144. Ibid., I.191.7.

insect), *starī*[145] (barren cow), *haya*[146] (horse), *hariṇa*[147] (gazelle) and *hastin*[148] (elephant) are included in the *Ṛgveda*. Among the birds present in the Ṛgvedic environment, the most common are *ulūka*[149] (owl), *kapota*[150] (pigeon), *gṛdhra*[151] (vulture), *cakravāka*,[152] *takvān*[153] (swiftflying bird), *ropaṇāka*[154] (thrush), *vartikā*[155] (quail), *vāyasa*[156] (crow), *śakunti*[157] (bird of omen), *śāri*,[158] *śyena*[159] (eagle), *haṁsa*[160] (gander) and *hāridrava*[161] (water wagtail). Besides, we find references like *pakṣin*, *śakuna*, *śakuni*, *śakunta* and *śakuntaka* which denote birds.[162] Existence of four-footed and two-footed animals in the environment are also noticed from the words *catuṣpāda* (quadruped) and *dvipāda* (biped) mentioned in the *Ṛgveda*.[163] All these creatures

---

145. Ibid., I.101.3; I.116.22; I.117.20, etc.
146. Ibid., V.46.1; VII.74.4; IX.107.25.
147. Ibid., I.163.1; V.78.2.
148. *Vedic Index of Names and Subjects*, pp. 501-02.
149. *Ṛgveda*, X.165.4.
150. Ibid., I.30.4.
151. Ibid., I.118.4; II.39.1; VII.104.22; X.123.8.
152. Ibid., II.39.3.
153. Ibid., I.66.2.
154. Ibid., I.50.12.
155. Ibid., I.112.18; I.116.4; I.117.16; I.118.8; X.39.13.
156. Ibid., I.164.32.
157. Ibid., II.42.3; II.43.1.
158. Ibid., I.112.16.
159. Ibid., I.32.14; I.33.2; I.118.11; I.163.1; I.165.2, etc.
160. Ibid., I.65.5; I.163.10; II.34.5; III.8.9, etc.
161. Ibid., I.50.12; VIII.35.7.
162. *Vedic Index of Names and Subjects*, vol. I, p. 465 and vol. II, pp. 347-48.
163. Ibid., vol. I, pp. 254, 386.

including human beings maintain the environmental equilibrium.

Climate

The climate, the fertility of the soil and beautiful and bounteous nature have induced the Indian people to take to agriculture and other peaceful pursuits. The geography of India presented by Vedic texts depicts a monsoon climate in those early days as at present. *Rajas*[164] found in the *Ṛgveda* denotes the region of the atmosphere between heaven and earth. The atmosphere like the sky (*div*), is divided into three regions,[165] but more normally into two, the "earthly" (*pārthiva*)[166] and the "heavenly" (*divya* or *divaḥ*).[167] In some passages,[168] the word refers in the plural to the dusty fields on earth.

Fire, Air and Water

Ṛgveda eulogizes the glory of fire in its Agni Sūkta[169] and that of air in its Marūt Sūkta.[170] Both fire and air help lives to exist. They occur in nature. They are personified and worshipped as gods. Agni is the master of great sovereignty. It is praised to bestow a longer life to living world and its creatures.

Marūt in the *Śatapatha Brāhmaṇa*[171] denotes *vāyu* (air). Air is the main component of our environment which provides oxygen for breathing and burning the fire. The plants prepare

---

164. *Ṛgveda*, I.56.5; I.62.5; I.84.1; I.124.5; I.168.6; I.187.4; II.40.3; VI.62.9, etc.
165. Ibid., IV.53.5; V.69.1; IX.74.6; X.45.3; X.123.8.
166. Ibid., I.81.5; I.90.7; I.154.1; VI.49.3; VIII.80.5; IX.72.8.
167. Ibid., IV.53.3; I.110.6. Cf. Macdonell, *Vedic Mythology*, p. 10.
168. *Ṛgveda*, I.166.3; III.62.16; X.75.7.
169. Ibid., IV.12.
170. Ibid., VII.56.
171. *Śatapatha Brāhmaṇa*, III.6.1.16.

their food by taking carbon dioxide from air. This helps the growth of the plants and hence production of biomass for energy. So *vāyu* (air) is also prayed to in the *Ṛgveda*.[172] In the Rudra Sūkta,[173] *Ṛgveda* describes the god of supplying water, whereas in its Varuṇa Sūkta,[174] the god of water (*jaladevatā*) is depicted. Macdonell and Keith opine that *jalāṣa* mentioned in the *Ṛgveda*[175] is an epithet of Rudra. Geldner[176] thinks that *jalāṣa* means rain-water which is conceived as urine.

Thus, air, water and fire though personified as gods in Vedic literature, are the chief natural environmental components primarily required for life to sustain.

The Earth in Ṛgveda

Pṛthvī denotes the "earth" as the "broad" one in the *Ṛgveda*[177] and later,[178] being often personified as a deity[179] both alone, and with *div*, "heaven" as *dyāvā-pṛthvī*.[180] Mention is often made of three earths,[181] of which the world on which we live is the highest.[182] The earth is girdled by the ocean, according to the *Aitareya Brāhmaṇa*.[183] The word also occurs in the *Ṛgveda*,[184]

172. *Ṛgveda*, Vāyuḥ Sūkta, I.134.
173. *Ṛgveda*, II.33.
174. Ibid., VII.86; VII.89.
175. *Vedic Index of Names and Subjects*, vol. I, p. 279.
176. Ibid., p. 280.
177. *Ṛgveda*, VII.7.2.5; VII.99.3; V.85.1, 5; VIII.89.5, etc.
178. *Atharvaveda*, XII.1.1 ff., *Vājasaneyī-Saṁhitā*, XI.53, etc.
179. *Ṛgveda*, IV.3.5; IV.51.11; V.49.5; V.84.1 ff.; VI.50.13-14; VII.34.23, etc.
180. Ibid., IV.56.1; VII.53.1, etc.
181. Ibid., I. 34.8; IV.53.5; VII.104.11.
182. *Atharvaveda*, VI.21.1; XIX.27.3; XIX.32.4; XIX.53.5.
183. *Aitareya Brāhmaṇa*, VIII.20.
184. *Ṛgveda*, VI.12.5; X.187.2.

though rarely, in the form of *pṛthvī*.[185]

As viewed from the above environmental aspects of the *Ṛgveda,* the nature and its creations form various components of our environment doing good to the living world, as a result of which, the earth, water, air, fire, etc. are personified as gods and goddesses and different hymns are chanted in honour of them.

Part II : Ecology

Introduction

The human beings have close relations with the biosphere in which they live. The whole environment and ecology consisting of the earth, air, water, the plants and the animal provide the necessary and sufficient conditions for sustaining human life. Darwin's theory of evolution goes a long way in this respect in explaining this creation of bio-world which embraces the man as a constituent part. The environment portrayed in the Vedas and the Vedic texts focuses a strong relationship between man and the bio-world. The object of this paper is to unfold the very relationship that existed between man and the biosphere in the perspective of the Vedic literature adhering to the ecology and environment of ancient times.

An extensive physical account of the world in general and India in particular is encountered in our four Vedas, viz. *Ṛg, Sāma, Yaju* and *Atharva* and other Vedic texts like Brāhmaṇas, Kalpasūtras, Āraṇyakas, Upaniṣads and the Vedāṅgas. The physical facts and the natural history of our subcontinent, which have been directly or indirectry referred to by the Vedic hymns are the country, the holy places, mountains, rivers, lakes, forests, flora and fauna and finally the people. Vedic names and places have their identification with the present

185. The regular adjectival feminine form of *pṛthu,* "broad."

cities, towns, mountains, forests, ocean, seas and rivers and hence their study reveals the cultural history and the traditions of the ancient man. The biosphere which consists of the animals, the birds, the insects and the plants that are reflected in the Vedas assists the man in sustaining his life. The earth,[186] the air[187] and the water[188] referred in the Vedas provide the chief requirements for the entire bio-world. The climatic conditions as understood from the Vedic verses and *sūtra*s throw some light on the social life of the people.

In connection with the building of a house, the *Gr̥hyasūtra*s mention soils of different colours, namely white, red and black. Physical environment outlined in the Vedic hymns and *sūtra*s plays an important part in shaping habits, customs and manners of the people.[189] The pattern of culture is largely determined by the biosphere around us. An adequate knowledge of the biosphere and the physical conditions of the world is, therefore, a *sine qua non* for the proper understanding of the relationship between man and the bio-world consisting of the animals and the plants. Ostensively, the Vedic knowledge of the ecology and the environment enables us to bring the man-and-the-biosphere relations to light.

Ecology of Matter, Energy and Life

Scholars of linguistics, mathematics, physics, philosophy and astronomy have tried to interpret the Vedic hymns from the point of view of their particular discipline. Dr. Marta Vannucci,[190] a biologist, has turned her attention to ecology of

186. *R̥V*, V.84.1.

187. Ibid., X.168.5; X.151.4.

188. Ibid., VII.86.2; X.137.6-7.

189. *Go. Gr̥hyasutra*, IV.7.5-7; *gaurapāṁsu brāhmaṇasya, lohitapāṁsu kṣatriyasya, kr̥ṣnapāṁsu vaiśyasya.*

190. M. Vannucci, *Ecological Readings in the Veda*, New Delhi: D.K. Printworld (P) Ltd., 1994, Foreword, p. 7.

matter, energy and life as reflected and articulated in the Vedic corpus. The purpose of the present work is to explore the close association of human beings with the plants and animals in the Vedic context. Such interpretations of the Vedic verses have not been so far by any researcher.

Matter and energy as personified by the Vedic God is easily recognized as Agni.[191] The relationship of Agni with Savitṛ[192] symbolizing life and hope is very intense. The *Ṛgveda*[193] begins with that memorable verse — "we worship Agni, the Purohit, God, minister of sacrifice . . . " and throughout this Veda as also the *Sāmaveda*[194] and *Atharvaveda,*[195] Agni is the primary concern of man as a species. The Vedic approach to the principle of energy and fire is related to the evidence of similar preoccupations of early man in sources as far apart as those of Stonehenge and the Greek myths of Prometheus. The Agni manifested in solar energy as well as domestic fire has been recognized as the premodial element for maintaining cosmic order (*ṛta*).[196] This is where the conception of Agni and the notion of ecological balance become relevant. As there is relationship between Agni (fire) and Lord Savitṛ (life), there is closeness between Savitṛ and Varuṇa (water). Savitṛ is on the one hand an aspect of Varuṇa[197] (water) and on the other, life itself. Savitṛ is the source of life and the same life that he ceaselessly regulates. The relationships of Agni and Savitṛ is at multiple levels of fire and water, of energy and life.

---

191. *ṚV*, 1.1.9; 1.31.3.
192. Ibid., III.38.8.
193. Ibid., I.1.1.
194. S.V. Ganapati (ed.), *SV*, New Delhi: MLBD, 7, 1992, pp. 162-63, and *SV*, D.VI.790-92.
195. *AV*, XI.1.3; IV.39.9; III.20.21.
196. *ṚV*, I.44.14; IV.3.9.
197. *ṚV*, VII.86.5.

Relationship of Organic Matter with Environment

The small treatise points at the interrelationships of organic matter and energy of living being among themselves and with the environment. The environment in turn comprises both organic and non-organic matter, i.e. both living and non-living. The Vedic man's preoccupation is deeply concerned with the nature of matter, organic or inorganic, and the nature of interrelationships of all living beings, human, and animal, plants, i.e. all biological species. In the *Ṛgveda,* man reflected on the very question of what was the relationship between him and the life around he saw? This conception is purely based on his observations, experiences with ignorance of the dynamics of structures of each species of organic matter.

Man and Biosphere Relations

The ciritical ideas, thoughts, concepts, conclusions and technicalities of the ancients are present in every verse of the Vedas. Indian tradition admits of three distinct ways in which the Vedic hymns may be interpreted. These are:

(a) *Ādhibhautika,* the material objective way,

(b) *Ādhyātmika,* the inner subjective way,

(c) *Ādhidaivika,* the godly or spiritual way.

Swami Satya Prakash Saraswati and Satyakam Vidyalankar have analysed *Ṛgveda* emphasizing on the *ādhidaivika* aspect as well as the *ādhibhautika*. Other scholars like Loude, Lievre and Robertson have also attacked the problem fundamentally to trace out the relationship between Vedic man and the environment around him. Their observations along with the others are invaluable source for ascertaining the way of living of Vedic people. According to *Ṛgveda,* Vedic people were one with nature.[198] "One is that which manifests in all." In

198. *ṚV*, VII.58.2-3.

contemporary ecological terms, it is expressed as "everything is related to everything else."[199]

A strong feeling of man's involvement in the universal order pervades the Veda; man is inseparable from his cosmic environment. Fire as energy is present in movable and immovable natural things. Agni, the original power or God is present everywhere at all times, even in stones.[200] Agni expresses and manifests itself in many forms. Energy and matter as well as the essence of God and man are one, the same and interchangeable. When bodily life ends, man, like other movable and immovable things merges with infinity. M. Vannucci, in modern ecological terms, analyses it as "matter is recycled and energy is one, under many interchangeable forms. In fact, even human mind is considered as a part of the cosmic soul or energy."

Clearly the ancients saw that there was a relation of cause and effect in everything, even if man the seers themselves could not always perceive all the hidden meanings, purposes and relations among the multiplicity of natural phenomena that they observed.

In conclusion, the study of a natural cycles of living and non-living things, the analysis and measurements of the multiple aspects of *ṛta* in space and time, is the true meaning of the word Ecology.

Of all natural cycles, the diurnal or circadian rhythm is the most readily perceived. It is the first one to which newborn babies coming from the uniformly dark and warm environment of the mother's womb must adapt. *Ṛta* is manifested concretely in cycles of summer and winter, rain and drought, cycles of the flowering and fruiting of plants, of

199. M. Vannucci, *Ecological Readings in the Veda,* New Delhi: D.K. Printworld (P) Ltd., p. 67.

200. *AV*, III.21.1.

shedding of leaves, and of animal reproduction, nesting of birds and emergence of butterflies, migration and hibernation of all kinds of animals from insects to mammals. The Vedas refer to the five traditional elements of Eastern and Western Indo-European tradition — earth, water, air, fire and void or *ākāśa*. Mother earth, *pṛthvī*, often identified with Aditi, the infinite, the "free from bonds," as well as with water, air, fire and *ākāśa* proceeds from the down-to-earth beginning of everyday reality to the imponderable, present but intangible space or void. The earth is referred to in the *ṚV* and *AV* mostly for the ecological traits where the central figure is, of course, man. For man's survival, there is a constant preoccupation with food and medicinal plants. Vedic people were closely associated with forests.

The sacredness of the cow was an ecological imposition. The greatest praise to Aditi goes like this — "Aditi, the cow, the sinless, injure it not."[201] Agni becomes the associate of water for the creation of plant and animal life.[202] Thus, identifying, the ancient man with the world around him throws light on the man-and-biosphere relationship in the Vedic perspective. We may interpret it as the ecological aspects of manifold environments colonised by man.

---

201 *ṚV*, VIII.101.15.

202. *ṚV*, X.142.3-4.

10

Science and Technology

INDIAN philosophical system clearly reveals that our ancient thinkers were familiar with materialism, which was really originated from oriental idealism. From the study of the history of philosophy, it is ascertained that materialism is the earliest philosophy. According to Professor Stace, "Materialism is ingrained in all men." We, Easterns and Westerns, are born materialists,"[1] Undoubtedly, it can be said that materialism had its root in India.[2] Uma Gupta[3] remarks that Indian philosophy has had an extremely long and complex development, much more complex and probably a longer history of continuous development than any other philosophical tradition. Varieties of thoughts like scepticism, materialism, pluralism, dualism, naturalism, along with idealism of different forms are prevalent in Indian philosophy. From the early stage to date man has been trying to unveil the ultimate reality through his philosophical thoughts and interpretations. Thus, the interpretations of the entire Indian philosophical heritage from uncompromisingly idealistic standpoint have achieved the widest popularity and publicity both inside and outside the academic circles. Scholars like

---

1. W.T. Stace, *A Critical History of Greek Philosophy*, London: Macmillan, 1953, p. 11.
2. S. Radhakrishnan and C.A. Moore (ed.), *A Source Book of Indian Philosophy*, Princeton University, N.J., 1957, p. xxiii.
3. U. Gupta, *Materialism in the Vedas*, New Delhi: Classical Publishing Company, 1987, pp. 1-2.

Damle,[4] Seal[5], Sircar,[6] Riepe,[7] etc. opine that the study of Indian philosophy will become incomplete without reconstructing Indian materialism.

Ancient Indian materialism was in no way inferior to that of Greece. Similarly, ancient Indian Science probably surpassed that of all other ancient civilizations. The wonderful developments of Hindu medicine, astronomy, chemistry and mathematics again project the insights of the Indian scholars in understanding the external world besides the internal. The "objective" side of Indian thoughts was also accepted by the idealist Radhakrishnan.[8] Thus, it can be said that materialism is the oldest known philosophy. Russell goes a step further and identifies this earliest philosophy with science. He, however, claims that materialism and science were born together at the beginning of the sixth century BCE as the products of speculations of the Greek philosophy.[9]

It is also observed that the Vedic religion was blended with materialism. The Vedas focus on three main objectives, namely, magic, religion and science, which together form a complex phenomenon. The earliest attempt of man to interpret nature and to search for causes of natural phenomena was made in the Vedic period. The conception of the cosmic order,

---

4. P.R. Damle, *Philosophical Essays,* Asia Publishing House, 1954, pp. 177-91.
5. B.H. Seal, *Positive Sciences of the Ancient Hindus,* Longmans, London, 1915.
6. B.K. Sircar, *The Positive Background of Hindu Sociology,* Book I, 1937.
7. D. Riepe, *The Naturalistic Tradition in Indian Thought,* Delhi: MLBD, 1964.
8. S. Radhakrishnan, *Indian Philosophy,* vol. I, New York: Macmillan, 1951, p. 29.
9. B. Russell, *A History of Western Philosophy,* London, 1954, p. 21.

ṛta in the Veda implies that the Vedic people were aware of the law-bound universe. These ancient generations had beliefs in the magical efficacy of *mantra*s and *yajña*s, which they took as the means to have control over the courses of nature and even over gods. All such consciousness expose the attitudes of the Vedic Āryans akin to that of Science. In this respect, Frazer[10] describes magic as the "next kin to Science," because both have in common "the general assumption of a succession of events determined by law." Both magic and science start as necessities for man's survival in the struggle for existence. But, magic fails to identify the causes imaginary and real. Science, on the other hand, has been able to do so only through a process of unfolding the reasoning faculty of man along with the accumulation of the a posteriori facts of experience in the course of a long period of history.[11]

The inception of science always lies in the outlook of an individual or the society towards the creation of the world of living (*cetana*) or non-living (*jaḍa*) things. All the innovations, inventions or discoveries in the field of science and technology emerge from the philosophical hypothesis formulated by only an individual or the society towards the origin or formation of the world. In the realm of metaphysical viewpoint, the entire world evolved from the union of *puruṣa* (self) and *prakṛti* (matter), or emerged out of the accident of *puruṣa* and *prakṛti* caused by the will of almighty *Brahman*. Vedic science was also developed from the philosophical innovations of the Vedic seers, who conceived that the world was not the composition of matter only, it was considered to have been represented by *prakṛti, puruṣa* and *Brahman* in various capacities.[12] According

10. J.G. Frazer, ed., *The Golden Bough, Abridged* London: Macmillan, 1959, quoted in Uma Gupta's Materialism in the Vedas, p. 128.

11. U. Gupta, op. cit., p. 128.

12. *Ṛgveda*, I.26.4.

to *Ṛgveda,* two beautiful friendly birds (*ātman* and *Brahman*) are sitting together on a tree (*prakṛti*). One of them tastes the sweet fruits and another sits looking at or acts as a mere witness to the former.[13] *Chāndogya Upaniṣad* holds that *prakṛti* existed before the creation. *Ātmā* (*puruṣa*) and the *Brahman* existed too before something is brought about. Upaniṣads, further, state that the accident of the *puruṣa* and *prakṛti* was materialized by the will (*saṁkalpa*) of the *Brahman.*[14] *Bhagavad-Gītā*[15] also says, "All things should be known to have been created by the will." Sāṁkhya Darśana opines that the accident of *puruṣa* with *prakṛti* is the name of the equilibrium of *sattva, rajas* and *tamas* qualities,[16] and which brings about the disequilibrium among these three qualities (*guṇatraya*) that results in *vikṛti* of *prakṛti,* and thus causes the evolution of matter. Modern science also believes that the creation has sprung from the chaosness or the great disorder. Ostensibly, *sṛṣṭi* (creation) emanated from *pralaya* (destruction). As there are three theories of creation like *prakṛti tattva, ātma tattva* and *brahma tattva,* three possible stages of evolution are forwarded by metaphysical or scientific thoughts, viz. sensory perception (the stage of ignorance); understanding the role of *ātma tattva* and *Brahman* in the creation of the world (the stage of freedom from the bondage of ignorance); and *asamprajñāta samādhi* (the stage of identification of oneself with the Almighty, i.e. the stage of self-perception). The third stage is the stage where everything of this creation unites with the *Brahman* who actually brings about the creation. As per the narrations of the Upaniṣads, all that is visible is *Brahman,* nothing here has a different identity. Further, if absolute is taken out of absolute, the remaining

13. Ibid., and R.P. Arya, *Vedic Meteorology,* Delhi: Parimal Publications, 1995, p. 163 and fn. 1.

14. R.P. Arya, op. cit., p. 163 and fn. 2.

15. *Bhagavad-Gītā,* 6.24.

16. *Sāṁkhya Darśana,* 1.1.

will be the absolute one.[17] This concept of "absolutism" in modern science is equivalent to the term "infinity." Addition or subtraction of anything to or from the "infinity" does not alter the quantity or quality of it. It still remains as infinity.

In the Vedic perceptions and speculations, the illusory technique of magic is a necessary stage for the development of the real technique of science. Vedic bards visualized the laws of nature beyond time and space. They had tried to understand each and every aspect of the creation and thus ransacked all the nature of science by declaring laws underlying the discoveries in various fields of science. Not a single aspect of science is left unstudied by them. Consequently, the Veda is the store-house of all true sciences. Only by exploring the Vedic thoughts and ideas, the genesis and growth of science can be well understood. The four Vedas, *Ṛg, Sāma, Yaju* and *Atharva* adequately help us in formulating various theories, laws and hypotheses to understand the world around us. The subject matter of the Vedas can be perfectly known by the meticulous interpretation of their archaic language. On the other hand, misinterpretation can cause blurred vision of the Vedic conceptions and speculations. Thorough and passionate readings of the Vedic *mantra*s can evolve the real meaning of the scienctific terms and explanations that lie underneath them. Hence, reappraisal of the Vedic terminology and metaphysics in the realm of fresh analyses can no doubt broaden the limits of our knowledge in the Vedic science and technology. Scholastic expositions are actually the need of the moment for the betterment of life on earth. Each and every contribution in this field — how small or big does not matter — throws light on the true intention of the Vedic seers who are the primary builders of our society. More and more investigations in the field can open up many aspects of the Vedas, that are still in the dark. All the Vedic *mantra*s signify to *ādhyātma,*

17. R.P. Arya, op. cit., p. 168.

ādhidaivata and *adhibhūta* which further support the concept of *mantra, tantra* and *yantra* respectively.[18] Later Vedic literature, e.g. Brāhmaṇas, Āraṇyakas, Upaniṣads and Sūtras, was shaped in view of the above notion.

Science did originate from the practical problems faced by human beings. Again, science and technology are correlated. The theoretical knowledge and its technical application are inseparable. The results of scientific knowledge are only realized through practical experiences. Hence, Farrington has rightly pointed out that techniques are a fertile seedbed of science. In his version, "The process from pure empiricism to scientific empiricism is gradual and therefore imperceptible."[19] Analysing the historical sequence between theoretical and practical aspects of science, it seems that technique developed before theory which owes its origin to the former. This fact is evident from the relation between magic and science. Through a long process of trial and error to devise methods for solving the problems faced by life, man reached at some conclusions and imprinted the background of the solutions he got, which he designated as "theory" of that practice. Thus, every achievement in science has two limbs, theory and application. In Vedic hymns, we also trace these two aspects of science to which our Vedic visionaries were quite familiar. Now, we will focus on the scientific achievements made the Vedic people on diverse fields of science, which are being unveiled day by day to our utter surprise. The ancient Indian sciences, rich in quality, quantity and variety and even comparable to those of the ancient Greeks,[20] took their origin directly from their Vedic germs. Vedic sciences deal with different aspects of science as

18. Ibid., p. 169.
19. B. Farrington, *Science in Antiquity,* Oxford, London, 1947, p. 13.
20. B.K. Sircar, *Hindu Achievement in Exact Science,* New York: Longmans Green and Co., 1918.

categorized today. Such branches latent in the Vedas are cosmology, cosmogony, astronomy, astrology, physics, chemistry, geology, mathematics, biology, medicine, seismology, meteorology, environmental science, agricultural science, etc. as already discussed.

Bibliography

Primary Sources

THE VEDIC SAṀHITĀS

Ṛgveda Saṁhitā with Sāyaṇa's Commentary, 5 vols., Pune: Vedic Saṁśodhana Maṇḍala.

Sāmaveda Saṁhitā, Delhi: Parimal Publications.

Yajurveda Saṁhitā, Delhi: Parimal Publications.

Atharvaveda Saṁhitā, Delhi: Nag Publications, Delhi.

Jaiminīya Saṁhitā, ed. W. Caland, Breslau, 1907.

Kāṇva Saṁhitā, ed. S.D. Satavalekara, Aundh, 1941.

Maitrāyaṇī Saṁhitā, ed. S.D. Satavalekara, Aundh, 1942.

Paippalāda Saṁhitā, ed. Raghuvira, Delhi, 1979.

Taittirīya Saṁhitā, ed. S.D. Satavalekara, Pardi, 1957.

Vājasaneyī Saṁhitā, ed. Vasudeva Laxmana Śāstri Pansikar, Bombay, 1929.

THE BRĀHMAṆAS

Aitareya Brāhmaṇa with the Commentry of Sāyaṇācārya, Poona, 1896.

Gopatha Brāhmaṇa, ed. D. Gastra, Leiden, 1919.

Jaiminīya Brāhmaṇa of the Sāmaveda, ed. Raghuvira and Lokesh Chandra, Delhi: MLBD.

Pañcaviṁśa Brāhmaṇa, ed. Vedāntavāgīśa, Calcutta, 1869-74.

Śatapatha Brāhmaṇa, ed. Vidyadhara Sarma Acyuta, Varanasi: Granthamālā, 1937.

Taittirīya Brāhmaṇa with Sāyaṇa-Bhāṣya, An. S.S., Poona, 1934-38.

THE ĀRAṆYAKAS

Aitareya Āraṇyaka, ed. A.B. Keith, Oxford, 1909.

Śāṅkhāyana Āraṇyaka, An. S.S., Poona, 1922.

Taittirīya Āraṇyaka with Sāyaṇa-Bhāṣya, An. S.S. Poona, 1926-27.

THE UPANIṢADS

Aitareya Upaniṣad *Bṛhadāraṇyakopaniṣad* *Chāndogyopaniṣad* *Kaivalyopaniṣad* *Kaṭhopaniṣad* *Kauśitakī Upaniṣad* *Kenopaniṣad* *Mahānārāyaṇopaniṣad* *Māṇḍukyopaniṣad* *Śvetāśvataropaniṣad* *Taittirīya Upaniṣad*	*One Hundered and Twelve Upaniṣads and Their Philosophy*, A.N. Bhattacharya, Parimal Publications, Delhi, 2nd edn., 1999.

THE ŚRAUTA-SŪTRAS

Āpastamba Śrauta-sūtras with Rudradatta Bhāṣya, ed. R. Garbe in Bibliotheca Indica, 1882-1902.

Āśvalāyana Śrauta-sūtras with Siddhāntic Bhāṣya, ed. Mangal Deva Shastri, Varanasi, 1938.

Baudhāyana Śrauta-sūtras, ed. W. Caland in Bibliotheca Indica, 1904-1913.

Bhāradvāja Śrauta-sūtras, ed. with English tr. C.G. Kashikar, Poona, 1964.

Hiraṇyakeśī Śrauta-sūtras, with Sanskrit Commentary, An. S.S., Poona, 1907-32.

Jaiminīya Śrauta-sūtras, ed. with Dutch tr. D. Gaastor, Leiden, 1906.

Kātyāyana Śrauta-sūtras, English tr. H.G. Ranade, Poona, 1978.

Mānava Śrauta-sūtras, ed. J.M. van Veldor, New Delhi, 1961.

Śāṅkhāyana Śrauta-sūtras, English tr. W. Caland, Nagpur, 1953.

THE GṚHYA-SŪTRAS

Āpastamba Gṛhyasūtra, ed. M. Winternitz Zeemza, 1887.

Gobhila Gṛhyasūtra with the Commentary of Bhaṭṭanārāyaṇa, ed. Chintamani Bhattacharya, Calcutta, 1936.

Hiraṇyakeśī Gṛhyasūtra with Mātṛdatta Vṛttisāra, ed. J. Kriste, Vienna, 1889.

Kāṭhaka Gṛhyasūtra, ed. W. Caland, Lahore, 1925.

Khādira Gṛhyasūtra with Rudraskandavṛtti, ed. A. Mahendra Śāstrī and L. Srinivasacharya, Mysore, 1913.

Mānava Gṛhyasūtra with Aṣṭavakra Bhāṣya, ed. Ramakrishna Harishaji Śāstrī, Baroda, 1926.

Sāṅkhyāyana Gṛhyasūtra with extracts from Nārāyaṇa Bhāṣya and Ramachandra Paddhati, ed. S.R. Sehgal, Delhi, 1960.

THE DHARMASŪTRAS

Baudhāyana Dharmasūtra with the Commentary of Govindasvāmin, ed. A.C. Shastri, Varanasi, 1934.

Viṣṇu Dharmasūtra (alias *Viṣṇu Smṛti*) *with Extracts from the Commentary of Nanda Paṇḍit*, ed. J. Jolly, Calcutta, 1981.

THE PURĀṆAS

Agni Purāṇa, A.S.S., Poona, 1900.

Brahma Purāṇa, A.S.S., Poona, 1895.

Garuḍa Purāṇa, tr. J.L. Shastri, Delhi: MLBD, 1978-80.

Nārada Purāṇa, Bombay, 1905.

Padma Purāṇa, A.S.S. Poona, 1893-94.

Skanda Purāṇa, Bombay, 1910.

Viṣṇu Purāṇa, Bombay, 1910.

THE UPA-PURĀṆAS

Devī Bhāgavata, English tr. H.P. Chatterji, MLBD, 1986.

Kālikā Purāṇa, Hindi tr., Varanasi: Choukhamba, 1993.

MĀHĀTMYAS AND STHALA PURĀṆAS

Bāmadeva Saṁhitā, Puri, 1972.

Nīlādri Mahodayam, ed. and English tr. B.L. Ray, Delhi, 1998.

Puruṣottama-Kṣetra Māhātmyam, Manuscript Section, Orissa State Museum Catalogue, No. p./21, Bhubaneswar.

ĀGAMAS AND TANTRAS

Ahirbudhnya Saṁhitā, Adyar, 1916.

Bṛhadbrahma Saṁhita, An. S.S., Poona, 1912.

Prapañcasāra, Calcutta.

Rudrayāmaḷa Tantra, Bombay.

Śāradātilaka Tantram, Calcutta.

Viṣṇu Saṁhitā, Trivandrum.

DHARMAŚĀSTRAS

Bṛhaspatyasūtram, Text with English tr. F.W. Thomas, 1922.

Dharmaśāstra Saṁgraha, Varanasi.

Vṛddhahārīta Smṛti, Calcutta.

EPICS

Mahābhārata with the Commentary of the Nīḷakaṇṭha, Poona, 1955.

Rāmāyaṇa of Vālmīki, Sanskrit Text with English tr., Delhi: Parimal Publications.

OTHER WORKS

Abhidhānacintāmaṇi, Hemachandra, Varanasi: Chaukhamba.

Ahirbudhnya Saṁhitā, Poona, 1912.

Aṣṭādhyāyī, Paṇini, Varanasi: Chaukhamba.

Bhāgavad Gītā, English tr. and Commentary N. Douglas P. Hill, London: Oxford University Press.

Bṛhat Saṁhitā, Varāhamihira, with Commentary of M.M. Sudhakara Dvivedi, Benares.

Jātaka, Trans. V. Fausboll, London, 1877-1897.

Kauṭilya Arthaśāstra, Varanasi: Chaukhamba, 1909.

Kṛṣṇa Yajurvedīya Taittirīya Saṁhitā, S.D. Satavalekara, Paradi, 1990.

Mahābhāṣya, ed. Kielhorn.

Manusmṛti, Varanasi: Chaukhamba.

Nirukta, Yāska, Varanasi: Chaukhamba.

Prema Bhakti Brahma Gītā, Yaśovanta Dāsa.

Sāralā Mahābhārata, ed. A.B. Mahanty, Bhubaneswar, 1965.

Śukra Nīti, ed. & tr. B.K. Sarkar, New Delhi: Munshiram Manoharlal Publishers Pvt. Ltd., 1975.

The Vedas, R.R. Mohan Roy, Delhi: Nag Publishers, 1977.

Vedic Hymns, 2 vols., English tr. Max Müller and H. Oldenberg, SBE, 32, 46.

Secondary Sources

BOOKS

Acharya, R.K., *Ṛg-Sūkta Samuccaya,* Agra: Vinod Pustak Mandir, 1976, p. 353.

Agrawal, V.S., *Matsya Purāṇa — A Study,* Varanasi.

Ali, S.M., *The Geography of the Purāṇas,* New Delhi: People's Publishing House, 1983.

Bagchi, P.C., *Pre-Aryan and Pre-Dravidians in India,* tr. of articles of S. Levi, etc., Calcutta, 1929.

Baldawa, B.S., *Theory of Orient or Study in Indian Civilization,* Latur, Maharashtra, 1997.

Basham, A.L. ed. *A Cultural History of India,* Oxford: Clarendon Press, 1975.

Bhandarkar, K.G., *Vaiṣṇavism, Śaivism and Minor Religious Systems,* New Delhi: Asian Education Service, 1983.

Bhat, R.M., *Varāhamihira's Bṛhat Saṁhitā,* Delhi: MLBD, 2 vols., 1986.

Bhattacharji, S., *Literature in the Vedic Age,* Calcutta: K.P. Bagchi and Company, 2 vols., 1986.

Bhattacharya, D.M., *Paippalāda Saṁhitā,* Introduction.

Bloomfield, M., *The Religion of the Vedas,* Delhi: Indological Book House, 1972.

Chakravarti, S.C., *The Philosophy of the Upaniṣads,* Calcutta: University of Calcutta, 1935.

Chakravarti, P., *Origin and Developement of Sāṁkhya System of Thought,* New Delhi: Munshiram Manoharlal, 1967.

Cunningham, A., *The Ancient Geography of India,* Delhi: Indological Book House, 1979.

Chatterji, S.K. et al. (eds.), *The Cultural Heritage of India,* Calcutta: The Ramakrishna Mission Institute of Culture, 1937.

Das, A.C., *Ṛgvedic Culture,* Delhi: Indological Book House, 1974.

Das, M.N. (ed.), *Sidelights on History and Culture of Orissa,* Vidyapuri, Cuttack, 1977.

Dandekar, R.N., *Exercises in Indology,* Select Writings III, Delhi: Ajanta Publications, 1981.

Deussen, P., *The Philosophy of the Upaniṣads,* Delhi: Oriental Publishers.

Devasthali, G.V., *Religion and Mythology of the Brāhmaṇas,* Poona: University of Poona, 1965.

Dey, S.K., *History of the Vaiṣṇava Faith and Movement in Bengal,* Calcutta: Firma K.L. Mukhopadhyay, 1961.

Dikshitar, V.R.R., *Some Aspects of Vāyu Purāṇa,* Madras: University of Madras, 1933.

Dongre, N.G., *Physics in Ancient India,* New Delhi: New Age International Publishers Ltd., 1994.

Eschmann, A., H. Kulke and G.C. Tripáthy, *The Cult of Jagannatha and the Regional Tradition of Orissa,* New Delhi: Manohar Publications, 1978.

Faddegon, B., *Studies on the Sāmaveda,* Amsterdam, 1951.

Farrington, B., *Science in Antiquity,* London: Oxford, 1947.

Fay, E.W., *The Ṛgveda Mantras in the Gṛhya-Sūtras,* Roanoke, 1899.

Fick, R., *The Social and Economic Condition of North-East India in Buddha's Time,* Varanasi: Indological Book House, 1978.

Freund, P., *Myths of Creation,* London, 1964.

Galloway, G., *The Philosophy of Religion,* Edinburgh: T. and T. Clark, 1960.

Ganapati, S.V. (tr.) *Sāmaveda,* Delhi: MLBD, 1992.

Ganguli, M.M., *Orissa and Her Remains,* Calcutta, 1912.

Garbe, R., *Philosophy of Ancient India,* Chicago, 1897.

Ghurye, G.S., *Vedic India,* Bombay: Popular Prakashan, 1979.

Gonda, J., *Vedic Literature,* Wiesbaden: Otto Harrasowitz, 1975.

———, *Epithets in the Ṛgveda.*

———, *The Vision of the Vedic Poets,* The Hague, 1963.

Gopal, Ram, *India of Vedic Kalpasūtras,* Delhi: MLBD, 1983.

Goode, W.J., *Religion Among the Primitives,* USA: Free Press, 1951.

Griffith, R.T.H., (tr.) *The Hymns of the Ṛgveda,* 2 vols, 2nd edn., Benares: E.J. Lazarus and Co., 1896-97.

———, *The Hymns of the Atharvaveda,* 2 vols, Benares, 1916-17.

Griswold, H.D., *The Religion of the Ṛgveda,* London: Oxford, 1927.

Gundry, D.W., *Religions,* London: Macmillan, 1958.

Gupta, U., *Materialism in the Vedas,* New Delhi: Classical Publishing Company, 1987.

Gyani, S.D., *Agnipurāṇa — A Study,* Varanasi: Chaukhamba Sanskrit Series, 1964.

Hiriyanna, M., *The Essentials of Indian Philosophy,* London: George Allen and Unwin, 1949.

———, *Indian Philosophical Studies,* Mysore: Kavyalaya Publishers, 1957.

Hopkins, E.W., *Origin and Evolution of Religion,* New Haven: Yale University Press, 1923.

———, *The History of Religions,* New York: Macmillan, 1928.

———, *The Religions of India,* London: Ginn and Co., 1895.

———, *Ethics of India,* New Haven: Yale University Press, 1924.

Hoyle, F., *Frontiers of Astronomy,* London, 1957.

Hume, R.E., *The Thirteen Principal Upaniṣads,* Oxford University, 1949.

Hunter, W.W., *Orissa,* vol. I, London, 1872.

Iyengar, P.T.S., *Life in Ancient India,* Madras, 1912.

Jain, J.C., *Ancient India as Depicted in the Jain Canon,* Bombay, 1947.

James, E.O., *Prehistoric Religion,* London, 1957.

Jeffrys, H., *The Earth,* Cambridge, 1924.

Jensen, A.F. (ed.), *Myth and Cult Among Primitive Peoples,* Chicago: University of Chicago Press, 1963.

Jha, D.N., *Ancient India — An Introductory Outline,* New Delhi: People's Publishing House, 1977.

Jolly, J., *Hindu Law and Custom,* Calcutta: Bharatiya Publishing House, 1975.

Joshi, J.R., *Minor Divinities in Vedic Mythology and Religion*, Poona: University of Poona, 1970.

Kaegi, A., *Studies in Ṛgvedic India,* Delhi: Indological Book House.

———, *Life in Ancient India,* tr. R. Arrowsmith, Calcutta: Susil Gupta, 1950.

———, *The Ṛgveda,* tr. R. Arrowsmith, Boston: Ginn and Co., 1886.

Kane, P.V., *History of Dhamaśāstra,* vols. I-V, Poona: Bhandarkar Oriental Research Institute, 1930-62.

Kashikar, C.G., *A Survey of the Śrautasūtras*, Bombay, 1968.

Keith, A.B., *The Religion and Philosophy of the Veda and the Upaniṣads,* Harvard Oriental Series, vols. 31 and 32, Cambridge, Massachusetts, 1925.

———, *Introduction to the Taittirīya Saṁhitā,* Harvard Oriental Series, 1914.

———, *Ṛgveda Brāhmaṇas,* HOS, vol. XX, 1920.

———, *Ancient India,* Cambridge History of India, vol. I: *India,* 1955.

Kochhar, R., *The Vedic People, Their History and Geography,* Hyderabad: Orient Longman Limited, 1999.

Kosambi, D.D., *An Introduction to the Study of Indian History,* Popular Prakashan, 1975, 1st edn., 1956.

———, *The Culture and Civilization of Ancient India in Historical Outline,* London: Routledge and Kegan Paul, 1965.

Kramer, S.N., *Mythologies of the Ancient World,* New York, 1960.

Kummel, B., *History of the Earth,* New Delhi: Eurasia Publishing House, 1961.

Law, B.C., *Tribes of Ancient India,* Poona, 1926.

———, *Geographical Aspects of Kālidāsa's Works*, Delhi: Bharatiya Publishing House, 1976.

———, *Historical Geography of Ancient India,* Paris, 1954.

———, *Geography of Early Buddhism.*

Levi, S., *La doctrine du sacrifice dans les Brāhmaṇas,* Paris, 1898.

Loeuw van der, C.W.J., *The Concept of Deva in the Vedic Age,* Utrecht University Press, 1954.

Lommel, H., *Symbolism* (*Ṛgveda Brāhmaṇas*), Stuttgart, 1964.

Macdonell, A.A. and A.B. Keith, *Vedic Index of Names and Subjects,* 2 vols. Delhi: MLBD, 1982.

Macdonell, A.A., *A History of Sanskrit Literature,* Delhi: MLBD, 1986.

———, *Vedic Mythology,* Delhi: MLBD, 1981.

Mahapatra, G.N., *The Land of Viṣṇu,* New Delhi, 1979.

Majumdar, R.C., *Vedic Age,* London, 1951.

Max Müller, F. (ed.), The Sacred Books of the East, Delhi: MLBD.

Milier, J., *The Vedas, Harmony, Meditation and Fulfilment,* London, 1974.

Mishra, K.C., *The Cult of Jagannātha,* Calcutta: Firma K.L. Mukhopadhyaya, 1971.

Mitra, V., *India of the Dharmasūtras,* New Delhi, 1965.

Moeller, V., *Die Mythologic der Vedischer Religion and des Hinduismus,* Stuttgart, 1966.

Mookerji, R.K., *Hindu Civilization,* London, 1936.

Morgan, R.W., *The Religion of the Hindus,* New York, 1953.

Mukhopadhyaya, G., *Studies in the Upaniṣads,* Calcutta: Sanskrit College, 1960.

Murthy, S., *A Study of Important Brāhmaṇas,* Mysore, 1974.

Murthy, S.R.N., *Vedic View of the Earth,* New Delhi: D.K. Printworld, 1997.

Nakamura, H., *Religions and Philosophies of India,* Tokyo, 1973.

Needham, J., *Science and Civilization in China,* 2 vols., London, Cambridge, 1956.

Nikam, N.A. and R. Mckeon, *Ten Principal Upaniṣads,* Bombay, 1974.

Oldenberg, H., *The Religion of the Veda,* Berlin, 1890.

———, *Ancient India,* Calcutta, 1962.

———, *Die Religion des Veda,* Berlin, 1894.

———, Sacred Books of the East, vols. XXIX and XXX, Delhi, 1975.

Otto, R., *The Idea of the Holy,* London: Oxford, 1924.

Padhi, B.M., *Dāru-Devatā,* Cuttack, 1964.

Parab, A.B., *The Miracle and the Mysterious in Vedic Literature,* Bombay, 1952.

Pargiter, F.E., *Ancient Indian Historical Tradition,* Delhi: MLBD, 1972.

Patil, D.R., *Cultural History from the Vāyu Purāṇa,* Delhi: MLBD.

Piggot, S., *Prehistoric India,* Penguin, 1961.

Pillai, G.K., *Vedic History Set in Chronology,* Kitabistan, 1959.

Potdar, K.R., *Sacrifice in the Ṛgveda,* Bharatiya Vidya Bhavan, 1953.

Raman, B.V., *Astrology in Predicting Weather and Earthquakes*, Bangalore, 1993.

Rapson, E.J., *Ancient India from the Earliest Time to the First Century* CE, Indological Book House, 1981.

Ray, B.L., *Studies in Jagannātha Cult*, New Delhi: Classical Publishing Company, 1993.

———, *Jagannātha Cult*, Delhi: Kant Publications, 1998.

———, *Studies in Sanskrit, Indology and Culture*, New Delhi: Classical Publishing Company, 1998.

———, *A Critical Edition of Nīlādri-Mahodayam*, New Delhi: Classical Publishing Company, 1998.

———, *A Concise History of Vedic Literature*, Delhi: Kant Publications, 2000.

———, (ed.), *Facets of Vedic Studies*, New Delhi: Kaveri Book Service, 2000.

———, *Kaivalyaru Kaṇikāe*, Nayagarh: Dārubhūta Sāṁskṛtika Pariṣad, 1992.

Renou, L., *Vedic India*, Delhi: Indological Book House, 1971.

Renou, C.A., *The Astronomers*, London, 1964.

Sahu, N.K., *History of Orissa*, Bhubaneswar: Utkal University, 1964.

Sampurnanand, *The Atharvaveda*, Madras: Vrātya-Khaṇḍa, 1956.

———, *Evolution of the Hindu Pantheon*, Bharatiya Vidya Bhavan, 1963.

Sarkar, G., *Mandirera Kathā*.

Sarton, G., *A History of Science : Ancient Science through the Golden Age of Greece*, Cambridge, Mass.: Harvard University Press, 1959.

Satavalekar, S.D., *Atharvaveda Saṁhitā*, Gujarat, 1944.

Satyaprakash, S.S., *Founders of Sciences in Ancient India*, Delhi.

Schagal, P., *Śāṅkhāyana Śrautasūtra*, Delhi, 1960.

Schroder, L. Von, *Mysterium und mimus in Ṛgveda*, Leipzig, 1908.

Schrader, F.C., *Introduction to the Pañcarātra and the Ahirbudhnya Saṁhitā*, Madras, 1916.

Seal, B.N., *The Positive Sciences of the Ancient Hindus*, Bombay, Calcutta and London: Longmans, 1915.

Sharma, K.L., *Kalpasūtras* (Hindi), Hoshiarpur, 1981.

Shamasastry, R., *Vedāṅgajyotiṣa,* Mysore, 1936.

Shende, N.J., *Religion and Philosophy of Atharvaveda,* Poona, 1952.

Singh, J.B., *Social Life in Ancient India,* New Delhi, 1981.

Singh, M.R., *A Critical Study of the Geographical Data in the Early Purāṇas,* Calcutta: Punthi Pustak, 1972.

Singh, Pt. U.N., *The Siddhāntaśīromaṇi,* Bombay: Golādhyāya, 1905.

Sircar, D.C., *Studies in the Geography of Ancient and Medieval India,* Delhi: MLBD, 1971.

———, *Studies in the Religious Life of Ancient and Medieval India,* Delhi, 1971.

Subbarayappa, B.V. and K.V. Sarma, *Indian Astronomy — A Source Book,* Bombay: Nehru Centre, 1985.

Thibaut, G., *Baudhāyana Śulbasūtra,* New Delhi.

Thibaut, G. and S. Dwivedi, *Pañcasiddhāntikā of Varāhamihira,* Varanasi, 1968.

Tilak, B.G., *The Arctic Homes in the Vedas,* 1903.

Tsuji, N., *Studies in Indology and Buddhology,* Tokyo, 1955.

Upadhyaya, B.S., *Women in the Ṛgveda,* Lucknow, 1933.

Upadhyaya, S.S., *The Nāradīya Purāṇa — A Philosophical Study,* Muzaffarpur: Jnananidhi Prakashan, 1983.

Vannuci, M., *Ecological Readings in the Veda,* New Delhi: D.K. Printworld, 1994.

Venkatasubbiah, A., *Vedic Studies,* vol. 2, Madras: Adyar Library, 1968.

Veron, Arnold E., *Vedic Metre in Its Historical Development,* Delhi: MLBD.

Weber, A., *The History of Indian Literature,* Varanasi: Chaukhamba, 1967.

Weber, M., *The Religion of India,* Illinois, 1958.

Wheeler, J.T., *India: Vedic and Post-Vedic,* Calcutta, 1952.

Whitney, A.B., *The Atharvaveda Prātiśākhya,* Chaukhamba, 1962.

Winternitz, M., *A History of Indian Literature,* vol. III, pt. II., Calcutta University, 1963.

Zimmer, H., *Philosophies of India,* London: Routledge and Kegan Paul, 1951.

———, *Altindisches Leben*, Berlin, 1879.

ARTICLES

Alsdorf, L., "Gleanings from the Atharveda", *Adyar Library Bulletin*, 25, 1961.

Apte, V.M., "Ṛgveda Mantras in Their Ritual Setting in the Gṛhyasūtras", *Bulletin of Deccan College Research Institute*, vol. I, pp. 14-44, 127-152.

Bhave, S.S., *The Soma Hymns of Ṛgveda*, M.S. University Research Series, No. 6, 1962.

Bloomfield, M., "Contribution to the Interpretation of Veda", *American Journal of Philosophy*, vol. 17, 1896.

Brown, W.N., "The Beginnings of Civilisation in India", *Journal of American Oriental Society*, 1959, (Supplement), 1939.

———, "Theories of Creation in the Ṛgveda", *JAOS*, 1965, pp. 23-24.

Chakravarti, D., "Occultism in the Atharvaveda", *Summary of Proceedings, 26th All-India Oriental Conference*.

Dandekar, R.N., "Some Aspects of Vedic Mythology", *University of Ceylon Review*, vol. XII, no. 1.

Deshpande, I.C., "Philosophical Thoughts in the Āraṇyakas", *Dandekar Felicitation Volume*, 1969.

Devasthali, G.U., "The States of the Atharvaveda", *Kaviraj Felicitation Volume*, 1967.

Elizarenkova, T.Y., "Notes on Contents in the Ṛgveda", *ABORI*, 68, 1987, pp. 99-109.

French, H.W., "The Place of the Sacrifice in the Upaniṣads", *Bulletin of Ramakrishna Mission Institute of Culture*, 22(5), 1971.

Ghosh, E.N., "Studies in Ṛgvedic Deities — Astronomical and Meteorological" *JASB*, 28, 1932.

Gonda, J., "Epithets in the Ṛgveda", *Dis. Rheno. Traj.*, IV, 1959.

Herbert, J., "The Hindu Myth", *Asia*, no. 7, 1952.

Jordens, J., "The Development of the Idea of Immortality in the Upaniṣads", *Journal of the Oriental Institute*, Baroda, 16(1), 1966.

Kashikar, C.G., "A Critical Study of Ritualistic Sūtras", *Gode Commemoration Volume*, 1960.

Mezger, F., "Gothic Managei", *Lg* 22(4), pp. 348-53.

Pandey, J., "Non-Aryan Elements in the Ṛgveda", 26, *AIOC*, 1972.

Rajaram, V.S., "Vedic and Harappan Culture, New Findings", *JMS*, vol. 84, Bangalore, 1993.

Ray, B.L., "Geographical Aspects of the Vedas", Abstract, IXth World Sanskrit Conference, Melbourne, 1994.

———, "Physical Geography of Ancient India in the Vedic Perspective", *Kṛṣṇamādhavacintāmaṇi*, Bihar, 1999.

———, "The Concept of Earth in the Veda", *Prof. K.V. Sharma Felicitation Volume*, Chennai, 2000.

———, "Vedic View of the Ratha", *Orissa Review*, June, 1998.

———, "The Antiquity of the Chariot", *The Green Lotus*, A Journal of Life of Letters, vol. I, no. 3, July, 1999.

———, "Environment in Ṛgveda : A Study", AIOC, 36th Session, Pune, 1993.

———, "Vedic Women : Their Status and Position", AIOC, Hardwar 35th Session, 1990.

———, "Exploring Man and Biosphere Relationship in Perspective of the Vedic Environment", Xth World Sanskrit Conference, Bangalore, India.

———, "The Concept of Matter, Energy and Life in the Vedas", AIOC, 38th Session, Jadavpur University, Jadavpur.

———, "Ṛgvedic Flora and Fauna", *VIJ*, vols. XXXI-XXXII, pts. i-iv, June-December, 1993-94.

Renou, L., "Cosmogonie et Mythologie", *Orientales Critique*, 16 (156), 1960.

Shende, N.J., "The Ṛgveda and the Atharvaveda", *JAS*, Bombay, no. 41-42, 1966-67.

Soundara Rajan, K.V., "The Cakravarti Concept and the Cakra (Wheel)", *JORM*, 27, 85-90.

Thite, G.U., "Elevation of the Sacrifice in the Brāhmaṇas", *Dandekar Felicitation Volume*, 1969.

Varma, S., "Vedic Stylistics", *VIJ*, vol. XV, pt. II, 1977.

Verma, V.K., "Is There Cosmology in the Metaphorical Episode of Indra-Vṛtra in Ṛgveda?", Sp, 31, *AIOC*, Jaipur, 1982, pp. 76-77.

Wijesekera, O.H. de A., "The Symbolism of the Wheel in the Cakravartin Concept", *Belvalkar Felicitation Volume*, 1957, pp. 262-67.

JOURNALS

Adyar Library Bulletin, Madras.

American Journal of Philology, USA.

Allahabad University Studies, Allahabad.

Annals of the Bhandarkar Oriental Research Institute, Poona.

Bulletin of the Deccan College Research Institute, Poona.

Bulletin of the School of Oriental and African Studies, London.

Harvard Journal of Oriental Studies.

Indian Antiquary.

Indian Historical Quarterly, Calcutta.

Indica, Heras Institute of Indian History and Culture, Bombay.

Journal of the Americal Oriental Society, New Haven, USA.

Journal of the Asiatic Society of Bengal, Calcutta.

Journal of the Bihar and Orissa Research Society, Patna.

Journal of the Bombay Branch of Royal Asiatic Society, Bombay.

Journal of the Ganganatha Jha Research Institute, Allahabad.

Journal of the Kalinga Historical Research Society, Orissa.

Journal of the Oriental Institute, Baroda.

Journal of the Royal Asiatic Society, London.

Journal of the Vedic Studies, Lahore.

New Indian Antiquary, Poona.

The Orissa Historical Research Journal, Bhubaneswar.

Proceeding of the All-India Oriental Conference, Poona.

Quarterly Journal of the Mythic Society, Bangalore.

Saptagiri, Tirupati.

Vedavāṇī, U.P., India.

Vishveshvaranand Indological Journal, Hoshiarpur, Punjab.

Viśva Jyoti, V.V.R.I., Hoshiarpur, Punjab.

Index

Āditya, 25-26, 28, 133

Agni, 1, 6, 25-26, 29-30, 50-52, 54-56, 62, 64-65, 68-69, 72, 75, 76, 124, 133, 176, 180-81, 184, 194, 200, 215, 219

Agniṣṭoma, 5

agriculture, 3, 88, 153-174, 198

air, 1, 23-25, 44, 48, 52, 54-55, 59, 63, 65, 76-77, 87-90, 183, 200-201, 215-217, 222

anatomy, 104, 109, 150-151

animal, 77, 88, 101-105, 137, 140, 148, 151, 159-161, 165-179, 196, 210-211, 218, 220, 222

antarikṣa, 24, 54, 76, 194

anthropology, 2

Āpaḥ, 54-55, 58, 62, 194, 199

archaeology, 2

Archery, 7

Astrology, 33, 76, 229

astronomy, 12, 18, 76, 192, 218, 224, 229

asuras, 8

Aśvamedha, 4, 5

atmosphere, 53-55, 194

Āyurveda, 1

bīja, 85

balāsa, 124

beast, 172

belief, 2, 15, 106, 110

Big-Bang, 45

biology, 18, 104, 229

biomass, 216

biosphere, 217-218, 220, 222

birds, 77, 88-89, 96, 101, 103, 150, 164, 200, 210, 214, 218

Botany, 77-86

Brahman, 2, 225-226

bronze, 3, 43

calendar, 4, 22

Candramā, 26

carbon dioxide, 216

cattle, 171-173

charge, 55-56, 60-62

charms, 117, 125, 129, 130, 134, 136, 139-140, 146-147, 149-150

chemistry, 18, 39-41, 224, 229

circle, 179, 180, 223

cities, 1, 77, 88, 200, 206, 218

climate, 1, 77, 88, 180, 200, 215

cloud, 54-56, 58-65, 68-69, 157, 178

colour, 40, 68, 167, 196, 218

copper, 3, 41, 43, 185

corn, 83, 169
cosmic cycle, 27, 46
cosmic law, 16
cosmic order, 34, 183, 219
cosmogony, 1, 18, 24, 28, 76, 186, 198, 229
cosmology, 1, 2, 18, 76, 198, 229
countries, 77, 88, 200, 206
cow, 3, 24, 38, 70, 89, 95, 96, 150, 165-170, 172, 210, 213
creation, 1-2, 10, 24, 26, 34, 44-46, 210, 217, 226
creeper, 82, 84, 87
crop, 155, 159, 160, 162, 165
cultivation, 152, 155, 157, 160, 169
cycle, 220-21
cyclone, 55-56

dāna, 8
dāru, 85
dayā, 8
demon, 6, 27, 110-112, 118, 121, 124, 126-131, 144
desease, 6, 87, 102, 110-112, 115-124, 126, 128-132, 134-35, 139, 146-47, 170
deva, 8
dharma, 8
dimension, 192
doctrine, 9, 10

earth, 1, 10, 19, 22-29, 44, 47-65, 67-70, 76-77, 87-88, 105, 133, 147, 155-156, 174-179, 182-188, 191-200, 215-219, 222
earthquake, 50, 67-68, 70-75
eclipse, 188-89
ecology, 1, 2, 200, 217-218, 221
education, 1, 7
embryology, 104, 150
energy, 1, 27, 43, 46, 50, 51, 56, 218, 221
environment, 1-2, 108
ether, 44
ethos, 2
etymology, 12

famine, 70
farm, 169-170, 173
farmer, 154-158, 160, 163-165, 172
fauna, 1, 88-89, 103, 176, 210, 217
fever, 69, 105, 116, 125-26, 128
fire, 44, 48, 50-51, 54-55, 58, 65, 67-69, 71, 77, 87-88, 115, 163, 181, 189, 196, 200, 210, 215, 217, 219, 221-22
flora, 1, 76, 88-89, 106, 148-150, 176, 210, 217
flower, 77, 81, 84, 87
food, 39, 70, 103, 154-55, 162, 164, 222
force, 8, 35, 50-51, 55-56, 65, 110, 126, 134, 136, 177, 180, 195, 197
forest, 1-2, 9, 69, 77, 87-88, 103, 155, 176, 200, 210, 217-218, 222
fort, 207-208
fruits, 77, 84, 87, 161, 211

geography, 76
geology, 55-56, 175-190, 192, 199, 229
geometry, 6, 12, 39
germ, 115
glass, 41-42
gold, 43
golden Egg, 45-46
grain, 82-83, 87, 154, 161, 163-164, 169, 173, 202, 210
grammar, 12
grass, 81-82, 210
gravitation, 35, 46-50, 180, 185, 192
guru, 7

hair, 144, 146
hṛdroga, 122-23
heat, 182, 190
heaven, 22-23, 27-29, 53-54, 58, 71, 147, 177, 184, 186, 216
heliology, 187
herb, 77, 82, 87, 111-113, 117-118, 128, 143, 146, 148-49, 150, 197, 211
hill, 208-209
history, 2, 76, 112, 217, 223
hut, 81

Indra, 72, 75, 76, 176-178,, 190, 200
inertia, 195
infinity, 227
injury, 140
insanity, 135-36
insects, 77, 88, 98, 103, 145
iron, 3, 42-43, 115, 163, 177, 185
irrigation, 156

jñāna-mārga, 9
Jaundice, 123-24

karma-mārga, 9
Kāsā, 128
kṛmi, 136-38
kṛṣi, 87
King, 69-70, 155
kingdom, 89
knowledge, 2, 9-10, 15, 18, 26, 39, 83, 89, 106, 110, 228
kuśa, 81
Kuṣṭha, 105-106, 117, 120, 122, 128

lake, 1, 69, 77, 87-88, 103, 176, 200, 217
law, 35-36, 49-50
lead, 43, 146, 160
legends, 8, 10
length, 38
life, 1-3, 6, 10-13, 16, 44, 65, 112, 132, 215-16, 218-19, 221
light, 52-53, 70, 111, 210, 218, 222, 227
lightning, 62-63, 68, 126, 181
lily, 81
livestock, 165
lotus, 81

magic, 16-17, 110, 124, 224

mantra, 2, 5, 9, 111, 225, 227
manure, 160
maṇḍala, 76, 176
Marut, 54-56, 61, 64, 176, 182, 199, 201, 215
Mass, 38, 72-73, 186
mathematics, 6, 18, 36-37, 39, 174, 218, 224, 229
matter, 1, 10, 13, 19, 33-34, 43, 46, 56, 186, 218-220, 225, 227
medicine, 105-152, 225, 229
metal, 3, 42-43
metallurgy, 18
metaphysics, 10, 227
meteorology, 50, 53, 198, 229
milk, 70, 159, 170, 173
minerals, 181
momentum, 73-75
Moon, 8, 20, 26, 47, 59-60, 67, 177, 188
mountain, 1, 28, 77, 87-88, 102-103, 105, 155, 176-77, 179, 185, 200, 209-210, 217
Myth, 8
mythology, 2, 7-8, 29

nakṣatra, 18, 22, 77, 176, 192
nature, 8, 16, 51, 53
nectar, 154
niṣka, 3, 38

ocean, 1, 27, 67, 76, 87, 155-56, 179, 183, 190, 200-202, 216, 218
oil, 84, 135
ores, 43, 186
organs, 109
ox, 165
oxygen, 215

paddy, 83-84
patient, 110-111, 125, 128-130, 136
petrology, 182
philosophy, 2, 7-8, 11, 17, 34, 43-44, 49, 76, 199, 218, 223
physics, 43-52, 229
physiology, 104, 150-151, 175
planet, 22, 46, 57, 64, 67, 73, 174, 176, 183, 186, 198
plant, 77-78, 80, 83, 87-89, 102-103, 105, 112-13, 115, 118, 127-128, 132, 134, 140, 146, 148-150, 165, 171, 210-11, 215, 217-18, 220-21
ploity, 1
presssure, 54, 72, 181
prosody, 12
psychology, 10
pṛthvī, 1, 23, 29, 47, 51, 53, 199, 217, 222
puruṣa, 26, 44, 225
puṣpa, 84

Quakes, 72, 176, 179, 182-83, 186, 196, 199

radius, 73
rain, 50, 56, 58-60, 63, 65, 68, 70-

71, 126, 157-58, 164, 178, 181-82, 198, 216
rainbow, 189
Rājasūya, 4-5
rāpas, 121-123
relativity, 46, 48
religion, 2, 7, 9, 16-17, 34, 110, 159, 175
reptiles, 100, 210
rice, 83, 84, 161-164
ritual, 8, 12, 148
river, 1, 28, 58, 71, 77, 87-88, 103, 155-56, 176, 183, 190, 200, 202-203, 205-206, 217-218
ṛṣi, 2
ṛta, 16, 27, 30, 34-36, 183, 185, 221, 225

sāmans, 4-5
sāṁkhya, 10-11
sacrifice, 8, 12, 20, 107, 114, 151, 210, 219
Savitṛ, 1, 19, 219
science, 1-3, 7, 15-18, 28, 34, 43, 48, 53, 76, 110, 114, 175, 225-231
sea, 1, 24, 28, 60, 76, 87-88, 103, 201, 218
seed, 83-85, 87
seismology, 50, 67-76, 175, 179, 198, 229
selenology, 188
skin, 142-144
sky, 22-25, 29-30, 47-48, 63-64, 68, 76, 177, 181
smṛti, 2
society, 1, 76, 103, 225, 227
sociology, 2
soil, 81, 154-55, 185
solar system, 74
soma, 5, 39, 133, 154, 164, 201, 209, 211
Somayāga, 5
sound, 45, 63, 71, 111, 130, 187
space, 51-59, 73, 76, 174, 177, 185, 198, 201, 221-22, 227
śruti, 2
star, 18-19, 189, 190
sun, 18, 19, 25-28, 46-47, 49, 59, 61, 68, 74, 76, 124, 130, 178, 181-82, 186, 188-89, 197-98, 201
sūtra, 12, 207, 218

tantra, 111
technology, 1, 223, 225
temperature, 54
theory, 10, 71-75, 175, 180, 184-188, 195-98, 217, 228
thought, 2, 104, 224, 226
thunder, 55-58, 60-63, 71
time, 3, 33, 38, 53, 73, 75, 105, 108, 173, 178, 197-98, 221, 227
tin, 43, 186
Tṛṇa, 81

town, 1, 77, 88, 200
toxicology, 104-105, 151
trade, 56, 202
tree, 85-88, 148, 200, 210, 226
uncertainty principle, 75
universe, 26-27, 30, 34-35, 44-45, 48-50, 54, 57, 75-76, 176-178, 183, 186, 189, 191-92, 195, 225
urine, 138-39, 147-48, 216
Uṣā, 76, 201
Uṣas, 133

vaccuum, 54.
Vājapeya, 4
vajra, 138
vapour, 54, 58-59
Varuṇa, 50, 55-56, 61, 72, 75-76, 134-35, 176, 183, 184, 190, 199-200, 219
Vasus, 57
Vāyu, 25-26, 30, 47, 51, 54-56, 63-64, 67, 72, 75-76, 176, 182, 189, 194, 199, 201, 215
vegetables, 77
velocity, 53, 73
void, 222
volume, 54
vyoma, 23

warfare, 1, 110
water plants, 80, 211
water, 1, 24, 44-45, 48, 51-60, 63-64, 69, 72, 80-81, 88, 102, 122, 135, 139, 146-47, 157-58, 171, 179, 181, 183, 186, 190, 195, 197, 200-201, 213, 215-219, 222
wave, 196
weapon, 138
weather, 53
weeds, 77, 80, 81
weight, 38
wind, 54-56, 60, 64-71, 146, 158, 163, 182, 189, 190
wolf, 137
wood, 85, 210
wool, 213
world, 22, 25-26, 44, 50, 105, 107, 178, 226
worms, 101-103, 136-37

yakṣmā, 116-118, 121-123
Yama, 201
yantra, 225
Yoga, 11
yojana, 70

zodiac, 184
zone, 186
zoo, 103
zoology, 89-104